Decentering Citizenship

Decentering Citizenship

GENDER, LABOR, AND MIGRANT
RIGHTS IN SOUTH KOREA

Hae Yeon Choo

STANFORD UNIVERSITY PRESS
STANFORD, CALIFORNIA

Stanford University Press
Stanford, California

Portions of Chapter 6 previously appeared in the article "In the Shadow of Working Men: Gendered Labor and Migrant Rights in South Korea" in *Qualitative Sociology*. It is reprinted here with permission.

Portions of Chapter 7 previously appeared in the article "The Cost of Rights: Migrant Women, Feminist Advocacy, and Gendered Morality in South Korea" in *Gender & Society*. It is reprinted here with permission.

Printed in the United States of America on acid-free, archival-quality paper

Library of Congress Cataloging-in-Publication Data

Names: Choo, Hae Yeon, author.
Title: Decentering citizenship : gender, labor, and migrant rights in South Korea /
    Hae Yeon Choo.
Description: Stanford, California : Stanford University Press, 2016. | Includes bibliographical
    references and index.
Identifiers: LCCN 2015044865| ISBN 9780804791274 (cloth : alk. paper) |
    ISBN 9780804799669 (pbk. : alk. paper) | ISBN 9780804799607 (e-book)
Subjects: LCSH: Women foreign workers—Civil rights—Korea (South) | Foreign workers,
    Filipino—Civil rights—Korea (South) | Women foreign workers—Korea (South)—
    Social conditions. | Foreign workers, Filipino—Korea (South)—Social conditions.
    | Citizenship—Korea (South) | Korea (South)—Emigration and immigration. |
    Philippines—Emigration and immigration.
Classification: LCC HD6057.5.K6 C46 2016 | DDC 323.3/224—dc23
LC record available at http://lccn.loc.gov/2015044865

For my parents

Contents

Acknowledgments   *ix*

1. Decentering Citizenship: Perils, Promises, Possibilities   1

2. The Journey of Global Women: From the Philippines
    to South Korea   19

3. Duties, Desires, and Dignity: South Koreans
    on Migrant Encounters   45

4. Everyday Politics of Immigration Raids in the
    Shadow of Citizenship   72

5. The Making of Migrant Workers and Migrant Women   93

6. Workers and Working Girls: Gendering the Worker-Citizen   118

7. Between Women Victims and Mother-Citizens   143

    Coda. Migrant Rights and a Politics of Solidarity   164

Notes   *173*
Works Cited   *181*
Index   *189*

Acknowledgments

This book project began in August 2007 with a simple question: How do migrant women navigate their lives in South Korea in the absence of ethnic nationhood, and how does their presence transform South Korea as a polity? For the next eight years, the question took me to many places—a Tagalog language classroom at the University of Wisconsin-Madison, migrant rights marches in downtown Seoul, an immigrant detention center in South Korea—then followed me as I moved to Toronto, Canada. Although the project certainly involved many hours of solitude in front of a computer screen, it also opened up countless new encounters and dialogues. Some of them can be found in the pages of this book, but others remain in my heart. For those who guided and supported me along the journey, thank you.

First and foremost, I thank the people I met during my field research in South Korea, especially in the two places I call Factorytown and Basetown. Although I am unable to name them here, I express my deepest gratitude to and respect for all those who allowed me into their homes, chapels, and workplaces, as well as the many migrants and South Koreans who generously shared their stories. I am grateful to the migrant advocates and activists who carry out challenging work for migrant rights and justice.

At the University of Wisconsin-Madison, I am deeply indebted to Myra Marx Ferree. Her passion for the pursuit of knowledge imbued both her research and her mentorship. Myra's unwavering faith in me, even as she challenged me, led me to think more deeply and freely. I also had the fortune of working with an amazing group of faculty mentors—Jane Collins, Julie D'acci, Chad Goldberg, Kirin Narayan, Pamela Oliver, Gay Seidman, and Leann Tigges—who shaped the project in memorable ways. I also thank fellow writing group members who read multiple drafts of this book, many of whom became friends: Wendy Christensen, Kristy Kelly, Shamus

Khan, Ayesha Khurshid, Chaitanya Lakkimsetti, Mytoan Nguyen, and Susan Rottmann.

For the past four years, University of Toronto has offered me a vibrant intellectual home, full of wonderful colleagues: Zaheer Baber, Jennifer Carlson, Clayton Childress, Jennifer Jihye Chun, Randol Contreras, Cynthia Cranford, Bonnie Fox, Takeshi Fujitani, Phil Goodman, Kelly Hannah-Moffat, Anna Korteweg, Neda Maghbouleh, Paula Maurutto, Ann Mullen, Jin-kyung Park, Ito Peng, Rania Salem, Scott Schieman, Erik Schneiderhan, Luisa Farah Schwartzman, Rachel Silvey, Jesook Song, and Lisa Yoneyama. Thank you for reading my drafts, sharing your insights over many coffees and dinners, making me laugh, and simply being there for me. You are the best colleagues I could ever hope for, and it is a tremendous joy to work with you and see you in the hallways. I also thank doctoral students Katelin Albert, Catherine ManChuen Cheng, Hyejeong Jo, and Yang-Sook Kim. I am privileged to be a part of their research projects, and their work has enriched my own.

Beyond Toronto, many scholars kindly shared their insights during various stages of this project over the years. I thank Kyeong-Hee Choi, Manisha Desai, Caren Freeman, Kimberly Hoang, Jaeeun Kim, Minjeong Kim, Nora Hui-jung Kim, Ching Kwan Lee, Yoonkyung Lee, John Lie, Joya Misra, Eileen Otis, Seoyoung Park, Hyunjoon Park, Mi Sun Park, Rhacel Parreñas, Bandana Purkayastha, Raka Ray, Rachel Rinaldo, Benita Roth, Elena Shih, Mangala Subramaniam, Hung Cam Thai, Jaeyoun Won, and Jun Yoo for their feedback, encouragement, and inspiring scholarship. I also thank colleagues at University of Illinois Urbana-Champaign, University of Wisconsin-Madison, University of Southern California, University of Pennsylvania, University of Virginia, University of Michigan, Pomona College, Columbia University, University of California at San Diego, University of Pittsburgh, and McGill University, where I shared my research.

Nancy Abelmann, Jennifer Jihye Chun, Nicole Constable, Pei-Chia Lan, Namhee Lee, and Rachel Silvey read an earlier version of the book in its entirety, and their thoughtful and sharp critiques left a mark on every page. Thank you for your generosity in sharing your gift of intellect. Hyejin Jeon and Yang-Sook Kim provided valuable research assistance for the follow-up research, and Katelin Albert and Kusang Burgess helped me with preparation of the manuscript. Jessica Cobb, a fabulous professional editor, read through multiple versions of the manuscript and brought out the best in my writing.

I thank many organizations for providing financial support for the research and writing of the book. For the field research in 2008–2010, I received support from the Social Science Research Council International Dissertation Research Fellowship, the National Science Foundation Dissertation Improvement Grant in Sociology, the American Philosophical Society Lewis & Clark Fund, and the Hyde Dissertation Grant at the University of Wisconsin-Madison. The Social Science Research Council was instrumental in developing my work through the 2008 Korean Studies Dissertation Workshop and the 2013 Korean Studies Junior Faculty Workshop; in particular, I thank Nicole Restrick Levit, a brilliant organizer. For the field research in 2014 and manuscript preparation, I thank the Sociology Department at the University of Toronto, the Global Advisory Program of the Yonsei Sociology Department, the Academy of Korean Studies Research Grant (AKS-2014-R22), the Center for the Study of Korea at the University of Toronto, and the Social Sciences and Humanities Research Council (Canada) Partnership Grant (895-2012-1025).

I am very fortunate to have worked with Stanford University Press and an amazing editor, Jenny Gavacs. Thank you for guiding me through the long process of bringing this project to completion and offering encouraging and incisive feedback along the way.

And there are people I love: my academic sisters and fellow travelers, Chaitanya, Ayesha, and Minjeong, who sustain and nurture me through hours of conversations; my friends Erik, Phil, Anna, and Jesook, who make me call Toronto home; and Mi Sun, whose care and faith in me makes everything possible.

Lastly, I send special thanks to my late father, Choo Young Gil, and my mother, Chi Eun Hee. From them, I learned the importance of integrity, compassion, and justice, and it is their legacy that I do my best to carry on. It is to my parents that I dedicate this book.

Decentering Citizenship

ONE

Decentering Citizenship

Perils, Promises, Possibilities

"We Are Labor! We Want Labor Rights!"
"Don't Call Us Illegals! Stop Crackdowns!"
Loud chanting filled the busy streets of downtown Seoul one sunny afternoon in August 2008—only a few months into my fieldwork in South Korea—as people marched five hundred strong past skyscrapers and low-rise storefronts. Slogans recited in Korean and English were then repeated in Urdu and Nepalese, languages unfamiliar to most South Korean ears. As migrant union flags flew in the hot summer wind, South Korean activists joined the protest against "barbaric" immigrant crackdowns, standing alongside many migrants who worked in factories with temporary work authorization and a smaller number of undocumented workers. Together, they openly demanded that South Korea recognize migrants' presence and rights.

Through their public demands, these migrant protests challenge a long-held conception of South Korean citizenship. The rules governing citizenship operate as an instrument of exclusion, separating outsiders from those whom the state and society deem worthy of rights and dignity. In South Korea, with its myth of ethnic homogeneity, the migrant labor system was designed to keep migrants from becoming legal South Korean citizens while taking advantage of their labor, except in the limited cases of high-skilled professionals and coethnics.[1] Instead, it allows migrants only as part of a short-term rotation workforce, preventing migrant settlement by denying migrant workers any possibility of becoming long-term residents or naturalized citizens and prohibiting spouses or children from accompanying them.

Fervent public protests and a spirited migrant advocacy movement since the mid-1990s in South Korea brought significant legal and policy changes, including a 2004 reform of the migrant labor system that recognized migrant workers as workers under South Korean labor law. However, hundreds of thousands of undocumented migrants—who constituted two-thirds of the total migrant workforce between 1994 and 2002—still face aggressive immigration crackdowns and deportations. The demand for more radical migrant policy reform based in the claim "We Are Labor" continues to this day, with little promise of accomplishment in sight. Yet the migrant population in South Korea continues to grow: by 2014, it reached 1.57 million migrants—mostly from China and Southeast and South Asia—or 3.1 percent of the national population of 51.1 million.[2]

Women entered the circuit of short-term migrant work in the manufacturing sector alongside men, but they also pursued transnational mobility through cross-border marriages, often the only path that enabled permanent residency and legal citizenship in South Korea.[3] These marriages between rural and urban working-class South Korean men and women from China and Southeast Asia have steadily increased since the early 1990s, though fewer migrants came to South Korea through marriage (14.9 percent) than for work (34.3 percent).[4] Since 2006, government, corporate, and civil society funding flooded into immigrant integration projects for marriage-migrant women as Korean mothers and wives, under the rubric of "multicultural families" (*damunhwa gajok*). Migrant advocates were quick to criticize the "government's hypocrisy" in assimilating marriage-migrant women while denying migrant workers the right to settle, but they also actively applied for and received state funding for educational programs for migrant women.

In the shadow of vibrant mobilization for migrant workers' rights and efforts to integrate migrant wives, a third migrant group was excluded from claims-making in South Korea as either *migrant workers* or *migrant women*:

migrant hostesses in US military "camptown" clubs. Since 1996, the entertainer visa has been used to bring migrant women from the Philippines and the former Soviet Union into camptown clubs to cater to American soldiers. In 2004, South Korean feminist organizations successfully utilized US-led international antitrafficking directives to reform the antiprostitution law, redefining women engaged in sexual commerce not as criminals but as victims eligible for state protections under the new law.[5] With little involvement on the part of migrant advocacy groups or trade unions, South Korean feminist groups characterized the migrant hostesses not as migrant workers but as "victims of sexual trafficking."

Through a comparative examination of three groups of Filipina women in South Korea—factory workers, wives of South Korean men, and hostesses at American military camptown clubs—my ethnography interrogates the puzzling discrepancies between "citizenship on the books" and the realities of migrant lives. Law and policy in South Korea shape the conditions of migrant citizenship in a distinctive way for each group: short-term rotation and nonsettlement policies for migrant factory workers, multiculturalist integration policies for migrant wives, and antitrafficking law for migrant hostesses. However, the reality of migrant lives reveals other forces that subvert such legal and policy edifices. For example, how do migrant factory workers—including the 187,340 undocumented migrants among them in 2014[6] living and working in industrial towns all across the country—settle in South Korea? Why do migrant wives—who have a legal status or, in many cases, are even naturalized citizens—become targets of immigration officers in the town markets? And why do only an extremely small number of migrant hostesses seek protection as trafficked victims?

To answer these questions, this book moves beyond a state-centered approach to examine how migrant rights are enacted and challenged in the realm of daily life, as migrants and other civil society actors mobilize various material and moral resources to claim rights and belonging. Delving into the interactive process of claims-making, I situate migrants' struggles for citizenship within the larger pursuit of mobility and dignity, illuminating how social inequalities of gender, race, class, and nation operate on a global scale in the making of citizenship.

THE ALLURE OF CITIZENSHIP
AND ITS SHADOWS

In the contemporary global era, transnational migration has fostered new struggles around rights and citizenship. As the boundaries of nation-states become increasingly fluid, growing numbers of noncitizens reside side by side with citizens, providing a political impetus to extend citizenship rights to migrants on one hand and intensifying anti-immigrant sentiments and social inequalities on the other.

In recent years, scholars in the field of citizenship studies have discussed the emergence of "postnational citizenship," in which rights and provisions that were previously limited to citizens based on membership in a nation-state are now extended to noncitizen residents based on universal personhood and human rights.[7] The international appeal to human rights principles has produced a glimpse of such promises. In June 2014, the city of Toronto, where I live and work, declared itself a "sanctuary city." The city council voted to grant undocumented migrants access to city services such as the public library and public education without fear of immigration control and deportation. This move resulted from the long-standing mobilization of migrant justice organizations such as No One Is Illegal-Toronto. In South Korea, migrant advocacy organizations have, as a matter of basic human rights, teamed up with health care providers since 1999 to build a network to provide subsidized health care for undocumented migrants who are unable to benefit from the national health insurance.

These significant victories are the hard-won fruit of migrant advocacy efforts, yet they reflect only a small part of the contemporary migrant experience. With respect to migrant rights, the nation-state retains the exclusive power of sovereignty to determine borders and terms of membership.[8] Thus we hear news about the deportation of migrant families, the repatriation of refugee-claimants denied asylum, and the arrests of border-crossers far more often than stories of inclusion for undocumented migrants. Migrant exclusion also operates in less visible and dramatic forms, through the state's legal and institutional measures, which preclude migrant settlement and deepen migrant precarity. Temporary labor migration is on the rise, even in immigrant nations such as Canada and Australia that formerly accepted migrants predominantly as future citizens, intensifying the state of "transience" that characterizes the contemporary migration regime.[9]

Simultaneously, across the globe, the sweeping forces of neoliberalism are eroding the social rights of citizens and noncitizens alike. The application of market logics to all dimensions of social life has led to the privatization of state welfare services, bolstered by rising nationalist and anti-immigrant sentiments that limit migrants' political and civic rights. As Margaret Somers compellingly shows, *market fundamentalism*—the notion that market principles should govern society—has superseded the premise of citizenship, rendering even citizens stateless. The meaning of citizenship is increasingly separated from equal rights and recognition, becoming a commodity to be purchased by "flexible"[10] and "paper" citizens.[11] Somers illustrates the erosion of citizenship with the case of Hurricane Katrina rescue efforts in the United States that excluded people deemed unworthy according to market values. In light of this reality, Somers makes a call for reclaiming citizenship, highlighting the importance of a robust public sphere, civil society, and a social state.[12]

For South Koreans in the wake of the tragic *Sewol* ferry disaster, the promises of citizenship seem as elusive as ever. In April 2014, more than three hundred ferry passengers—many of them high school students on a field trip—drowned without any proper rescue effort. The accident involved multiple factors, including the deregulation of safety measures to maximize profit, but the most prominent issue it raised was the lack of state protection for common citizens. South Koreans wondered out loud whether the state would have let the passengers die if they had been the families of the rich or of high-ranking government officials. For many, this event was a solemn moment of awakening; in the words of Ham Jiyoung, a South Korean college student who volunteers to read storybooks to migrant children, "Seeing the *Sewol* ferry made me want to emigrate to another country. To live in our county, it seems like we need to have money. . . . Otherwise, we really don't seem to have protection for citizens." Jiyoung's statement resonated with the sentiment shared by many migrants to South Korea searching for security, mobility, and dignity in the face of weakening citizenship in their home countries. Their migration was an individual response to a lack of state accountability, one that propelled them abroad to fend for themselves and their families.

Migration in South Korea is part of a broader trend of inter-Asian labor and marriage migration that is increasing in scale and significance. The 1980s witnessed neoliberal reforms and the transition to a postsocialist economy, combined with deepening inequality and weakening social security in countries like China, Vietnam, and the Philippines, providing the conditions for emigration from what sociologist Robyn Rodriguez called "labor brokerage states."[13] Around the same time, the economic ascendance of the "Four Asian Tigers"—South Korea, Taiwan, Singapore, and Hong Kong—as well as the Gulf states, made these countries attractive new migrant destinations as the doors to historical receiving countries such as the United States, Canada, and Britain were rapidly closing. Distinct from the United States or Western Europe, where migrant settlement is still possible, migration regimes in Asia are characterized by a high degree of exclusion for labor migrants, except high-skilled professionals. It was an uphill battle for the Filipina women in my study to build a home in South Korea under a system that deterred migrants' settlement, or to realize their wish for transnational mobility to a country higher in the global hierarchy of nations.

This book explores the spaces—what I call the "margins of citizenship"—where migrants negotiate their rights, entitlements, and belonging. Margins are the spaces that defy a simple binary of inclusion and exclusion, occupying an uncertain and indeterminate edge. They are, feminist theorist bell hooks argues, "more than a site of deprivation"; margins are "the site of space of radical possibility, a space of resistance."[14] By bringing attention to the margins where claims for rights and belonging challenge and shift the borders of inclusion, I interrogate the paradox of citizenship: its duality of inclusion and equality for members and exclusion for nonmembers. Since its emergence as the predominant polity and as the guarantor of rights, the nation-state has produced citizens by constructing commonalities among its members as "imagined communities"[15] and actively excluding others, both physically and symbolically. Exclusion is at the heart of citizenship, operating as what Rogers Brubaker called "a powerful instrument of social closure and profoundly illiberal determinant of life chances."[16] In fact, as Evelyn Nakano Glenn compellingly showed, citizens and noncitizens are "interdependent constructions," and citizenship is used to "draw boundaries between those who are included as members of the community and entitled to respect, protection, and rights, and those who are excluded and thus not entitled to recognition and rights."[17]

I approach citizenship as full and equal membership in a polity, which is an ongoing project rather than an achieved status. Although citizenship is an expansive concept—referencing multiple dimensions of legal status, rights, political participation, and sense of belonging[18] arising from the liberal and republican origins of the term—using it as an all-encompassing concept for any type of inclusion and social change obscures more than it reveals. Instead, the project of citizenship needs to be specified and situated to uncover its dynamic operation in interaction with other projects. At the core of citizenship lies the work of building a polity that enables a project of equality.[19] Approaching citizenship in this way decenters the state as a taken-for-granted actor of citizenship and moves beyond a limited focus on the vertical relationship between the individual and the polity to bring attention to horizontal relationships among polity members that are premised on equality.[20] In this research, I examine citizenship as a meaningful language for social and personal transformation, but I also show that the project of citizenship is situated in a broader pursuit of dignity, security, and mobility. This broader pursuit is at times in concert and at times in conflict with the equality project of citizenship.

Citizenship holds a relentless allure because of its multifaceted and protean nature. The border of citizenship has never been static; rather, it is a productive site for the pursuit of equal rights in the face of exclusion. The boundary separating citizens and noncitizens, in this sense, is not fixed in law and policy; instead, it is permeable and negotiable in particular local contexts among concrete actors.[21] T. H. Marshall's classic study calls attention to the shifting borders of citizenship for the British working class during the eighteenth through twentieth centuries through the expansion of civil, political, and social rights.[22] South Korea's modern history is also characterized by the hard-won expansion of civil and political rights, with the transition from military authoritarian regimes to parliamentary democracy in the late 1980s. Even as the struggles for democratic citizenship continue in South Korea, as a recent migrant-receiving country, the nation-state is also grappling with how to position migrant newcomers within the new polity it has built. South Korea is embroiled in "classification struggles"[23] over who deserves belonging and rights as citizens. These struggles do not involve simply the inclusion or exclusion of new groups; in the process, the boundaries of citizenship are reconstituted, and existing citizens are remade anew.

The generative paradox that citizenship is both a means of closure and an impetus for inclusion has propelled many scholars to focus on the contested nature of citizenship, "as a relationship" that is "subject to active negotiation, and is therefore unstable."[24] Many scholars have highlighted the fluid and dynamic negotiations involved in citizenship, using court cases, survey data, and theoretical debates in which actors are involved in "disputing," "negotiating," and "contesting" citizenship.[25] This theoretical reconceptualization of citizenship provides a springboard for inquiry into the processes of contestation on the ground. Who can be a subject of negotiation and who cannot? How do local and transnational structures of social inequality affect negotiations of citizenship? Through a comparative study of migrant groups with divergent configurations of legal status, labor organization, and gendered morality in South Korea, this ethnography inquires into the politics of gender, race, and labor that shape dynamic processes of citizenship-making.

The case of migrant women in South Korea reveals a complex interplay between the perils and promises of citizenship. Migrant citizenship is not simply determined by legal status and political categories; it is also shaped by interactive processes of translating the formal rights into practice through encounters among migrants, civil society groups, and the state.[26] Since the mid-1990s, South Korean civil society has been actively involved in the process of negotiating citizenship for migrants. Although the South Korean state viewed "guest workers" as disposable labor, South Korean civil society actors had diverse alternative visions. Many faith-based migrant advocates approached migrant workers as the new *minjung* (common people) or the new poor, whose marginalization and rights violations were a shameful yardstick for South Korean democracy. Evangelical Christians saw migrants as an opportunity for global missionary work in their backyard, while Marxist student activists saw migrants as potential allies against global capitalism. In the case of migrant women in particular, some feminist groups viewed them as vulnerable victims needing protection, and social workers saw them as new clients whose integration required their professional expertise. Through government funding and service provision projects for migrants, many civil society organizations have become part of the state apparatus, even as they challenge the state's immigration policy. To claim rights and dignity, migrant women negotiated with these various state and nonstate actors as individuals, as members of ethnic and religious communities, and as workers and mothers. These encounters between migrants and diverse groups of South Koreans revealed and redefined the meaning of citizenship in contemporary South Korea and in a global world.

This book moves investigations of migrant rights beyond the realm of law and policy to examine day-to-day interactions and contestation among the state, migrant, and civil society actors in the receiving nation-state of South Korea. The successful mobilization of migrant advocacy groups and the migrant community in South Korea significantly expanded migrants' labor and social rights over the past two decades. However, access to rights in South Korea is distributed unevenly across different groups of migrants, who are affected by the dynamics of intersecting social inequalities. The dignity accorded to paid labor has been an important discursive resource for extending rights to migrant workers. This discourse is highly effective given the long-standing connection between work and citizenship globally[27] and the strong legacy of labor rights struggles in South Korea; however, its use also produced gendered consequences. Historically, the model of worker-citizen has long been associated with male workers, whereas maternal citizenship offered women limited access to rights and recognition because this discourse is constrained by its relationship to the domestic sphere.

When struggles for migrant rights are fought on the terms of the dignity of workers, they leave out other sectors of migration that do not offer the same level of societal and moral standing. While the feminized sector of carework is often devalued as not legitimate skilled work[28] and offers only "partial citizenship,"[29] work in sexual commerce poses moral risks under the discourses of human trafficking and sexual immorality[30] that may be even more detrimental to citizenship claims. For migrant women in the manufacturing sector and for those in the illicit and feminized service sector of hostess work, the distinct gendered symbolic politics of each sector plays a significant role in their differentiated access to rights. By examining how advocacy groups for migrant factory workers and hostesses are embedded in broader social movement legacies in South Korea, this study illuminates the significant role that gendered morality and symbolic politics play in the making of migrant rights.

Building on previous studies of gender and global migration that primarily focus on a single feminized sector of migration such as sexual commerce,[31] domestic work,[32] or cross-border marriage,[33] this book brings multiple sectors of migration into conversation to provide a unique analytic lens for considering variations in migrant inclusion and exclusion as well as the relational process of constituting migrant subjects. In South Korea, migrant factory workers secured rights as worker-citizens, and migrant wives secured a different set of rights as mother-citizens. Yet migrant hostesses were left out as subjects of rights as neither migrant workers nor migrant women but as victims in need of protection.

Despite their shared life trajectories in the Philippines and the migrant path and common experiences of migrant exclusion in South Korea, the three groups of Filipina migrant women in my study were included and excluded from the full and equal membership in South Korea in very different ways—not necessarily according to their legal status, but through the organization of their work, the mobilization of the migrant community and South Korean civil society, and the symbolic and moral boundaries that distinguished them from respectable citizens.

To demonstrate how rights and membership are negotiated on the ground, this book transports readers to less familiar destinations than parliaments or courts: the passenger seat of a van owned by a Korean migrant advocate as it rumbles through alleys in pursuit of immigration officers; a dimly lit booth in a club where an American GI and a Filipina hostess desperately seek a modicum of privacy to affirm their love; a classroom full of newly arrived migrant wives learning to cook Korean food from South Korean women volunteers at a migrant advocacy NGO. In these quotidian spaces, negotiations over citizenship emerge from the complex interplay of morality and the pursuit of mobility, which at times work in accordance with and in tension with the equality project of citizenship. It is on the margins of citizenship that migrants contest and sustain the borders of citizenship in South Korea, opening up new possibilities for the polity. By decentering and situating citizenship in the multiplicity of people's aspirations for rights, dignity, and belonging, this book delves into the paradox of seeking a full and equal membership in a deeply unequal world.

ETHNOGRAPHY OF THE MIGRANT ENCOUNTER IN SOUTH KOREA

This book is based on eighteen consecutive months of ethnographic research and interviews conducted between July 2008 and January 2010 and two return visits in the summers of 2012 and 2014. I conducted in-depth interviews with thirty-six Filipina women and twenty-four South Korean actors, such as NGO staff, social workers, Korean language teachers, volunteers, labor activists, and religious leaders involved in migrant advocacy in 2008–2010. These were supplemented by additional interviews with forty-two South Koreans and migrants involved in migrant rights activism and immigrant integration programs from April to October 2014.[34]

I conducted this research in two segregated migrant neighborhoods on the outskirts of Seoul, South Korea: an industrial town that I call "Factorytown" and an American military camptown called "Basetown." Because my ethnography focused on migrant encounters, I place the experiences and narratives of Filipina migrant women center stage and connect them to others who inhabited their lifeworlds: migrants from other ethnic groups; South Korean employers and migrant advocates; government officials; and the American, South Korean, and Filipino men with whom they formed romantic relationships and families. The focus on Filipina women, the only ethnic group in South Korea involved in all three sectors of migrant flow— factory work, cross-border marriages, and hostess work[35]—offered a unique vantage point for comparative analysis while encompassing other migrant groups and various South Korean actors. The multiple groups of people in my study, migrants and South Koreans, had conflicting interests and viewpoints, posing challenges for representation in the fieldwork and writing. In this book, I strive not to shy away from contradictions, but instead explore the site of conflicts and alliances for insights into the complexity of citizenship.

Factorytown

You can close your eyes and tell you are in Factorytown. The acidic smell of burned plastic assaults your senses as you walk past the slipper factory, and the dusty, almost spicy smell of wood particles signals that the furniture factory is near. From afar, you might hear people singing 1990s Korean pop songs in the karaoke pub while the grating sound of furniture being sanded raises goosebumps on your flesh. Surrounded by mountains and located on a hill, the factory complex is in the heart of Factorytown. Furniture showrooms and stores line the main streets, but when they close in the evenings and the Korean storekeepers and customers head home, the entire factory complex is left to approximately eleven hundred migrant workers from Bangladesh, the Philippines, Nepal, Vietnam, Thailand, and other Asian and African countries, some with legal working visas and others without, about 30 percent of whom are women. Four local South Korean migrant advocacy NGOs/church groups work with migrant workers in the area; two of the groups also work with migrant wives in surrounding towns. When I began my fieldwork in July 2008, I chose Factorytown because of the presence of a substantial Filipino community in residence (a population of 300–350), as well as active South Korean migrant advocacy NGOs and church groups that bring together additional Filipino and other migrants in the surrounding rural and industrial towns.

The presence of South Korean volunteers, activists, journalists, and researchers was common in Factorytown, and only a few weeks after my arrival, the Filipino migrants, even those I had not met personally, knew who I was and what I was doing there. As the "girl" from the United States who spoke "cute" Tagalog, I was warmly received. As a volunteer at Peace Center, a major local NGO in Factorytown, I observed and taught a Korean language class for migrant factory workers and migrant wives three times a week and participated in other educational programs, including classes in cooking, filmmaking, and flower decoration. I also participated in field trips and child-rearing education for migrant wives. Because of my fluency in Korean and English and my proficiency in Tagalog, I worked closely with staff members at Peace Center and other local NGOs, sometimes as a translator, other times assisting with labor counseling, hospital trips, and visits to the immigration office and detention centers.

Religious services and churches serving Filipino migrants were another critical venue for my fieldwork. Churches are the most important sites in the Filipino communities of Factorytown, and all five churches—spanning the Catholic, Protestant, and Unification faiths—offered focal points for community building.[36] I attended weekly worship services, Bible study meetings, and prayer meetings. And there were parties, parties, and more parties—birthdays, baptism celebrations, Christmas and New Year's parties, caroling, and basketball league games. The close-knit ethnic community and extensive migrant mobilization that existed in Factorytown stood in contrast to the weak and fragile migrant community in Basetown.

Basetown

In February 2009, I extended my fieldwork to Basetown, located about fifty kilometers from Factorytown. One of the oldest camptowns in South Korea, Basetown includes a US military camp of eleven thousand military personnel. Inside the camp is a small American town with military barracks, tanks, bowling alleys, and medical clinics. The influence of the US military does not end at the camp gate, but extends to all of Basetown, often superseding the influence of the South Korean nation-state. Since 1945, the beginning of the American military presence in South Korea, sexual commerce has proliferated in camptowns surrounding major US bases despite antiprostitution laws in South Korea, and the club district in Basetown, which was central to my fieldwork, was one such area of complicated sovereignty. Instead of Korean police officers, US military police (MPs) patrol the streets of Basetown and possess the power to shut down clubs that violate military policy. For what is often their first time outside their hometowns in America, young soldiers freely roam Basetown in and outside the military camp, drinking in the foreigner-exclusive clubs. The names of these clubs promise to treat the young men as "Kings," "VIPs," and "Pharaohs" as they seek refuge from their homesickness, fall in and out of love with Filipina women, and marry and have children in a residential area near the military base where many American GI and Filipina couples reside.

My introduction to Basetown was through a Filipino priest affiliated with the Migrant Mission of the Catholic Church, whom I met in Factorytown. By attending weekly mass in Basetown, I met Filipina women married to American GIs and those working in the clubs. To observe daily life there, I visited clubs in the early evening and met other club hostesses and managers. Some Filipina hostesses left the clubs and moved in with their American boyfriends and husbands, and I visited their homes and spent time with their partners, children, and friends. A second entry point that helped me learn more about women's troubles in camptowns was my volunteer work at Sisterhood Center, one of a few NGOs offering assistance to migrant women in the camptown clubs.

Unlike in Factorytown, my presence as a South Korean woman in her late twenties in Basetown was unusual, if not suspicious. The number of South Korean women willing to work in the camptown clubs decreased as South Korea entered its economic ascendancy, and since 1996, the vast majority of hostesses in camptown clubs have been migrant women from the Philippines and the former Soviet Union. Over 90 percent of the hostesses in the clubs I visited in Basetown were Filipina women. Linda, a Filipina woman who left the club to move in with her American GI boyfriend, tried to lightheartedly introduce me to the grocery store owner in her neighborhood, a middle-aged Korean woman. "She's my Korean friend! Take a guess—what do you think she does?" The owner looked me up and down with a disdainful gaze and said, "You are, what, a Jehovah's Witness?" In her experience, a South Korean woman who would associate with Filipina women in camptowns must be proselytizing her faith. Indeed, during my field research, I met several Jehovah's Witnesses, a rare group of South Koreans who learned migrants' languages—Mongolian, Vietnamese, Tagalog, and so on—for their door-to-door missionary work. Some Filipina women in the clubs half-jokingly told me that when we were seen together, others would think that I am a "madam," a manager of Filipina hostesses in the club. Despite the work of Sisterhood Center, outreach efforts from feminist organizations or any other migrant advocacy groups in Basetown were few and far between; most Filipina hostesses did not know about them, and club owners were hostile toward such "outsiders."

Comparing Factorytown and Basetown offered me insight into the distinctive formation of migrant community and citizenship in each local site. While these two towns were central to my research, I also conducted fieldwork in similar industrial and military camptowns with high numbers of migrants in the Greater Seoul area (Seoul, Incheon, and the surrounding Gyeonggi Province), including Ansan, Suwon, Incheon, Osan, and Uijeongbu, where 63.1 percent of the migrant population in South Korea resides. In addition, I participated in meetings and events organized by national organizations and alliances for migrant workers and migrant wives.[37]

Since I started my fieldwork in 2008, some things have changed in South Korea, while others remain the same. Migrants and migrant advocates still repeat the same slogans in their protests as they respond to the erosion of migrant rights under two consecutive conservative governments. Many migrants I met left South Korea and returned to the Philippines, Nepal, and Bangladesh, or moved on in their transnational journeys to Dubai, the United States, and Canada; others were so firmly grounded in their community that they could not imagine anywhere else as home. Whatever their individual trajectories, this book hopes to bring light to migrants' continuing struggles for rights, dignity, and belonging in South Korea and beyond.

Being in the Field

I could not tell her age. I guessed somewhere between forty-five and fifty-five, but I did not dare ask. "Don't drink that. It does nothing good," Ms. Han told me in a firm voice after I ordered an amaretto sour, my usual. "Just get coffee for her," she ordered Dinah, a Filipina hostess behind the bar. I was not much of a drinker, but I was compelled to order something to be allowed to sit in the club, *her* club, in an American military camptown on the outskirts of Seoul. After my third visit, Ms. Han noticed that I never finished even a quarter of a drink and refused to sell me another. I quietly wondered if she was implying that I should stop coming.

But from that day on, every time I came in to sit in a corner with the Filipina hostesses, Ms. Han brought me free coffee and found moments to chat with me—about the weather, customers, hostesses ("the girls"), the camptown—in the Korean language that no one else in the club understood, neither the American GI customers nor the Filipina hostesses. Ms. Han rarely talked about her personal life or asked about mine. She knew I was a student in the United States writing about Filipina women in South Korea, but she was not keen on knowing anything more. She was not a woman of many words, but once in a while she poured a fragment of her thoughts out to me. One evening, leaning on the bar, she said:

> People say it is sinful to run this kind of a business. Even people at the [Catholic] church, they whispered when I took part in communion, and so I stopped. Maybe they are right. Who knew I'd be doing this for so long? Even my mother says, "Don't do it for a long time." People come in with a clear mind and go out stumbling, so what's there to feel good about? I kept saying, "Just one more year," and it's already been twenty years.

The door opened, bringing sunlight into the dimly lit interior. She greeted the two GIs who entered, and hastily served them beer. Then she came back to my corner to continue:

> Although I think I don't do anything that I should be ashamed of—like making the girls prostitute—sometimes I catch myself yelling at the girls to sell more drinks. They all come here because they want to earn money. That's fine, but when I hear how they lived [in the Philippines], it's just too sad, these young girls. Then I wonder, bringing them here, making them work like this, making them drink more, sell more drinks, isn't this all sin?

I rarely knew how to respond to moral queries like these, but my response hardly seemed necessary. Perhaps my naïveté made me a good listener in her eyes, and she welcomed my visit during down times at the club.

At times, Ms. Han's penetrating eyes made me nervous, as if she was looking into and through me, at the moral questions I had of my own.

Foremost on my mind was my ongoing conversation with Rachel, a Filipina hostess working for Ms. Han, whom I met through the Tagalog mass in the church. Rachel had initially invited me to this club, and we connected well. Rachel sought my advice about running away from the club, though she changed her mind every week. She generally liked Ms. Han's club and that she was not pressured to go out with customers at night, though she had many complaints about the working and living conditions. Moreover, she was uncertain of whether her contract would be renewed and afraid of where she would be sent next. Rachel asked if I could help her find a factory job, and I hesitated. The boundaries of involvement during fieldwork aside, my worry was personal: What if I helped her run away and Ms. Han found out? Would I be able to look her in the eye?

My second ethical dilemma regarded my volunteer work with Sisterhood Center, a feminist organization in a contentious relationship with some club owners because of the Center's work assisting runaway migrant hostesses and its opposition to the camptown club industry as a site of trafficking and violence against women. Although Ms. Han was not involved in any direct disputes with Sisterhood Center during my fieldwork, I knew what she thought about "those women's organizations who don't know anything and just blame us," and I did not tell her about my involvement with the group. Just a week earlier, I had accompanied a Sisterhood Center staff member and a runaway hostess to meet with the owner of a club a few doors down the street from Ms. Han's to retrieve her passport. The thought of running into Ms. Han while I was with him had made me uneasy.

My fieldwork as a participant observer was full of seemingly mundane interactions fraught with dilemmas and contradictions. Similar tensions also existed in Factorytown, as I was involved both with various migrant communities with internal hierarchies and conflicts, and with multiple migrant advocacy and church groups that did not always see eye to eye. In various situations, I presented myself to research participants like Ms. Han, Rachel, Sisterhood Center activists, pastors and priests as a naive and eager student from the United States, as a South Korean insider with shared progressive or feminist leanings who wants justice for migrants, as a lapsed Catholic open to returning to the faith, and as a second-generation daughter of a "multicultural family." While I truly was all of these things, I might disappoint those who believed that I shared their worldviews wholeheartedly and would therefore be a good interlocutor for their stories. I hope they know that I have tried to represent their perspectives truthfully and faithfully, even when they think I have failed. It is with this wish that I narrate the stories of Factorytown and Basetown.

THE JOURNEY OF THE BOOK

This book unfolds by moving through Filipina migrant women's global journey, from their departure from the Philippines to a series of short-term labor contracts in East and Southeast Asia and the Middle East, and to South Korea. Chapter 2 shows how Filipina women use transnational migration to pursue mobility through multiple border-crossings and encounters with migration law and policy regimes in South Korea. It asks what South Korea means for Filipina women in their broader migrant trajectories and situates migrant women in South Korea within a transnational landscape in which working-class women's mobility is encouraged for their labor, but citizenship and rights are held out of reach. Chapter 3 flips the gaze of Chapter 2 to ask what the migrant encounter means for contemporary South Koreans, exploring such diverse groups of South Koreans as migrant activists, volunteer Korean language teachers, and pastors of migrant churches. It highlights the gendered and generational aspirations that led these individuals to work with migrants as they search for a sense of national belonging, new forms of sociability, and membership in global South Korea.

The next part of the book turns to the task of decentering the state as a primary actor shaping migrant citizenship. Chapter 4 examines immigration raids as the state's regulation of legal status not simply as a force of exclusion but also as a strategy to regulate and discipline migrants physically and socially. By taking a close, personal look at how documented and undocumented migrants negotiate the rules of immigration raids, this chapter illustrates that the containment of migrants involves not only state actors but also the South Korean advocates and migrants who challenge and bargain with the state's exclusionary force. Chapter 5 critically examines the formation of migrant subjects who challenge their exclusion in South Korea, demonstrating how migrants embedded in ethnic and religious communities in South Korea are constituted as separate subjects of migrant workers and migrant women through day-to-day interactions with South Korean civil society actors.

Chapters 6 and 7 take readers deeper into the dynamic process of making migrant rights in South Korea, highlighting intersecting inequalities that produce uneven rights for different migrant groups and the exclusion of migrant hostesses. In Chapter 6, I interrogate why migrant factory workers and hostesses are offered differentiated rights despite their common status as migrant workers. Migrant factory workers mobilize the support from South Korean civil society embedded in the legacy of trade unionism, and advocacy for the dignity of workers for the expansion of labor and social rights, but migrant hostesses in camptown clubs are excluded from this civil society mobilization and the organization of work that fosters self-mobilization. Finally, Chapter 7 explores the divergent paths to rights and dignity for women in feminized sectors of migration: cross-border marriage and hostess work. Migrant wives used their moral status as mothers as a basis to claim citizenship and belonging in South Korea, but all that migrant hostesses had was limited access to the discourse of gendered victimhood, which prevented their inclusion as either *migrant workers* or *migrant women*. These chapters show how migrant women negotiated their respective subject-positions within the discourses of human rights, labor rights, and gendered victimhood.

The Coda then takes up the question of why decentering citizenship in the larger pursuit of dignity and security is important in discussions of migrant rights and justice. As the promise of equal rights and full membership in a polity is swiftly eroding in the face of increasing global inequalities, this decentering illuminates contestation at the margins of citizenship. This contestation shifts and remakes the borders of citizenship, reimagining new possibilities for solidarity.

The Journey of Global Women

From the Philippines to South Korea

Loyda Del Rosario's transnational journey as a migrant worker began at the age of eighteen. She was the mother of two young children and the wife of a man from her neighborhood in Baguio, in the northern Philippines. Born the third of four children to a motorized tricycle driver father and laundry woman mother, Loyda was the first in her family to work abroad. One morning in 1986, she left her hometown to meet a labor broker who could help her secure employment as a domestic worker in a foreign country. Loyda spent the next ten years journeying back and forth between the Philippines and Southeast and East Asia before coming to South Korea.

Twenty-three years later in 2009, Loyda's memory of her first migrant destination, Singapore, was still vivid. Under a bright fluorescent lamp in a two-hundred-square-foot shipping container that served as her studio apartment, she recalled crying every night, missing the family she had left behind. But she was also excited to be in a foreign country that seemed "clean and very nice." Her first boss was "very strict," giving her few days off and even following her on the weekends, but Loyda still managed to explore the city and make friends. After this first experience in Singapore, all the other countries where Loyda worked blurred together in her memory: Malaysia, Hong Kong, mainland China, Macau; one year here, two years there.

During the time she was abroad, Loyda's relationship with her husband slowly fell apart. He started seeing other women, and eventually they separated. While working in Taiwan, she met her current husband, Victor, a Filipino migrant factory worker. Her eyes sparkled as she remembered their courtship:

> I was very lucky because a single man, a handsome man, chose me! Back then, I didn't have this belly; my teeth was all straight, original, very pretty. That's why although other women courted him, I was the one he chose, and we went back together to his family in Manila and stayed there until 1999. That's when we had our son.

As soon as the baby was born, Victor traveled to South Korea on a tourist visa, following his cousins who already worked in Factorytown. As soon as she stopped breastfeeding, Loyda joined him in South Korea, where they both worked at a furniture factory, leaving her children behind with her parents. Ten years later, Loyda and Victor were still in Factorytown. Their migrant work in South Korea improved their family's living condition considerably; they were able to support their children's education and small businesses and provide financial support for relatives to migrate to South Korea and other Asian countries. With their savings, they purchased land in Baguio, where they were building a four-bedroom house. But Loyda and her husband did not know whether they would ever return to the Philippines to live in that house. She told me that plans for return would have to wait; although her first daughter was married and had a stable business, her second child had just graduated from college and wanted to study further to become a lawyer, and her youngest was only a third grader.

It was not just concerns about money that kept them in South Korea. Loyda was the center of the Filipino community in Factorytown, where she had a rich social and church life. She and her husband both had more relatives living in Factorytown—including her sister, brother-in-law, nephew, cousins, and second cousins—than in their hometown in the Philippines. During her stay in South Korea, Loyda's father passed away in 2001, and then her mother in 2004. She was unable to attend their funerals because of her undocumented legal status in South Korea, which would prevent her reentry. She no longer had many immediate family members in Baguio because all her siblings worked abroad in South Korea, Hong Kong, and Saudi Arabia after Loyda paid their placement fees. "All thanks to me!" she proudly exclaimed.

Life in Factorytown was not perfect. Loyda and Victor were haunted by the fear of immigration raids, and her coughing—a common condition for workers surrounded by debris and wood particles in the furniture factory—kept her awake at night. After ten years, Factorytown was home, but Loyda was acutely aware that her future in South Korea was uncertain: the country's immigrant policies did not allow the settlement of migrant workers. Loyda and Victor planned to stay in South Korea as long as possible before they were deported. If she were deported alone, Loyda planned for Victor to stay in South Korea and send money home so that she could open a restaurant in Baguio.

Loyda is an exemplar of a "global woman,"[1] or "a servant of globalization," as sociologist Rhacel Parreñas would say.[2] Her labor was in demand throughout Asia, but there was little room for Loyda and her children to build a home together in the Philippines or abroad. As a migrant domestic worker, she was welcome only if she migrated alone on a year-to-year basis and restricted her mobility to the private homes where she worked, at times without even a day off. Facing the exclusionary migration regime in Asia, Loyda ultimately made a choice to leave what Pei-Chia Lan called "legal servitude"—the legally sanctioned restriction of rights experienced by migrant workers with short-term contracts—and to opt into "free illegality," which allowed her relatively long-term settlement in South Korea but without legal freedoms.[3]

Like most Filipina migrant women in my study, Loyda did not fit the common portrait of transnational migrants who are firmly grounded in both host and home societies and who maintain transnational political, social, and economic ties.[4] Although she maintained connections to her family members in the Philippines via remittances and Internet chats, Loyda had not seen them face-to-face for more than a decade, not even when her parents passed away. As Parreñas rightly noted, much of the scholarship on migrant transnationalism is based on the experiences of permanent and long-term migrants in North America. This literature does not account for the experiences of short-term "circular" migrants in Asia, whose settlement is heavily constrained by restrictive legal and institutional frameworks.[5]

Yet unlike the Filipina hostesses in Parreñas's study, the migrant women I met in South Korea were rarely "homeward bound," either. Although many of these women experienced limited integration in South Korea—to varying degrees depending on their legal status and immersion in the community—and maintained a transnational connection with their families in the Philippines, few held on to the notion that the Philippines was a "home" where they would soon return. In fact, the erosion of security, livelihood, and community that Filipina women experienced in the Philippines propelled their perpetual migration across multiple destinations. As sociologist Robyn Rodriguez argued, rather than implement structural measures to address social problems such as unemployment and poverty, the Philippine state of the 1970s instituted a labor export policy and bureaucracy. Since then, the state has effectively mobilized Filipino citizens for migrant labor to the extent that "membership in the Philippines is increasingly construed as actually requiring employment overseas."[6]

How do Filipina women like Loyda navigate a migrant journey of multiple border-crossings, promoted by the Philippine state, under the exclusive migration regimes where migrant women are valued only for their labor and where their citizenship and belonging are severely curtailed?

CONVERGING PATHS FROM THE PHILIPPINES TO SOUTH KOREA

South Korea is one of the "Four Asian Tigers" alongside Taiwan, Singapore, and Hong Kong, and migrants viewed entry into the country as a "stepping-up" experience, either as their first opportunity to leave the poverty and insecurity of the Philippines or following low-paid employment in domestic and factory work elsewhere in Asia. Before entering South Korea, many women previously worked as domestic workers in Hong Kong, as factory workers in Taiwan, as service workers in China, and as hostesses in Japan. Filipina migrant women's choice of South Korea as a migrant destination accorded with their perception of a global hierarchy of nations, but it was also contingent on personal circumstances. This was true not only for migrant factory workers and hostesses on short-term labor contracts but also for migrant wives who came to South Korea as a place of permanent settlement. They could just as easily have landed in another country of similar economic standing; their trajectories might look entirely different if the migration broker had instead suggested Hong Kong, if they had happened to see a newspaper advertisement for international matchmaking with Taiwanese men, or if had they received a work referral from a cousin in Singapore.

South Korea held various meanings for Filipina women. To some, it was a "god-given opportunity" where "hard work pays off," an escape from fear and insecurity, a home for their families—albeit one where they suffered daily indignities. To others, it was a "second-best place" for now, a stepping-stone to future migrant destinations. While in South Korea, migrant women remained intimately connected to the Philippines through monetary remittances and regular communication, not only to support their family members' daily subsistence but also to enable their transnational labor and marriage migration out of the Philippines. Some made a temporary destination into a place of settlement and created a home and a community, even in the face of hostile legal and social conditions in the host society, while others aspired to move on to the next step in their migrant journey to the United States, Canada, or Europe,[7] where they hoped to achieve greater mobility, permanent residency, and family unification. This chapter follows these migrants' transnational journeys from the moment of departure to their temporary settlement and continuing pursuit of mobility.

In South Korea, even as these women lost their visa status as tourists, spouses, industrial trainees, factory workers, and entertainers, their labor remained in demand in small-scale factories, domestic homes, and camp-town hostess clubs. This chapter examines how migration law and policy of South Korea governed their labor and migrant trajectories, and situates South Korea and the home country of the Philippines in the global pathways of Filipina migrant women in three distinct sectors. Although it is impossible for any narrator to capture the fullness of their lives, I hope the narratives presented in this chapter offer a glimpse of the complex desires, history, quirks, and global aspirations that shaped these women's migrant journeys, beyond their legal status as migrant workers or migrant wives.

Becky: Bahay Kubo under a Storm

In the Philippines, Becky Concepcion built her first home with her husband, Aaron, whom she married right after high school. Their house was a *bahay kubo,* a small bamboo hut. "You know, like in the song '*Bahay kubo, kahit munti,'"* Becky chuckled, as she sang the well-known Filipino folk song out of tune. But their *bahay kubo* was not as idyllic as in the song; it was easily destroyed by storms and took days to repair. Raising four children on the income from a small coconut farm and piggery was also a challenge. Becky recalled a moment when she was washing the children's dirty clothes by hand—a washing machine was an unattainable luxury—and she suddenly burst into tears because she realized she had no more soap. Running out of daily necessities like soap or rice was a routine occurrence, and Aaron's unstable employment and their agricultural work provided no way out.

"Thank Lord, then my brother took a pity on our family and helped us," Becky recalled fondly. Her brother, who had been a migrant factory worker in South Korea for several years, paid a placement fee for Aaron to join him in South Korea. Two years later, Becky followed Aaron and settled in Factorytown, and they worked together for nine years in a shoe factory from 8:30 a.m. until 6 p.m. six days a week, with frequent additional overtime. Their new home in the Philippines was not a *bahay kubo,* but "a real house with cement"; in fact, by 2008, they owned three homes: one in Manila for her daughter who was starting nursing school, and two near the coconut farm in the province of Quezon. Her sister lived in one of these homes with Becky and Aaron's three younger children, and they rented out the other. Becky whispered to me, "Don't tell others here that we have three houses because people think that we are boasting. We are not rich; I wouldn't say we are rich. But we are better than before, that's for sure."

For Becky, now thirty-seven years old, migration to South Korea was a "godsend," an opportunity to give her immediate and extended family a modicum of security and mobility. It was a way for her to be a good Filipino citizen by contributing to the national economy; she and her husband were praised as "national heroes," actualizing what Rodriguez called "migrant citizenship" in the Philippines.[8] But their financial security also came with a lengthy family separation. Both Becky and Aaron were undocumented after their tourist visa expired and could not visit the Philippines. If they left South Korea, they would have to wait ten years before they could even apply for another visa. During their nine years in South Korea, Aaron had visited home only once in 2002 when the South Korean government gave temporary amnesty to undocumented migrants for one year, and Becky had never visited at all. Like many migrant women, Becky engaged in "transnational mothering," relying on phone calls, Yahoo chats, remittances, and *balikbayan* packages—large cardboard boxes filled with gifts from Filipino migrants to families and friends back home—to maintain her connection to her children.[9] Becky believed that their children were mature enough to understand why they were away:

> They know because we are here, we are able to support their education and better life. We explain this, and they say, "Okay, Mom. You stay there." It was not always easy. There were times when they said, "Just come back, Mom. We don't need good schools; we don't need this and that. So just come back." But now they know.

Aaron felt more strongly about the separation. Now that Becky was pregnant with their fifth child, he wanted her to return to the Philippines because he thought that their children needed their mother's guidance, reflecting the particularly gendered anxiety surrounding women's migration from the Philippines.[10] Becky said, "It is hard for Aaron. Our fourth child hardly remembers him. Once he asked on the video chat, 'Is my father tall?' You see, he had only seen his father's face because he's sitting down for the chat. And that made Aaron very sad, his child not knowing what his father looks like." But she was still uncertain about the possibility of return:

> After having this child in July, we will see. I might return home, but I don't know. Pastor Paul says, "Don't go back" because he's afraid if Aaron is here without me, he might see another woman. You know how it is with Filipinos here in Korea—so many *couples* [extramarital affairs]. And who knows, he might start gambling again. When he was here by himself for two years, he gambled a lot because he was all alone. But when we started attending Jesus Church, he slowed down and stopped. Thank Lord. So I am thinking, okay, Pastor has a point. Maybe I will stay with him. It's difficult to be separated from your husband. I did it for two years, and I don't want to do it again.

For Becky, returning to the Philippines and leaving her husband alone seemed risky. She had to choose between going to her children or staying with her husband, because she could not see any job opportunities in the Philippines that could provide for their family. She said,

> If you don't have work experience, you can't get a job in the Philippines, even though you are professional. But here, if you are a hard worker, you are good. And we are here for a long time; we are used to the culture here, met good people, and we like it here. You go tell the president: give visa to the Filipinos because they love Korea.

Although Becky missed her hometown, especially during harsh winters, South Korea provided economic opportunities that helped her family move out of poverty, and a place where she and her husband formed a closer bond. Leaving South Korea altogether was not an easy choice for Becky. Her dream was to stay in the country long term and to settle there with her children. This dream contrasted with the reality of life in South Korea as an undocumented migrant under constant threat of immigration raids; Becky had little recourse to protect her own position in South Korea, let alone to bring her children over. When I asked what she would do if she were deported, she hesitated and said after a long pause, "Nothing really. Perhaps a little business, something like selling rice, and taking care of my children for a bit. But soon, probably I will apply to go abroad again, Spain or Canada, try something new." If South Korea did not work as a destination to reunite her family, Becky would not give up; instead, she would try her luck in other places. For Becky, the "home" she left behind in the Philippines became a place for a temporary return before seeking another opportunity abroad to support her family.

Becoming Migrant Factory Workers in South Korea

Becky's story of becoming a factory worker in South Korea after entering with a tourist visa was not unusual, especially prior to the reform of migrant labor policy in 2003–2004. Labor migration in South Korea began in the late 1980s as migrants from China, Southeast Asia, and South Asia came to South Korea to fill the demand for workers in the manufacturing sector.[11] Without a formal infrastructure for migrant labor, most migrants in this early phase entered the country with a tourist visa and overstayed. Recognizing the need to institutionalize the migrant flow in response to increasing demand, the South Korean state implemented the Industrial Trainee System (ITS) in 1994, under which migrant workers were treated as "trainees" and precluded from exercising the labor rights accorded to South Korean workers, such as minimum wage. Many workers who experienced repressive working conditions under ITS-assigned employers left their workplaces to work without legal authorization, contributing to a further increase of undocumented migrants, who constituted two-thirds of the total migrant workforce between 1994 and 2002.[12] Using the metaphor of "human slavery," migrant activists in South Korean civil society protested human rights abuses and demanded that the South Korean state acknowl-edge that migrant workers are "workers" with labor rights, not "trainees."

The call for reform from migrant activists led to a partial success in 2004 with the implementation of the Employment Permit System (EPS). The EPS provided migrant workers the same labor rights as South Korean citizens, such as workers' compensation, severance pay, and minimum wage—at least on paper. However, the EPS continued the policy of allow-ing migrants as part of a short-term-rotation workforce only, denying migrants any possibility of becoming long-term residents or naturalized citizens and preventing spouses or children from accompanying migrant workers. And it still bound migrant workers to a particular workplace—be it a factory, a farm, or a butcher shop—and constrained their freedom to change employers.[13] The transition from ITS to EPS also came with height-ened immigration raids against undocumented migrants, which brought increased fear into the everyday lives of migrant workers like Becky.

Under the new EPS, Joyce Basa came to South Korea with a three-year visa, contingent on her employment, that could be renewed for another two years. For Joyce, a single woman in her mid-thirties, migrant work was an opportunity to experience independence and new places. Prior to coming to South Korea, Joyce worked in Hong Kong as a domestic worker, and she fondly recalled the new food, friends, and "adventures" she experienced there.

For some migrant women like Joyce, the freedoms associated with living in a foreign land had strong appeal. When Joyce came back from a month-long vacation in the Philippines between labor contracts, I asked what she had done at home. She answered, "Nothing! It was so boring, and I just wanted to come back earlier!" Joyce elaborated:

> The problem back home when I return is, like this time, many relatives—even the ones you don't even know well—come and ask to borrow money from you. They think if you went abroad, then you are rich, and they come with all kinds of stories—like someone is sick, so and so needs to pay debt, and so on. It is so hard not to give. This time, I went and just laid low. I just stayed at home, cutting the coconut tree in the backyard. Noth-ing to do. I'd much rather stay here [in South Korea] and have my life.

Part of the reason Joyce felt such boredom at home was that so many peo-ple she cared about were out of the country on their own migrant path. As increasing numbers of Filipinos pursued their mobility overseas, their home communities in the Philippines became globally dispersed. During Joyce's most recent visit, the only close friends and family who remained in her hometown were her father, with whom she never got along, and an ex-girlfriend whom she had supported through college but now would much rather avoid. Her mother and good friends were all abroad as migrant domestic workers in East Asia and the Middle East. Joyce was still surrounded by relatives—who demanded money and favors—but she no longer felt at home in the Philippines.

Joyce's migrant life in South Korea was not dictated by personal sacrifices to send money back to the Philippines. She explained:

> Because the dollar [the exchange rate of the US dollar with Korean currency] is so high these days, the money I earn here is not that different from what I can make in the Philippines, if you consider the living expenses. If I work in the Philippines, like a call center agent or something, I can get similar money. But here I am more free.

In South Korea, Joyce had friends and co-workers to rely on for practical assistance and companionship. In her automotive accessory factory, she worked together with other EPS workers from the Philippines, but also with other Filipina women who came to South Korea with a spousal visa, as well as undocumented migrants from the Philippines and other Asian countries.

While working in her factory, Joyce joined the Migrants' Trade Union in South Korea. Joyce started attending the local union meetings and learned about migrant rights and labor laws. Even among the union members, Joyce's passion and high energy stood out, and other Filipino workers in another factory in the area brought her questions about workplace issues. She was proud of the nickname she earned: *abogado* (lawyer).

On one occasion, a co-worker approached Joyce for advice about sexual harassment after their factory manager invited her to his office in the late evening, made sexually suggestive comments, and tried to kiss her. Joyce and her co-workers organized a sit-in, and the manager finally apologized. With other union members and South Korean activists, Joyce created a brochure about sexual harassment that they distributed outside the local Catholic church during Tagalog mass. Although migrant factory work was sometimes tiring and frustrating, Joyce's life in South Korea gave her excitement and a sense of purpose beyond economic considerations. This was where she felt she belonged, much more so than her hometown in the

Philippines where she had little more to do than cut the coconut tree in her yard.

Even as the EPS recruited new migrant workers every year, migrants continued to enter South Korea for factory work without legal authorization, using the established network of migrant workers and wives in South Korea. Florence Ocampo, a Filipina woman in her late twenties, came to South Korea with a tourist visa to work in a furniture factory after being employed as a domestic worker and service worker in other countries in East Asia. Growing up, Florence spent little time with her mother, who, like Joyce's mother, had been a domestic worker in Saudi Arabia. She resented that her mother was not there when she graduated from high school or college, on her wedding day, or when she gave birth to her two children. Her mother took a vacation every few years and visited home, but over time, her parents grew apart and separated. What hurt Florence the most was the thought that she was doing the same thing to her two sons, whom she left behind in the Philippines under the care of her mother-in-law. She was glad that at least she and her husband were able to live together in Factorytown, unlike when she was alone in Taiwan as a domestic worker, but she missed her sons.

The hope of living together with her children propelled Florence not toward the Philippines but toward another migrant destination where permanent settlement and family unification were possible. She said, "Canada is great! The most important thing for me is that I can bring my children there. We can all live together as a family. I couldn't do that with my mother, and that's what I am doing now to my children—to be separated from them to support them. But in Canada, everything would be different!" In her free time from factory work, Florence regularly checked the website of the Canadian Immigration Bureau and asked other migrants about their pending applications for Canadian immigration. Florence was hesitant to tell her relatives in Factorytown about her dream, because she thought that "they'd laugh at it," considering it unrealistic. Florence was aware that she and her husband had limited social and financial capital to connect them to a job placement in Canada, pay for expensive certificate training, or settle a high placement fee. But she was not willing to give up.

Florence was not the only Filipina migrant in Factorytown with a dream of migrating to Canada, the United States, or Western Europe. For these women, South Korea was just a stepping-stone on that journey. Some resented their relatives in the United States and Canada who showed no intention of sponsoring their immigration or finding employers on their behalf. But Florence had a few "lucky" friends who migrated to Canada as live-in caregivers or restaurant workers, and this knowledge fueled her desire to do the same. Lhisa, an acquaintance of Florence's, left South Korea after only a year after finding a job as a domestic worker in Vancouver, Canada, through the Live-in Caregiver Program (LCP). Unfortunately for Florence and other Filipino migrants, later that year, the Canadian embassy in South Korea stopped accepting applications from undocumented migrants, instead urging them to return to their home countries to file for immigration. Florence waited to see if the policy would change back, but it did not seem likely. She needed to earn more money before she could return to the Philippines and pay the placement fee for a job in Canada, but she was determined to pursue her dream. For Florence, neither the Philippines nor South Korea offered a place where she and her husband could build a home and reunite their family.

More than seven years after I first met Florence in South Korea, she was still in Factorytown, hoping to eventually move to Canada. During that same time period, I finished my PhD, took a faculty job in Canada, and became a permanent resident. When I told her I was moving to Toronto, she asked me to find an employer willing to hire her through the LCP, which would make her eligible to apply for permanent residency. I asked my faculty colleagues with small children whether they might be interested, but received no positive answers. As a newcomer to Canada at the time, I was not yet aware of long-standing immigrant activism to reform or abolish the LCP or of critical scholarship on LCP, including geographer Geraldine Pratt's *Families Apart,* which argues that LCP requirements inflict the "trauma" of family separation and place migrant women in vulnerable conditions.[14] Yet despite all its limitations, many migrant women like Florence, who had worked under various migration regimes in East Asia and the Gulf states, viewed the LCP as a way out of the short-term migrant cycle and long periods of family separation. The LCP was an option that would require both high costs and luck, but these women dreamed that someday it would be theirs. Although not all migrants in South Korea planned to migrate elsewhere as Florence did, many aspired to find a country where they could settle without the insecurity of being undocumented or the constraint of labor contracts tying them to a particular employer or labor market sector. Thus it is important to recognize the global conditions that give rise to such aspirations, in addition to the institutional and legal barriers that make actualizing their dreams a rare occurrence.

Lupe: Running away from Ghosts

"You just don't feel safe there," murmured Lupe Enriquez, who went by the Korean name of Park Gahee. As a young woman in her hometown of Ilocos, Gahee was very afraid of walking alone, having heard many stories about street muggings at knifepoint. "Here in Korea," she asserted, "it's different. You can take a taxi at night, walk by yourself, and you don't feel fearful." Basic security could not be taken for granted back in the Philippines, she warned me, a point that was driven home by the tragic death of Gahee's best friend, Jhanine. Jhanine was a hospital nurse on a night shift. According to Gahee, a mutual friend with psychic powers called Jhanine to warn her that something bad might happen after a troubling dream. But Jhanine just laughed it off as superstition. Soon after, Jhanine disappeared on her routine walk home from work in the early hours of the morning. Her body was discovered a few days later; Jhanine had been sexually assaulted and murdered.

Jhanine's death was a breaking point for Gahee. She never again felt safe in her hometown, as if her friend's ghost were haunting her. She searched for a way to go abroad, and her first opportunity took her to Taiwan for three years as a migrant worker at an electronics factory, where she lived in a dormitory together with more than three hundred Filipina women. Although the work was hard, she preferred factory work to domestic work, which she viewed as demeaning, and she felt safer living with many others.

After her contract in Taiwan ended, Gahee sought a way to permanently leave the Philippines. Because she was not a professional who could qualify for a skilled worker visa, the only option she saw was marriage. Her older brother was an undocumented factory worker in South Korea, and he told her about the country's safety and prosperity. She started dreaming about marrying to migrate to Korea, but her brother refused to act as a match-maker, saying that Koreans were not warm or nice people and that living in South Korea would be a struggle. But Gahee ignored her brother and responded to a newspaper advertisement from the Unification Church, a religious organization based in South Korea that offered cross-border mar-riage matchmaking as a way to promote world peace. A very small number of South Korean men and Filipina women in my study who married via the Unification Church did so for religious reasons; the vast majority of the couples—including Gahee and her husband—used the Church solely as a matchmaker.

After meeting her husband once in the Philippines, Gahee married in 1997 and, after a year of waiting in the Philippines, came to South Korea and settled in Factorytown, where she had three sons. She entered South Korea with a spousal visa that needed annual renewal with the husband's sponsorship, but after the two-year residency requirement was fulfilled, she applied for South Korean citizenship and naturalized. Her husband worked in factories and gas stations; he often changed jobs or experienced bouts of unemployment. He stopped attending the Unification Church as soon as the marriage was finalized, but Gahee participated in the local church community of migrant women from the Philippines, Japan, and Mongolia and attended services quite regularly. Gahee also integrated into the Filipino ethnic community in Factorytown through friendships with her Filipino co-workers on the beaded jewelry assembly line where she worked before she gave birth to her first child. Her husband left all the housework and child rearing to Gahee—even when he was unemployed. She wanted him to "help out a bit more," but she felt lucky that at least she did not have to live with her parents-in-law and take care of them, as did some of her Filipina friends.[15] Although she was busy raising three children almost by herself, she still engaged in sporadic part-time employment, such as cooking Filipino food for delivery to Filipino migrant workers, selling international phone cards, and teaching English in a kindergarten. Neither Gahee nor her husband was very involved in the children's schooling; in South Korea, school interaction is considered the mother's job, but because of persistent racism, Gahee thought it would be better if the school didn't know her children's mother was a foreigner.

Gahee and her husband had a limited income, so she could not provide financial support to her natal family in the Philippines. Instead, she fulfilled her duty to her family by sponsoring her younger brother and niece to come to South Korea on a visitor visa, which they overstayed to work in the factories. Gahee had mixed feelings about South Korea, especially after her brother and later her niece were arrested in immigration raids and deported. "It was terrible to go see my brother in the detention center," said Gahee: "His face became almost half the size, because he couldn't eat the food there. They fed him worse than to a pig. Seeing him like that, I didn't know what to say. What did he do wrong, really?" South Koreans often treated Gahee with disrespect, even though she was a legal citizen. She complained, "Because we can't speak Korean well, Korean people think of us like ants. Down below. They step on you so easily. When I take a taxi, the driver says, 'Where to?' in *banmal* [an informal mode of speech]. I have fights with those Korean people so many times."

Gahee's membership in the Unification Church was another target for South Korean derision. Many South Koreans, especially Christians, perceived the Unification Church as a cult rather than as a legitimate religion. When her neighbors asked which church she attended, Gahee always answered frankly; some responded by trying to "teach" her how "sinful and dangerous" the cult was—talking down to her as an ignorant foreigner—and others by cutting off all communication. Gahee defended her church fiercely to these neighbors, but she also held her own resentments against the Unification Church. She felt that the South Korean church leaders respected Japanese women, who had sacrificed their nation's relative prosperity to migrate to South Korea for religious reasons, while looking down on Filipina and other women "from the poor countries," despite the Unification Church's rhetoric of equality among nations and peoples.

Even with her experiences of discrimination and exclusion, Gahee said that she never regretted leaving the Philippines. She remembered her life in the Philippines as one filled with insecurity and violence. It was a life she had consciously chosen to leave behind. Referring to the everyday indignities in South Korea, Gahee said, "It is just what it is. But what can you do when you don't feel safe to even walk outside after the sun goes down? How can I raise my children there [in the Philippines]? That's why, although I really wanted them to see where I come from, I've never returned."

When her marriage went through difficult times—often caused by her husband's suspicion that Gahee was seeing other men—she sometimes considered divorce, but even then, she did not imagine returning to the Philippines. Reflecting on her life, she said, "I think my choice, a choice to come to South Korea, was a great one. My husband has a temper and gets angry easily, and sometimes scary, but he is a warm-hearted guy, and responsible, and handsome! And I have my cute children here."

Becoming Migrant Wives in South Korea

Gahee was one of the migrant women who came to South Korea via cross-border marriages between rural and urban working-class South Korean men and women from China and Southeast Asia after meeting their husbands through kinship networks, the Unification Church, or commercial matchmaking agencies. These marriages had steadily increased since the early 1990s, when urban growth and women's employment produced a "bride deficit" for such men in South Korea.[16] Rather than treating the women like migrant factory workers, as temporary residents who were expected to return after their labor contracts expired, the South Korean state opened the door to permanent settlement and naturalization for these women,[17] who would become South Korean mothers, daughters-in-law, and wives.

Gahee's story of choosing cross-border marriage after years of migrant contract labor was common among migrant wives in South Korea, though there were also those for whom marriage was their first opportunity to go abroad. Sociologist Nicola Piper argues that cross-border marriages for women like Gahee stem from the desire to opt out of the labor migration circuit through a more secure legal status in the receiving country; and once married, migrant wives are not limited to domestic roles at home but participate in the labor market as well.[18] Thus, treating migrant women as either "wife or worker" does not capture the complexity of migrant experiences that are embedded in women's multiple social locations as wives, mothers, workers, and citizens.[19] In South Korea, especially in urban areas with a significant migrant population like Factorytown, migrant women who entered via marriages were an integral part of the migrant coethnic community along with migrant factory workers. Although fewer migrants came to South Korea through marriage than for work, the distinction between marriage migration and labor migration blurred as some migrant workers married South Koreans and as those who came through marriage worked side by side with other migrant workers in the factories.

Yet in 2006, with the initiation of multiculturalism policy, migrant wives—and their Korean husbands and children—were constituted as a distinct group in South Korea in need of policy intervention and social welfare provisions separate from migrant workers or nonmigrant South Koreans. The policy brought a flood of government, corporate, and civil society funding to immigrant integration projects for marriage-migrant women under the rubric of "multicultural families" (*damunhwa gajok*), a new term for families consisting of a South Korean spouse, a "foreign" spouse, and their children—technically a gender-neutral term, yet commonly referring to migrant wives and their Korean husbands. Under the multicultural policy, educational programs for migrant wives sprung up in various locales, teaching Korean language and cooking, and offering other job training. At the same time, multicultural education for the South Korean public also emerged, teaching South Koreans the value of the diverse cultures present in South Korea. Such programs did not eliminate deeply entrenched xenophobia overnight, but some migrant women reported positive changes since the introduction of multiculturalism policy.

Sung Nayun (the Korean name of Filipina Wilma Santiago) came to South Korea in 1998 to marry a South Korean man, a cook in a small neighborhood restaurant on the outskirts of Seoul. She decided to marry after spending a few years as a domestic worker in Southeast Asia, when she realized she was "becoming too old for marriage" and "too tired of going back and forth" for migrant work. When she first arrived in South Korea, as one of a few migrant women in town, she remembered being stared at on the bus and the streets. Unlike Hong Kong where she had worked before, she was struck by South Koreans' lack of familiarity with foreigners and how little English the South Koreans she met spoke on a daily basis, "even those who went to college." At the time, well before "the multicultural boom," there were no Korean language classes or immigrant integration programs, and she learned Korean through self-study, watching TV, and asking her neighbors for help. Nayun changed her first name to a Korean one and took her husband's last name. She had two sons and one daughter, naturalized, and acquired South Korean legal citizenship.

Like Nayun and Gahee, other migrant women who came before the multicultural shift talked about experiencing blatant hostility toward foreigners and strong pressure to assimilate into Korean culture based on a patriarchal conception of family in which women enter into the husband's family. Most migrant wives I met during my field research had changed their names to Korean ones, rarely spoke their native language with their children, and cooked the food they grew up with. Like Gahee, who wanted to hide her Filipina identity, many migrant women felt the pressure to hide and assimilate, so that their husbands and children would not feel "ashamed," or so that their children would not be discriminated against because of their migrant mothers. Their stories of imposed secrecy resonated with me because my grandmother, a Japanese woman who married a Korean man during the colonial period in the 1930s, hid her identity to avoid anti-Japanese sentiment after Korea's independence. She assimilated to the extent that even her children—my mother and uncle—discovered her ethnicity only in their late teens; I learned about it after she passed away, despite living with her for more than ten years.

Following the growth of multicultural initiatives, Nayun saw some differences in the attitudes of South Koreans. Although after several years in South Korea she had learned to speak Korean, Nayun was still uncomfortable with formal reading and writing, and she enrolled in a free Korean language class for migrant wives at Peace Center, a local migrant advocacy NGO. There she met migrant women from across Southeast and East Asia, as well as a Filipina woman from her hometown, with whom she became close friends. She was able to borrow Tagalog and English books from the Center's multicultural library. Unlike Gahee, who was afraid to reveal her Filipina identity, Nayun volunteered in her children's school as a "multicultural educator," visiting the classroom with a Filipino dress and flag to teach about Filipino culture. She told me that her son's homeroom teacher wrote a thank-you note after her presentation, stating that her visit prompted another student in the class to tell his classmates that his mother was from Vietnam.

The marginalization that migrant wives experienced in South Korea resulted from their race, legal status, or being "multicultural families," but it also intersected with social class. Although a majority of marriage-migrant women achieved secure legal status, including permanent residency and legal citizenship, working-class and rural families faced precarious economic conditions that posed challenges to everyday belonging. Nayun prided herself on being a good mother, and she was very critical of the South Korean educational system. She claimed:

> The schools in South Korea are not good, because you have to send kids to all these private institutes [cram schools] and after-school programs. I wanted to talk to somebody about this. The problem with the school is that because school ends at 2:00 p.m., kids go to these private institutes, and those are very expensive. What should those of us without money do? In the Philippines, kids go to school, come home for lunch, and the

teachers teach them until 5:00 p.m.—math, language, everything. I will write to the Ministry of Education about this.

Nayun's "problem with the school" was related to her status not just as a migrant woman but also as one of "those of us without money" in South Korea. Many migrant wives whose families belonged to rural and urban working classes faced similar problems. Her husband's small income as a cook meant that their finances were always tight, and Nayun worked in factories to bring in additional income. When her children were young and she could not leave them to work, she brought assembling work back home. They lived in a four-hundred-square-foot two-bedroom apartment, and all three children shared a room. Nayun and her husband's dream was to have their own business, a small restaurant that they could run together. But her husband had growing doubts about whether they could achieve their dream in South Korea and had started looking into immigration opportunities in Australia or New Zealand, where he had heard he could apply for immigration as a skilled worker. Nayun said, "He said that here in South Korea, people don't respect you if you don't have a college degree, but in the West, that is not true. Here, we have no future. But there, if you have skills, they respect you and you can earn a good amount of money." "Do you want to live there?" I asked. "Maybe," said Nayun, without much hesitation. "I don't mind. If we can have our own business and have a good living, it doesn't matter if it is a different country. Maybe that's better for our children."

Over the course of my research, I heard many Filipino migrants describe the Philippines in relation to South Korea as a place where hard work was not met with recognition, reward, and respect; Nayun's husband used these same terms to describe South Korea in comparison to the West. Other working-class South Koreans shared a similar sentiment. In particular, after the Asian financial crisis of the late 1990s, labor market opportunities for the working class deteriorated in South Korea, a phenomenon sociologist Yoonkyung Lee referred to as "the birth of the insecure class," comprising irregular workers and petty entrepreneurs.[20] South Korea's turn toward globalization in the 1990s increased cross-border mobility in a nation that already had a long emigrant history, so it was not unusual for South Koreans like Nayun's husband to look overseas for better opportunities. Some of these men used kinship networks to emigrate to Australia or the United States, while others used their migrant wives' networks in the Philippines,

Vietnam, or China to start an import business to South Korea or other businesses catering to South Koreans abroad. This type of emigration caused some Filipino migrants to joke, "South Koreans seem to like the Philippines so much, and we like it here—why don't we just switch our countries?" Although Nayun originally came to South Korea with a plan to settle permanently, she was now considering extending her transnational journey to an unknown destination because of the stunted opportunities for economic mobility in South Korea.

Cecille: The Second-Best Choice

Cecille de la Cruz entered South Korea with an entertainer visa on a one-year contract with a South Korean promotion agency and was assigned to work as a hostess in a club in Basetown. Before her eleven-year-old son was born, Cecille had spent three years working at hostess bars in different cities in Japan on six-month contracts. She remembered her days in Japan fondly; one club *mama-san* (manager) was particularly nice, allowing the hostesses plenty of freedom and taking them sightseeing on their days off. Cecille's migrant work in Japan provided a safety net for her family and her son. She proudly told me,

> When I worked in Japan, my salary was two, three times higher than now, and I saved up and bought land and a small house in Manila. My big brother is living on the first floor, my sister used to live on the second floor but now we are renting it out, and on the third floor, I lived with my parents and my son.

While working in Japan in her twenties, Cecille met a Filipino factory worker and fell in love. When she became pregnant, she returned to the Philippines to give birth to her son, but she and the baby's father separated soon after. He sent money from time to time, but he stopped after he married another woman and had other children. Cecille had a few part-time jobs in the Philippines selling perfume and makeup, but the income was "nothing" compared to her earnings in Japan and not enough to support her family and her son. Her mother encouraged her to go abroad again. But when she tried, she was given the disappointing news that she could no longer take her pick of where to go and would have to accept "the second best": "The agency said if you are over thirty, you are too old; Japanese clubs would not take you. But they can send me to Korea instead."

During the eight months she worked in clubs in South Korea, Cecille was disappointed that she could not save as much money as in Japan. She was sorry that unlike in Japan where she was able to tour the local tourist sites, such as Japanese castles, she hardly set foot outside of the club district where she lived and worked in a dilapidated camptown, away from the metropolis of Seoul. She worked as hard as she could, flirting with American GI customers at the club until 2:00 a.m., texting them sweet messages, and even listening to them on the phone until 6:00 a.m., but her drink sales and tips weren't as high as she would have liked. Although her club did not have the "bar fine" system, whereby customers pay the club owner to take the hostesses out for the night, Cecille thought the customers still hoped to have sexual relations when they met her outside of the club during the day. She said sullenly, "I have no customer now because I don't sleep with them. They would buy me a drink a couple of times and expect you to go out with them. They are all the same. They want the same thing." But having sex with customers was something she was morally opposed to, and she wasn't about to change that, despite the financial disadvantages.

As the end of her one-year contract approached, Cecille started to think about what she would do after she left the club. Many of her co-workers planned to find an American GI boyfriend and emigrate to the United States, and two Filipina women in her club had already received marriage proposals from their regular customers/boyfriends.[21] But Cecille was not interested in marriage. Like other hostesses, she had a "special friend," an older American GI who came every evening to buy her drinks, and they certainly had feelings for each other, but he was a married man with two daughters. "If only he was a single man!" she said before letting out a deep sigh. "But that's how life is. You know, I was married once. I don't want to do it again just to get married, or to go to the US. I don't know what is the right thing to do. If I run away, it wouldn't be for marriage but to work, maybe in a factory."

Cecille's family members back in the Philippines made it clear that they wanted her to stay abroad to send remittances. She said, "This morning, my mom said, 'Stay there as long as you can. Go TNT [undocumented] if you have to.' She was like, 'If they don't extend the contract and if you come home, how are we going to live?' My son says the same thing. He said, 'Don't come home, Mom. I think it is better that you stay.'"

It made practical sense that she should stay as her mother and son suggested, but their words hurt Cecille. Their phone conversation drove home the reality that a life together with her mother, son, and siblings in the Philippines was not possible, and that she would continue to be separated from them unless she took drastic measures. She was tired of the insecurity that accompanied short-term contracts or undocumented status, of not knowing when she would return home, and of supporting her family only from afar. Her precarious position caused her to consider marriage as a way out: "If I marry an American and emigrate to the US," said Cecille, "then all this would be over. My son can come live with me there." Other times, she considered following her cousin, an elder-care worker in southern Europe who had secured stable immigration status. The feeling of uncertainty regarding her final destination was sometimes overwhelming, but Cecille was trying her best to take care of herself and save up as much as she could in South Korea.

Migrant Hostesses in Camptown Clubs

US military camptowns where Cecille and other Filipina women worked as club hostesses have been present in South Korea for more than sixty years, since the end of World War II. American military bases like the one in Basetown are a signifier of US power across the globe, and they are especially concentrated in the Asia-Pacific region.[22] American GIs entered South Korea at the height of the Cold War as a front line against the Communist bloc in the 1950s, the period during which South Korea experienced severe postwar poverty. The recent advancement of the South Korean economy is often understood as a product of the growth of the export-oriented manufacturing industry, but the service economies surrounding American military camptowns, including South Korean women offering sexual services to American soldiers, have also played an important role in the development of postwar South Korea since the 1950s.[23] The South Korean state, especially under the authoritarian regimes of the 1960s and 1970s, supported and regulated camptown sexual commerce as a source of foreign currency for the national economy, despite the antiprostitution law.[24] The camptowns have long been what Aihwa Ong would call "zones of exceptions."[25]

In the 1980s, when the South Korean economy began to globalize and to grow, the American military bases ceased to provide a lucrative source of income, and the camptown club industry experienced a labor shortage of

Korean women in the mid-1990s. Today, the clubs are filled with migrant women predominantly from the Philippines, with a small minority from the former Soviet Union.[26] Since 1996, the entertainer visa has been used to bring migrant hostesses into the country on six- to twelve-month contracts. In 2004, South Korean feminist organizations successfully utilized US-led international antitrafficking directives to reform the antiprostitution law such that women engaged in sexual commerce, who were previously considered criminals, were redefined as victims eligible for state protections under the new law.[27] Yet these protections were rarely enacted in camptowns.

As the number of migrant workers in South Korea increased in the 1990s, some camptown clubs expanded their clientele to include migrant workers from Southeast and South Asia, such as Bangladesh, Pakistan, and the Philippines, while others remained exclusively for GIs. Due to frequent fights among migrant workers and American GIs, clubs that served both groups would often temporarily segregate their clientele according to the curfew of the military camp. As one Filipina hostess explained, "Until 12:00 a.m., it is GI time, and afterwards, it's Asian time." Despite persistent hierarchies among American GIs and Asian migrant workers, these two groups of men were similarly contained as migrant labor in a space segregated from South Koreans.[28]

Ms. Han, the owner of the club where Cecille worked, was strongly opposed to allowing migrant workers into her club. She perceived "third world people" as scary—a particularly racialized and class-based distinction, considering that she welcomed American GIs of all races. Hostesses made similar distinctions based on personal experience. Linda Querobin, who had a few American GI boyfriends when she worked at the club, recalled her experience:

> GIs are good. Yeah, there are players and all, but some are very kind, and they understand it when you are out on a bar fine and you don't want to have sex. If you say you are just there because *mommy* [the club owner] forced you, but you would like to get to know each other first, they get that. They feel sorry for us and take you out to dinner, go club-hopping, and take you to a hotel and let you rest. But Pakistanis and Koreans![29] They are only into getting into your pants, and get really upset when you say no. They are like, "I paid all this money, what are you going to do to make up for it?"

Like Linda, many Filipina hostesses preferred having American GIs as regular customers or boyfriends. GIs had higher average incomes than migrant factory workers and visited the clubs more often (due to their curfew on the military bases, they could not travel far and often stayed locally). In addition, dating these men provided potential opportunities for marriage and migration to the United States. But even women who did not want to marry preferred American GIs because these men were more likely to "feel sorry" for the women and were therefore "easier to work with."

For Ramona Abundo, a twenty-three-year-old Filipina woman who had never left the Philippines before coming to South Korea, the Base-town club offered a way to emigrate to the United States, which would mean the end of the migratory cycle of temporary contract labor. Almost as soon as she started working in her club, she met a young American GI, Steven, who fell in love with her and visited her club almost every day. He came in the early evening and stayed until the club closed so that she would not have to sit with any other customers. Staying in the club was expensive; sitting with a hostess for even fifteen to twenty minutes required a $10 drink. One day, Steven proposed to Ramona, and they were excited to get married after her contract ended. But Ramona began to worry whether Steven would change his mind like the many American boyfriends of fellow hostesses who just stopped coming one day. As she put it, "It's not that I doubt him. Nothing like that. But he is young, and people say you never know about Americans. They are not like us; once they change their mind, that's just it."

Ramona did not want to tell Steven that she was unsure of his commitment and instead lied to him, saying that the club owner was forcing her to go out with other customers on bar fines. Steven was furious and wanted to fight the club owner, but Ramona managed to calm him down and told him she just wants to leave quietly. Yet leaving her assigned employment would void her work visa. Ramona would be undocumented and would even be deported if she were unlucky enough to be caught in an immigration raid. Steven suggested they should get married right away, so that Ramona would have a spousal visa in South Korea as a dependent of the American military. After a few days, Ramona left the club, married Steven, and moved into a rented apartment in Basetown. Because Steven and Ramona were both in their twenties and had not been previously married, the paperwork for a marriage license was not complicated; some other Filipina–American GI couples had to go through lengthy and expensive processes of divorce and annulment before they could marry.

After leaving the club, migrant hostesses like Ramona continued to per-form intimate labor. Ramona cooked, cleaned, served food, washed laun-dry, and cared for Steven, who paid the rent and provided living expenses. When Ramona became pregnant, and she told him she needed to work to send money to her family in the Philippines, he told her that he wanted her to stay home during her pregnancy, and committed to sending her fam-ily $200–$300 every month. When I met with them several months later, they were leaving soon to return to the United States, where Steven would be stationed at a military base. Ramona was one of a few Filipina women who made it to the United States. Others were not lucky enough to meet "the one" during their contract or were abandoned by their fiancés and husbands before leaving South Korea.[30]

For migrant hostesses like Ramona and Cecille—as well as migrant wives like Gahee and Nayun who married South Korean men—cross-border marriage was one of a few limited pathways to mobility and secu-rity, away from livelihood struggles in the Philippines and the seemingly never-ending cycle of short-term labor migration in Asia. However, instead of permanent settlement, marriage sometimes meant that migrant women found themselves on the move again. Women who married American GIs were bound to their husband's military contract, which might take them to new overseas deployments in Germany, Okinawa, or other parts of the world. Their uncertain futures reflect the challenges migrant women face as they seek a place to call home in a global world where stability is a rare commodity.

LOYDA, GLOBAL WOMAN STILL ON THE ROAD

Five years after Loyda first described her global journey across Asia to me, she posted a stock photo and quote on Facebook. The photo depicted a young white woman and a three-year-old girl with curly blond hair. They were walking down the street under autumn foliage, holding hands, wear-ing matching white casual dresses and smiling. The quote underneath read: "I don't want my children to follow my footsteps. I want them to take the path next to me and go further than I could have ever dreamt possible."

Looking at this Facebook post brought back my memories of the many pho-tos of Loyda's three children that hung in picture frames on the walls of her shipping container apartment in Factorytown. I am not sure what she saw in the photo of the white woman and girl holding hands, whose reality appeared to me as utterly distinct from that of the twenty-eight-hundred-kilometer separation between Loyda in South Korea and her daughter in the Philippines. But perhaps this separation was the best way that she could build a home for herself and her children, so that they could travel further, and perhaps this was why she was still on her own road, not knowing when she would return.

This chapter followed Filipina migrant women's journey in their transnational pursuit of mobility and security. Filipina women like Becky, Gahee, and Cecille began their migrant journeys for different reasons—to escape poverty, to find a safe place, and to enjoy personal freedom. Many women described the Philippines in terms of a lack of job opportunities, limited personal security, and interpersonal conflicts with families. Because of a global demand for Filipino migrant labor, few migrants in South Korea could return to hometowns filled with relatives and friends. Instead, it was common to hear about sisters, brothers, cousins, and close friends in South Korea, other parts of East Asia and the Middle East, or North America and Europe. For some, their own migrant journeys were part of a cycle that began when their parents or older siblings traveled to work abroad; others facilitated labor migration for their family members by paying their placement fees. While some Filipina migrants like Becky expressed the pain of family separation, for others like Joyce, being overseas provided a space for self-transformation and for exploring different kinds of intimacy and kinship. Whether they sought prosperity, safety, or freedom, these Filipina migrants came to South Korea on their migrant journeys from elsewhere in Asia and built their lives in the face of legal exclusion and discrimination.

As the Philippine state engaged in the "labor brokerage" of its citizens for migrant labor export,[31] these women left the Philippines to labor in various factories, hostess clubs, and private homes throughout Southeast and East Asia and the Middle East as contract migrant workers and wives. Some carved out a space in South Korea against a restrictive immigration policy, while others aspired to continue their transnational journey, planning their next step to an often unknown destination in the United States, Canada, or Europe, where they hoped to achieve socioeconomic mobility, permanent residency, and family unification. Through the narratives of Filipina migrant women, this chapter situates their seemingly never-ending journey within a transnational landscape in which working-class women's mobility is encouraged, but security and citizenship are held just out of reach.

THREE

Duties, Desires, and Dignity

South Koreans on Migrant Encounters

Without even a knock, a gray-haired man in a suit entered the classroom. He was a stranger to the beginner-level Korean language class I observed at Peace Center, a South Korean migrant advocacy NGO that offered educational programs for women who immigrated to South Korea via cross-border marriages. Pastor Kim Wonsik, the director of Peace Center, followed directly behind the stranger, commenting, "Here are our students. See, everyone is working hard from early in the morning, women from all over the world—China, the Philippines, Vietnam, even Mongolia." Pastor Kim turned to the migrant women, "Okay, everyone. Let's say our greetings and welcome our guest." Each woman greeted the gray-haired man in Korean, but he responded with only a curt nod before leaving the classroom with Pastor Kim. Class continued as usual until lunch, when a staff member of Peace Center informed teacher Hong Youngjoo that the man in the suit was a wealthy donor. Sitting at the lunch table with other teachers, Youngjoo exploded with anger: "They think they can walk in like that, just because they give the center money? They should have respect for our students and us! They know nothing about these women, and they think it's okay to barge in! I am so frustrated [*dapdaphaesô*], I'm going crazy." Nam

Sojeong, a younger woman volunteer, chimed in: "I know. I wish Pastor Kim could be just a bit more sensitive. We don't come here for that."

Youngjoo and Sojeong were among thousands of predominantly middle-class South Korean women who buttressed immigrant integration programs for migrant women across rural towns and industrial cities in South Korea, often as unpaid volunteers. The dramatic increase of cross-border marriages between Chinese and Southeast Asian women and South Korean rural and working-class men in the 1990s, the state-driven "multicultural boom" in 2006,[1] and a surge in state and corporate funding led various government and nongovernmental organizations to offer educational programs for migrant women. Through lessons in Korean language, culture, and cooking, these programs were designed to assimilate migrant women to a South Korean way of life.

This chapter tells the stories of South Korean actors like Pastor Kim, Youngjoo, and Sojeong who were involved in migrant advocacy and integration projects and who interacted with migrants on a daily basis, as a means of asking what migrant encounter means for everyday South Koreans. Scholars show that these local actors in the host society play a significant role in shaping migrant rights and citizenship through their advocacy work and service provision for migrants.[2] Yet rather than focus on their work for migrants, this chapter pays attention to the gender- and generation-specific motivations that propel diverse groups of South Koreans to come together at the site of migrant encounter. Building on Bonnie Honig's insight that encounters with "the foreigner" solved America's problems in the realm of symbolic politics,[3] I show how migrant encounters—not just as discursive symbols but as embodied experiences and sites of labor—"solved" distinctive problems for various groups of South Koreans and shaped their own citizenship projects.

These South Korean women and men occupied diverse roles as directors of multicultural education centers, volunteers, social workers, and migrant worker activists.[4] These individuals assigned heterogeneous meanings to their work with migrants, which they used to pursue their personal aspirations and their aspirations for the South Korean nation. Their narratives provide a glimpse into the social lives of South Koreans who came into direct contact with migrants through their gendered labor to delve into shifting meanings of citizenship and belonging in a globalizing South Korea.

I lay out South Koreans' multiple narratives based on the intersection of gender and generation. Members of the older generation of South Koreans who came of age in the 1960s through the 1980s were driven to the project of migrant advocacy and integration by a sense of duty. This duty varied by gender, as men took on the role of national protectors and women took on the role of mothers of the nation. For the younger generation who came of age after 1990 under parliamentary democracy and globalization, their vision of global cosmopolitanism and their search for a new sociability motivated them to work with migrants as peers in the pursuit of global mobility. Although gender differences among this group were less salient than for the earlier generation, women in particular tended to envision migrants as a bridge to "overseas" as an imagined space of personal freedom. These distinct motives brought men and women of different generations into the same spaces, united by their shared belief in the value of human dignity that transcended national borders or origins.

DRIVEN BY DUTY TO THE NATION: MEN OF THE DEVELOPMENTAL GENERATION

"A grave social problem."

"Crisis of the nation."

"We need to do something now."

When I asked South Korean men from the "developmental generation" to describe the state of South Korea in relation to its growing migrant population, they responded with a sense of urgency. These men came of age through their participation in movements for national development under the authoritarian regimes of the 1960s to 1980s. Their urgency was not rooted in anti-immigrant protectionism—quite the opposite. What they perceived as "a grave social problem" was not the presence of migrants per se but rather South Korea's incompetency in accommodating those migrants. In their view, South Korea was failing miserably to protect migrant workers' basic rights, to integrate migrants into neighborhoods, and to teach the children of migrants how to live in South Korea. They believed that these failures would lead to a "crisis" in the near future, and that it fell to them to prevent this crisis.

These men took diverse life paths to their positions as key actors in migrant advocacy movements, migrant integration programs, and religious missions for migrants. Almost all of these men were leaders of their own organizations, including a state-funded center for multicultural families, a migrant church, and a migrant advocacy organization. The events that led them to their current posts differed significantly: some participated in pro-democracy struggles against authoritarian regimes in the 1970s and 1980s as student or labor activists, others were members of the clergy serving the socially marginalized, and yet others had professional social work training and work experiences. Despite their diverse journeys, these men were united by their shared concern for the nation and their belief that they should intervene on behalf of the Korean nation through their hard work.

At fifty-two years of age, Do Hansuk was a director of a migrant advocacy center that also offered educational programs promoting multicultural dialogue between migrants and South Koreans. Hansuk was driven to this work by the rapid shifts he experienced in South Korea coming of age in the 1970s and by his decades-long involvement in the student and labor movements. He recalled growing up in a rural village in the developmental era of the 1960s:

> When I was little, until I went to high school, our society shared poverty [ganan] together in a similar way. Because it was all shared, I don't think we had much of a sense of deprivation due to poverty in our society. Instead of thinking of someone as lower class [hacheungmin], we thought of them as all common people, fellow nationals [kukmin].

At that time, consumer goods that visibly marked social class were limited. Hansuk's father was a schoolteacher, and his family was one of the first few in his village to own a TV at home. Until the 1960s, Hansuk did not feel as though being "poor" or "lower class" in his small town hindered one's sense of membership in the nation.

However, after entering an elite university in Seoul away from his rural hometown in the early 1970s, Hansuk joined a student movement and realized that the logic of national membership was shifting. Where previously someone who was poor was considered "a fellow national," poor people were now marginalized and subjected to exploitation under the military dictatorship. Hansuk joined the student-worker alliance in the 1970s as part of the emerging people's (minjung) movement, and like many other student activists at the time,[5] he dropped out of the university to become a factory worker and a union organizer at the age of twenty-one. Hansuk was involved with labor activism for more than two decades before he turned to migrant advocacy and integration, working with migrant factory workers and migrant wives.

Hansuk's previous work as a labor activist and his current work as the head of a migrant advocacy organization were both based on an acute sense of a social responsibility. He held a particular understanding of modern Korean historiography and the special role of "the socially underprivileged" (*sahoejôk yakja*) to bring about social transformation:

> At the time of my student activism, it was the workers who mattered. So when there was the movement into the "people" [*minjung*] from the late 1970s and early 1980s, it was about the working class. Before that, in the 1960s and 70s, it was about the farmers. Now in the contemporary society, it's about irregular workers and migrants. So when I started this work, I thought, now I have to stand with migrants. Not just to provide support for them, not just to support the socially underprivileged, but because I believed this would be a big impetus for the development of our society.

Hansuk emphasized the importance of migrants to national "development" and "progress." Migrants bring "fresh perspective and values" to ethnically homogeneous South Korea, helping cultivate multicultural sensibilities.

Pastor Choi Youngsik was a man in his sixties and one of the key leaders in the migrant advocacy movement. Pastor Choi echoed Hansuk's sentiments, claiming that his work for migrant workers was "for the benefit of our country." Like Hansuk's, Pastor Choi's migrant advocacy grew out of his previous activism for workers and the poor. He had been involved in the pro-democracy *minjung* movement since the 1970s, resulting in his imprisonment under the military regime. He was proud of the migrant advocacy movement's achievements in improving the working conditions of migrant workers. He believed that migrant workers enjoyed relatively "good conditions" in contemporary South Korea, especially in comparison to other migration destinations in Asia, such as Saudi Arabia, which he believed was "ten times worse than South Korea." In fact, for Pastor Choi, migrant workers symbolized the promise of upward mobility through hard work, a promise that was diminishing for South Korean workers. As he put it: "They [migrant workers] earn a lot of money! When they work today, they buy a house in their home countries! Frankly, for South Koreans, if they work today, it's hard to get even one room, let alone a house."

But the movement's achievements did not mean that his migrant advocacy work was finished:

> People ask me, "Pastor, if that's the case, why do you keep fighting for migrant workers' human rights?" I tell them, "When they discriminate against migrant workers and disabled people, would they discriminate against South Korean workers?" The answer is, "Yes, absolutely." When we have the three basic labor rights for migrant workers, the same is true for South Korean workers. When the most vulnerable group in South Korea is doing well, then everyone else is doing well. So I work for the South Korean people, not for foreigners, because when our society becomes one that does not discriminate against others, we will stop discriminating against South Koreans. That's why I am involved in the movement for migrants.

Both Pastor Choi and Hansuk drew on a developmental narrative in which the struggles of "the most vulnerable group" would bring about change in the society as a whole. At the heart of their work for migrants was the drive to transform the vertical relationship between the individual citizen and the nation-state to become more equitable and just. They believed that it was their duty to South Korea to advocate for migrants, just as it had been their duty to fight for workers and the poor when they were younger, despite their own status as university students, a marker of upward mobility and middle-class status at the time. Their work on behalf of migrants was driven by a sense of duty to protect South Korea as a nation and as a society, rather than to advocate for any particular group; as Pastor Choi put it, "I work for the South Korean people, not for foreigners."

Pastor Choi's hesitancy to claim that his migrant advocacy work was designed to benefit migrants as opposed to the nation as a whole was related to his perception of migration. Like many other South Korean men and women in his generation, Pastor Choi understood migration as displacement driven by economic need. He was skeptical as to whether migration was beneficial for migrants or for their families in the sending countries. He argued,

> From the perspective of migrant workers, a long-term stay in South Korea might bring them more money, but it doesn't bring a happy life. There was a TV program *Asia Asia* that invited families of migrants to come to South Korea for a visit. There was a woman from Mongolia, and her children visited her. Because it had been a long time since she met her children, she

really wanted to go home afterwards. So she called her husband and asked, "What should I do?" The husband simply said, "Do whatever you want"; they were a married couple, separated for seven to eight years at that time. What does that mean? Basically, he was saying she should keep making money. Twenty people in the in-laws and twenty people in her natal family live off her income—that's supporting forty people while the husband is staying at home. That is not a happy life.

Pastor Choi believed that migration was a desperate choice forced on people in the global South by global capitalism combined with the failures of migrant-sending nation-states. Pastor Choi's seeming anti-migration stance can be understood in relation to his generation's experiences with migration. When the developmental generation came of age, cross-border mobility was highly regulated under the authoritarian regime; the few South Koreans who migrated were deployed to earn foreign currency for national economic development as miners and nurses in Germany, construction workers in Saudi Arabia, and soldiers fighting in the Vietnam War. Pastor Choi, like many other men in his generation, perceived these forms of migrant labor as exploitative. Grounded in this understanding of migration as exploitation, he argued that global civil society had a duty to ensure the livelihood of people in the global South so that they would not have to migrate abroad:

> We can't do much about people who already came, but we should prevent more people from coming. . . . So far, we have tried various "happy return" programs like computer education and auto-mechanic training, but they all failed because the skills that migrants learn in South Korea are not useful in their home countries. Because of the lack of social infrastructure, they end up coming back to South Korea. If they can't come back here, they go to Japan or somewhere else. We call this the vicious cycle of migration. . . . So we argue that migrant workers should not come to South Korea, but instead we should engage in fair trade programs.

In addition to stopping the "vicious cycle of migration," South Korean men of the developmental generation believed that South Korea needed their help to deal with the migrant population already present in the country. They spoke at length about myriad social problems related to a lack of migrant integration. They perceived Western countries as cautionary examples of what the future might hold if South Korea did not improve its social provisions for migrants. In particular, they pointed to the temporary guest-worker program that led to "a separate Germany within Germany," to the recent conflicts in immigrant suburbs in France, and to Latino immigrants' lack of integration in the United States. In their imagination, the West exemplified a failure to integrate migrants, as evidenced by political unrest, racism, and hostility against immigrants, and they felt a duty to prevent a similar failure in South Korea.

Hansuk described South Korea as facing a critical moment of "crisis" (*gobi*). He elaborated on the dangers of segregation:

> For the next five years, we can't rule out the possibility that migrants will become a group, with the formation of slums, that they will become a group that is completely separated from South Korean society. Some harbingers are already here. Like Wongokdong in Ansan, which is almost 90 percent migrants, and the Chinatown with people who are not just from China but other countries, and Hwaseong also.

With a sense of urgency, Hansuk worried that without proper integration efforts and cross-cultural dialogue, slums housing a migrant underclass would develop, and anti-immigrant violence would increase.

Likewise, Suh Bongho, the fifty-six-year-old director of a center offering immigrant integration programs for marriage-migrant women, was worried about South Koreans' exclusionary attitudes, which could lead to segregation. Bongho did not share a background in the people's movement with Hansuk and Pastor Choi; instead, he had been a public servant and a businessman before taking charge of the multicultural center. But Bongho shared their rhetoric that approached migration as a serious social problem for South Korea. Speaking about the children of migrant mothers and everyday exclusions, he said,

> They [migrants] might end up becoming like the most problematic case in the US, Hispanics, who do not have a place to belong. We are witnessing it right now, but the government does not seem to feel the graveness of it, and just talks about budget issues. . . . If these people cannot be integrated, we as a whole will be destroyed. So if we are to lift them up together, we have to start with ourselves, open up and embrace them. Many say that they are embracing migrants but never do what they say. For example, when children play with a kid from a "multicultural family" without knowing, but when the word spreads, parents say to their children, "Don't play with that kid."

Pastor Bong Kyungsoo, a missionary in his fifties who offered assistance to migrant workers from China, expressed his concern that the mistreatment of migrant workers could lead to a serious problem for South Koreans. Motivated by an evangelical mission to spread the gospel overseas, he started working with migrants through a small church he opened for Chinese workers in South Korea, and later became involved with migrant advocacy in the surrounding area regardless of religion. He was particularly worried about the possible consequences for South Koreans of rising anti-Korean sentiment in migrant-sending countries. He recounted a story that he said was circulating among migrant advocates:

> This story is a bit old, but migrant workers from the Philippines were treated not like human beings before. Not all South Koreans were like that, but many swore at them and talked down to them. And Filipinos tend to be smaller than Koreans, so they were beaten. . . . So when these Filipino workers returned home after several years of abuse, they became so angry. At the airport in the Philippines, they recognized South Koreans and beat them up. The story goes, when the Filipino police came and arrested them, they told the police about what they had gone through in South Korea, and the police became angry too and beat Koreans up together. I think it's a totally plausible story in Southeast Asia. When there is such a strong anti-Korean sentiment, there's nothing you can do about it. Episodes like this can easily happen.

Pastor Bong believed that it was imperative for South Korea's government and its citizens to recognize the seriousness of the problem of migrant integration. He found it ironic that the South Korean government spent money to promote a positive image of South Korea overseas through advertising campaigns, while citizens' treatment of migrant workers actively harmed the country's image. He argued, "It's all useless to have that kind of positive image-making about Korea overseas. Instead, we should treat the people who come here better. I am not saying we should do something amazing— just treat them like human beings. It would be extremely effective to improve the national image."

These South Korean men emphasized their work to improve the treatment of migrants as driven by a sense of duty and social responsibility and as a personal sacrifice for the common good. Hansuk described his involvement in social movements:

I jokingly say I will start living my life after ten years. If I count the years of my life that I have dedicated, that's thirty years since the student movement days, so just ten more years. After forty years when I become over sixty, I would like to live my own life. But I don't know. Now this issue of migration is a "project" for our society. When I see migrant children and migrant workers who are segregated from our society and our culture, and marriage migrants who lack rights and equality within the family, I don't know whether I can leave it all. What I really want to do is to go back to nature [laughs]. I really like gardening and things like that, so whenever I travel, I visit botanical gardens and forests, but I don't know whether I'd be able to do that. I really wish that by that time, there would be diverse channels to work with migrants, so that I can do that.

Hansuk's sense of self-sacrifice and duty to society was also evident in his response to the tragic *Sewol* ferry disaster that took place only a few months before our interview in 2014. During the ferry disaster, the captain and crew members deserted the sinking ship, leaving many passengers behind to die. This event left a lasting scar not only on the families of the victims but also on many South Koreans as a symbol of the country's hopelessness. After the disaster, some South Koreans considered permanent emigration to another country. Hansuk poignantly said,

> This morning, I just read a newspaper column that said, "We do not deserve to talk about immigrating overseas," and it really resonated with me. . . . The author was writing about the *Sewol* ferry disaster, asking us: "Are you not guilty? You are also a crew member. You can't evacuate the ship of South Korea." And it made sense to me. Yes, we have that responsibility, those of us who are in our fifties and above. When you are fifty, you don't get to blame the older generation.

Drawing a contrast to the captain and crew of the *Sewol* ferry, Hansuk asserted the duty of the older generation not to abandon the ship of South Korea as it struggled to integrate new migrants. Even if it meant putting his personal goals on hold, Hansuk planned to work with migrants for the betterment of the nation as a whole, which he considered his duty as a citizen of South Korea.

CARING FOR THE NATION, CARING FOR THE
SELF: WOMEN OF THE DEVELOPMENTAL
GENERATION

The South Korean women who came of age during the developmental era
had a different understanding of the history of modern South Korea. Men
narrated the developmental era as a period of economic development involv-
ing class struggle and labor exploitation under the military regime, without
reference to gender. In contrast, the women of the developmental generation expressed the acute sense that gender shaped their everyday lives. In
contrast to the masculine version of modern Korean historiography, which
tracked shifts in marginalized groups from farmers to workers to migrants,
women provided clear narratives of marginalization based on gender.
Women in this era experienced discrimination and limited life chances and
trajectories. Kwon Inhye, a fifty-four-year-old volunteer who taught Korean
language for marriage-migrant women, explained her generation's experiences: "Our generation is a pitiful [*bulssanghan*] generation. . . . Certainly
among those who are now in their sixties, but even among us [in our fif-
ties], many gave up our lives for our brothers. There are so many around
me, and the generation above me, who went straight to factories [instead of
pursuing education]."

As members of "a pitiful generation" who made gender-based sacrifices,
the South Korean women who worked with migrants occupied different
positions than men and were accorded a different status. The leadership
of migrant advocacy NGOs, multicultural family centers, and migrant
churches were disproportionately male, but the rank-and-file staff members
and volunteers of these same organizations were predominantly women.
This was especially true of organizations or departments that worked specifically with migrant women; nearly every Korean language teacher and
counselor to migrant wives and migrant hostesses was a woman.

These South Korean women, who played diverse roles as rank-and-
file staff members, volunteers, and counselors for migrants, had dis-
tinctly gendered life trajectories. Coming of age in the social milieu of the
1960s–1980s, they reported that daughters in the family were expected to
give up their ambitions for higher education to support their brothers, and
many started working in female-dominated occupations as factory workers
or secretaries right after graduation from high school, if not earlier. While

a small number of the women said their own families did not discriminate between sons and daughters when it came to education, these women noted that their families were "unusual." Na Myounghwa was a forty-eight-year-old with a typical story. When she was young, she dreamed of becoming a writer and wanted to study literature in the university, but she faced economic and gendered constraints. She recalled,

> I am the third among eight siblings, so I have many younger brothers and sisters. So when I told my parents that I'd like to go to the university, they simply asked, "How many younger siblings do you have?" I cried and cried, so they let me go to a local [two-year] technical college instead, for transportation and industry, something like that. It was not a good fit for me at all, but I thought it was the only choice. . . . It was very tough.

Bitter about her unfulfilled dreams, Myounghwa watched her family support her brothers' higher education. But like many other South Korean women of the developmental generation whom I met through this study, Myounghwa pursued education later in life. Myounghwa ultimately earned a university diploma in literature through the distance-learning program at Open University (*bangsong tongsin daehak*) more than fifteen years after graduating high school.

These women's life trajectories resonated with the script of gendered labor and citizenship under the intensive drive for economic development in postwar South Korea. During Park Jung-Hee's authoritarian regime (1961–1979), the middle class was constructed as the model of national subjects,[6] and, in particular, middle-class housewives were glorified for their supportive roles as mothers and wives. All South Koreans were asked to contribute to the building of the South Korean nation, men as soldiers and workers and women as temporary workers before marriage and then as household managers and reproducers of the nation as mothers.[7] Most of the women in my study, including those with a university education, followed this gendered script and quit their jobs upon marriage, relocating to a different city away from their natal family to follow their husbands' job or their families-in-law. Many reported experiencing depression—postpartum or after another significant life event—and chose to volunteer in carework (for senior citizens, disadvantaged children, people with disabilities, migrant women, and so on), which they viewed as an extension of their maternal self and as a way to escape "the force of domesticity."[8] As Pyo Nanjung, a forty-three-year-old volunteer who helped migrant mothers with school-age children, put it, "I had to do something—otherwise, I felt like I was about to die."

South Korean women were propelled to work with migrant women by two primary factors: gender-based empathy as married women, and their sense of duty as mother-citizens. Myounghwa expressed her admiration for migrant women as a reason for her volunteer work:

> I think marriage-migrant women are incredible people. I use this expression to describe them: women warriors. When women living in Seoul get married and move to Busan or Daegu, it is tough to adjust. But these migrant women come to South Korea without knowing anyone, after having just met their husbands through an arrangement. That's very brave. Many of the women live well and are very active. At first, some of them have a tough time, crying, thinking about their mothers—some of them are quite young—but they take initiative in their lives, and it made me want to help out more.

Myounghwa understood migrant women's relocation to South Korea to follow their husbands as similar to the relocation experiences of many South Korean women, although their own migration away from their natal families took place within the nation's borders. Myounghwa's own experience of displacement caused her to sympathize with migrant women's "tough time" of isolation and loneliness in South Korea, and she wanted to help.

Likewise, Nanjung, who began her volunteer work as a way to cope with postpartum depression, recounted the experience she found most rewarding: helping a migrant woman whose struggles echoed her own. Nanjung spoke at length about a Vietnamese woman whose South Korean husband passed away. The woman was left alone with three children, and Nanjung was able to support her emotionally:

> She wasn't able to do anything. She just stayed at home. She came to South Korea when she was quite young and had three children, so didn't get to go out. And she didn't have much chance to make friends. Then she lost her husband, and had to go outside. How helpless must she have felt! It's not even her own country, but in a foreign country. . . . After she found out about this [mentoring] service, she started to talk and come out, to sit in the sun, like photosynthesis [gwanghapsông]. . . . She was the only one I met outside. Usually I visit them at home and look at children's books, but with her, we often met outside. She said, "Wow, there is a world out here." She was really thankful. It's not that I gave any concrete help, like economic help, but it seemed like she strongly felt, "Now I can come out and do something."

Nanjung felt a strong connection with this Vietnamese migrant woman based not only on their common domestic identity as wives and mothers but also on their shared experience of regaining energy—through "photosynthesis"—by coming out of an isolated domestic life that was limited to the home, to greet the "world out here."

Building on their empathy with migrant women, South Korean women expressed concerns about the controlling behaviors of South Korean mothers-in-law, a problem they often encountered during their interactions with migrant women and their families. Mothers-in-law were a frequent topic of discussion among volunteers; they were said to control the mobility of migrant daughters-in-law and to forbid them to meet with other migrants. Women believed that mothers-in-law worried that their daughters-in-law might have come to South Korea via "fake marriage" and would run away from home with the help of other migrants. Although South Korean women volunteers acknowledged that migrant women had material motives for entering into marriage, they also claimed that this was not a cause for concern; women in their generation, unlike the younger generation in their twenties and thirties, were accustomed to marriage by arrangement (*jungmae*) and approached heterosexual marriage as an economic as well as intimate arrangement. If anything, they argued, this was all the more reason for South Korean families and society at large to nurture migrant women, so that they would feel that they were a part of the family and would "put down their roots here, from deep in their hearts." Hong Youngjoo, a volunteer Korean language teacher for migrant women, said: "Even though they came with different motives, no woman thinks lightly of marriage. It is a very important decision for them, and unless they are treated really badly, they would not leave easily. But if the husband and in-laws treat them like they are always under surveillance, it's only going to make matters worse!"

In addition to gender-based empathy, many South Korean women drew on their own experiences of mothering as they worked with migrant women, and viewed themselves as the "maternal guardians" of migrant women whose natal mothers were far away in their home countries, and of migrant women's children as the next generation in South Korea.[9] Like South Korean men who talked about the failure of migrant integration as a national crisis, many South Korean women claimed that their work integrating migrants was necessary for South Korea. Unlike the men, however, they grounded the need for this work in a strong maternal rhetoric focused not only on the South Korean people as a whole but on the needs of children in "multicultural families."

Bae Yoonsook, a fifty-five-year-old volunteer teacher of Korean language for migrant women, drew on the mother-citizen rhetoric even though she was the only person of this generation in my study who did not have children of her own. Yoonsook grew up in a devout Christian family, and her mother was a housewife devoted in her role as a mother and a wife supporting her husband. Yoonsook grew up wanting to follow her mother's example. After graduating from the university, she became a schoolteacher, but gave up her teaching career when she married and moved to a different city. Yet Yoonsook's dream of becoming a good wife and mother was cut short when she was unable to conceive. For more than ten years, she and her husband tried multiple fertility options, but when she reached forty, they gave up. She did not go into detail on the topic, but even though she was active in her church community, Yoonsook felt that she did not fully "fit in" as a childless woman. To fulfill her goal of caregiving, Yoonsook eventually decided to "give back to the society" by volunteering to teach after-school programs for underprivileged children. This first volunteer position led to her current volunteer work teaching literacy to Korean seniors and the Korean language to migrant women.

Volunteer work became one of the limited pathways for Yoonsook to claim gendered national belonging, which she could not achieve through motherhood. She described her volunteer work teaching the elderly and migrant women as caring for those who are left behind in South Korea as well as caring for South Korea's future.

> For these elderly, they don't have long life ahead of them. When I hand out the books, some of them cry, holding the book. For the first time in their lives, they have a book that belongs to them. Since they didn't have any education, they never had their own pencils, notebooks, or books, so they are deeply touched. It's the most rewarding when they say, "Now I can ride the subway by myself" because they can read the signs. And they had to follow others before, pretending that they could read. Seeing them happy makes me feel proud.

Whereas Yoonsook was concerned with the emotional empowerment of senior citizens, in her work teaching migrant women, she focused on "doing it right" so that migrant women would be able to educate their children properly:

> Our second [future] generation is in their hands. So last year, when I taught the beginner-level Korean, I always emphasized that the basics are important. I told them, "Later when you give birth to your children, they ask you 'Mom, how do I do this?' You should learn the basics correctly now, so that you can teach them correctly." . . . It is in their hands that our future lies.

For Yoonsook, helping migrant women was contributing to "our future" because these women would become the new mothers of South Korean children. Through this work, Yoonsook was able to fulfill the role of mother-citizen, a particularly gendered path to citizenship in South Korea.

Many South Korean women like Yoonsook stepped up to help migrant women out of their shared concern for the children. Um Kyounghee, a fifty-three-year-old volunteer for a mentoring program for migrant women, was worried about these children's lagging school performance as an emerging social problem that would lead to juvenile delinquency and the formation of an underclass in South Korea. As part of her volunteer work, she visited migrant women's homes to teach Korean and to give advice about daily matters, but Kyounghee believed that the real purpose of her work was to help the family as a whole. She was especially concerned about migrant women and their marital families, who, in her eyes, were not equipped to educate the children properly. She claimed: "People who receive good education give good education. Among many migrant women I met, many graduated only from elementary schools and didn't go to middle schools, and not many went to high schools. Because they haven't received much education, the education they give their children is not proper."

Kyounghee believed that migrant women's marital families, including their South Korean husbands and parents-in-law, exacerbated the problem of poor education. She believed that because of their lower-class background, husbands were not able to support their children's education.

> They [the husbands] don't have a good background. It's not that they are bad people, but they just haven't learned; not in a sense of academic studies, but about how to interact with people. Because I am older than most husbands, I just scold them when they look down on their wives and say things like they find it embarrassing when they go outside and people recognize [that their wives are migrants]. I tell them, if the mother doesn't

receive respect at home, it will affect your children. In schools, other kids tease them, saying "Your mother is a foreigner." If the father does the same at home, the children will lose respect and love for their mothers, and stop listening to their mothers, so the problem grows. I tell them if you don't respect your wife, it will be a big problem.

Kyounghee believed that with the help of educated people like herself, South Korean husbands could learn the importance of treating their wives with respect for their children's sake. She acknowledged that the disrespect and discrimination that migrants experienced were not limited to their marital families but also present in their schools and neighborhoods. Yet she believed that it was the husbands' responsibility not to "[do] the same at home," and it was her responsibility as an older person to "scold" them for doing so, to prevent "a big problem" for their families and for South Korean society.

In addition to the husbands, the South Korean women also spoke about the problem of "uneducated" parents-in-law. Kyounghee argued,

> Among their families-in-law, many are not open-minded. For example, when you are doing bilingual education in early years, in many cases, mothers don't speak Korean fluently and switch between Korean and Vietnamese, and kids understand both and speak a bit of Vietnamese. When they go to day care and kindergarten, they speak Korean, but being exposed to Vietnamese does not hamper their Korean proficiency. But the in-laws often tell mothers not to speak Vietnamese at all. So if mothers can't speak Vietnamese and only speak fragmented Korean, children's Korean proficiency suffers even more. Then it becomes difficult for them to communicate with their mothers later, if they can't understand Vietnamese. So I tell them, "Teach your children Vietnamese." There is research showing that if children are exposed to multiple languages, it makes them smarter. What a great opportunity it is! These days, in college admissions, you can choose Vietnamese as a second language—it is a global era! If they speak fluent Vietnamese when they graduate from college, they will have good social standing.

Referring to "research" on the benefits of bilingual education, Kyounghee expressed her concern that families-in-law who had not caught up to the "global era" would discourage bilingual development and thus harm children's standing in South Korea. By taking up the role of maternal guardian for children whose full potential might not be realized under the inadequate care of migrant mothers and their marital families, these South

Korean women became national citizens, extending their gendered labor in the domestic sphere to claim a modicum of social standing for themselves through personally meaningful public service to the South Korean nation.

COSMOPOLITAN DESIRES AND THE REPOSITORY OF ALTERNATE DREAMS: THE GLOBAL YOUTH

> I had this wish [*somang*] that I shared with everyone else: "Oh, I want to live in a foreign country." I wanted to go abroad, away from nationalism and patriotism, and live freely and anonymously, away from people I know and broaden my perspective. I think all of us have this wish. When I was twenty-nine, I thought maybe in my thirties I can go abroad, even for a few years, or just leave South Korea and live elsewhere.

When Seol Yuna, a thirty-nine-year-old cultural activist and migrant advocate, spoke about wanting to go abroad and "live in a foreign country," she understood it as a "wish" that "all of us have." Indeed, her wish was widely shared among members of her generation, especially among women, who often expressed their aspiration to leave South Korea—temporarily or permanently—in pursuit of "curiosity" and "freedom." But this desire was not shared by the men and women of the developmental generation in my study, for whom transnational mobility was unfamiliar, and a sense of national belonging was central to their identities.

When the older generation of South Koreans came of age between the 1960s and 1980s, because of economic constraints and a wide-reaching overseas travel ban under military dictatorship, travel abroad was rare, enjoyed as a luxury by the highly privileged or enacted by the few migrant workers permitted abroad to earn foreign currency. Under such conditions, the members of the older generation understood migration as a tough decision driven by economic necessity, an act of self-sacrifice for family and nation, and an experience of displacement better avoided, rather than as a happy choice based in personal desires and the pursuit of freedom.

Younger-generation South Koreans like Yuna came of age between the late 1980s and early 2010s, a period signified by the achievement of parliamentary democracy and increasing transnational mobility into and out of South Korea. Unlike the women of the developmental generation who had to compromise their desire for higher education for the sake of the family, all men and women of the younger generation in my study were either in college or college educated, and many were pursuing a graduate degree. This is consistent with broader trends in educational expansion in South Korea, in terms of both the drastic increase in overall university attendance and changes in the gender composition of higher education in the second half of the twentieth century.[10] Since the overseas travel ban was lifted following the 1988 Seoul Olympics, foreign travel became a common aspiration of many South Korean youth, especially university students. As Yuna stated, for this generation, "overseas" symbolized a space of a liberal desire where one could realize her individual selfhood without the heavy constraints of "nationalism and patriotism" and where one could experience freedom from others' expectations.

Although the "wish" to go abroad and emergent sense of belonging beyond South Korea was widely shared among South Koreans of the post-authoritarian generation, the everyday cosmopolitanism they practiced was stratified by social class. Upper-class youth could easily act on their desire to travel abroad, routinely spending summers or a few years in the United States or Europe as tourists, for English study, or to pursue an advanced degree. For the less economically advantaged like Yuna, traveling abroad required lengthy planning and preparation to surmount the barriers of visa restrictions and lack of funds. Many South Korean youth in my study, predominantly from middle-class to lower-middle-class backgrounds, went to Australia or Canada on a "working holiday" visa combining manual labor and English study, or went on backpacking and overseas volunteering trips to Asian countries like China, Vietnam, Nepal, and Thailand. These experiences helped them feel a personal connection to migrants in South Korea.

Gong Hyojeong, now in her forties, reflected on her first sit-in protest with migrant workers against immigration crackdowns and labor rights abuses in 2003, when she was twenty-nine:

> When I look back, I think I had some sort of a desire. We all have this desire; if we don't like it here, then we want to go somewhere else and live there, right? When I put myself in their [migrants'] shoes, I thought they were the ones who made a different kind of choice [she used the English word *choice*] and changed their lives in a drastic way to come to a different country. If I were to go and live in a different country, I would go through the problems they have in a similar way. So I felt that kind of similarity and curiosity.

Hyojeong and her fellow South Korean youth participants in the sit-in protests were loosely organized to support progressive causes. These youth approached migrants as their peers, whose desires and "problems" echoed their own. Because she was between jobs at the time, Hyojeong was able to spend almost five days a week at the sit-in protest for several months. She spoke about "a friend" she met at the sit-in, a migrant worker from Bangladesh, with whom she kept in touch for more than ten years:

> Irfan was from a rural mountain village. You know, in South Korea, if you get into Seoul National University [a highly prestigious university] from a small town, the whole village puts up a banner to celebrate. He went to Dhaka University, which is like Seoul National, and afterwards came to South Korea to work. His dream was to build a solid bridge in his village, because the bridge at that time broke down whenever flood came. If you look at it this way, these are the people who had curiosity and made a choice to go abroad, and I was curious about the people taking initiative in their lives. He was a history major at Dhaka University, and it was lots of fun [jaemi]. Because I didn't know much about Bangladeshi history, I listened to him. I think it was out of intellectual curiosity for sure.

Although the economically conditioned goal that propelled Irfan to pursue migrant labor in South Korea—his desire to build a solid bridge for his village—was clearly different from Hyojeong's individual desire to "go somewhere else and live there," she still felt that they had much in common. They were both university graduates and young people with curiosity, and they took the protest as an opportunity to make friends, learn about the world, and have "lots of fun" while acting in solidarity for migrant justice.

It should not be surprising that Hyojeong and her peers at the protest site encountered some conflicts with South Korean activists who entered social movements under the authoritarian regime. Migrant worker protesters, largely in their twenties and thirties, did not have a problem with this new group of young South Koreans who showed an interest in learning Bangladeshi history and Nepalese folk songs. But the older generation of South Korean activists did not appreciate the lighthearted approach of the South Korean youth. As Hyojeong recalled:

> We had some tensions with South Korean activists. They tended to operate as a group, and if the leadership demanded certain things, those on the ground had to follow. But such logics might not have been important

for migrant workers. From the perspective of migrant workers, there was some discontent: "Why are these people forcing things on us? This person tells us to do one thing, and the other person another." And the culture of South Korean movement groups tended to be somewhat conservative. There was a younger woman in our group, and a South Korean male activist told her, "This sit-in site is a serious place. Don't come here in a short skirt and flip flops."

Hyojeong was resistant to such policing of bodies and outfits, which she experienced herself during her student activist days at the university. Although she did not belong to "the generation that learned feminism from the books," referring to campus feminist groups that emerged in the mid-1990s in multiple universities in Seoul, she was part of a growing contingent within student activism that challenged the "conservative" culture of social movements, which involved hierarchical structures, the regulation of women's bodies and sexuality, and the demand of "serious" devotion. The old movement culture was part of what South Korean youth like Yuna and Hyojeong wanted to leave behind when they expressed their desires to go abroad and be free "away from nationalism and patriotism." They wanted to create a new culture in which the collective pursuit of social justice could include having "fun" (*jaemi*), building personally meaningful "friendships," and practicing everyday forms of democracy and equity. Their citizenship project was not limited to transforming vertical relationships between the state and migrants but also included horizontal relationships among members of the polity, for migrants and South Koreans alike. Migrant protests were a site where the cosmopolitan desires of South Korean youth entered into tension with older modes of movement organizing, a tension I explore further in Chapter 5.

The younger generation of South Koreans involved in various sectors of migrant advocacy, activism, and integration programs shared the narrative that they were pursuing an alternative way of life, distinct from "the standard track" prescribed in South Korea. The standard track, as these young men and women described it, consisted of a narrow path toward success—excelling in school, entering a prestigious university, competing for a corporate job, getting married, and buying a house and raising children—which they found neither viable nor attractive. Following the Asian financial crisis in 1997, which South Koreans commonly referred to as the IMF crisis, neoliberal reforms dismantled the standard of lifelong employment through massive layoffs and reorganized the labor market to include irregular employment.[11] This led to the social problem of unemployment and underemployment, especially among youth,[12] as described by the best-seller *88 Manwon Sede* (the *880,000 Won Generation*). These South Korean youth benefited from their nation's global standing and the accompanying improvement in material conditions through an expanded ability to travel abroad and improved access to higher education and consumer goods, but they also experienced a heightened sense of insecurity in comparison to older generations.

Whereas all of my interviewees from the developmental generation were married, among the younger generation, only one was married, and the rest expressed no plans to marry. Chae Minseok, a twenty-seven-year-old migrant advocate, at times wondered whether he could get married with his income. He said: "When I see my friends who work at big corporations, they have something like three bank accounts, and something called a mortgage loan, and work with a fund manager. They say to marry, you need thirty million won (approximately US$30,000) or something, so they save up for three years." Yet Minseok was not envious of those friends; he found his current work meaningful and valued the opportunity to work with migrant workers from all over Asia, although his paycheck was below that of most migrant factory workers he worked with, his wage being just above the minimum wage without proper overtime pay. Like Minseok, the other South Korean youth I interviewed called life on the standard track too "intense" (*bbakbbak*), "fierce" (*chiyôl*), and "dry" (*gônjo*); it was a life filled with competition, overwork, and no "fun." For South Korean youth facing intense competition on the job market and shrinking employment opportunities, their aspirations to go overseas expressed their desire to pursue a life different from the one that society and family expected of them. Likewise, they saw their work with migrants as a bridge to a different way of life.

The younger generation of South Koreans projected their dreams and aspirations onto the space of "overseas." Some imagined overseas as a space of freedom, a narrative shared among young women more than men. Hyun Youngjung, a thirty-four-year-old migrant advocate, recalled a watershed moment in college that pushed her off the standard track. During her junior year, she read *I Am a Taxi Driver in Paris,* the best-selling memoir of Hong Sehwa, a South Korean antiauthoritarian dissident intellectual who sought asylum in Paris. This book served as a wake-up call or, as she put it, "a big blow to the head." Youngjung was deeply moved by the author's account of political repression in South Korea in contrast to the French value and practice of *toleránce* (tolerance). She said:

> Starting with the book, I read other books of his, and started feeling, "Was this country [South Korea] this messed up?" . . . After reading the book, I realized I could not get a job in a regular company. So instead of getting a regular job, I started thinking about other options, and KOICA [Korean Overseas International Community Development Agency] came to my mind, although it wasn't a perfect fit. I became someone who could not become a company employee.

After she realized that she did not want to join the common ranks of corporate jobs, Youngjung expressed her desire to work at KOICA—a South Korean government body, established in 1991, that sends one thousand long-term volunteers to various parts of the developing worlds in Asia, Latin America, and Africa, similar to the US Peace Corps. KOICA appealed to Youngjung as a way to combine her desire to go abroad with her desire to create social change. But when she told her parents of her plan, they adamantly opposed it, and she gave up the idea after her mother cried to dissuade her. Instead of joining KOICA, Youngjung began volunteering at a migrant advocacy NGO, offering labor counseling and teaching the Korean language to migrant workers and migrant wives, before becoming a full-time staff member. Unlike the older generation of South Korean migrant advocates who worked with a sense of duty to the nation, Youngjung enjoyed the experience itself: "I didn't think of it as helping migrants; rather, I was just having fun. Meeting migrant workers was fun, and other volunteers were fun people, because we had a similar outlook in life." Her work with migrants led her to pursue an advanced degree overseas to study migration-related issues. During the time she was away from South Korea, she realized that her belonging to South Korea was stronger than she assumed: "Wherever I was, my eyes were looking toward South Korea." After completing her degree, Youngjung returned to South Korea and rejoined migrant advocacy as a way to realize her global cosmopolitan desires in the comfort of home.

For Yang Hyesin, a thirty-seven-year-old Korean language instructor for migrant wives, working with migrants in South Korea was the final step in a path from a corporate job to volunteering in Indonesia and back home to find work that was more personally meaningful. Upon graduating from college right before the onset of the Asian financial crisis ("Thank God, the IMF hit the next year," she said), Hyesin found a job at a well-known multinational corporation that "paid more money than I ever need" and that came with many perks, such as luxury hotel stays during frequent work trips to Tokyo and Guam. When she heard about the opportunity to be an overseas volunteer through KOICA, she took a leave of absence and was sent to Indonesia as a computer teacher. In a rural village in Indonesia, she learned that "people don't live on money alone. Money is really nothing. So since then, I thought money was trivial, and I can be happy without it. I used to earn $3,000 per month, but in Indonesia, I received $310 per month, but the happiness that $310 brought was bigger than $3,000."

In contrast to her life in South Korea, which was too "intense," life in Indonesia made Hyesin rediscover the importance of "things that money can never buy." She characterized Indonesia as a place filled with intimacy and affection among people. She gave the following example:

> When I was returning to South Korea, I had to come to Jhakarta. So the women in the village got all my luggage in the car, like one in the 1980s in South Korea. When we became hungry, we stopped the car on the side of the highway, and all shared the food together with our hands. . . . In Indonesia, only people with flight tickets can enter the airport. But they came anyway and brought Indonesian food I liked, and the container was warm. So we ate together outside of the airport, and I didn't know whether I was crying or eating. They have so much affection [*jŏng*] like that.

Hyesin was among several South Korean youth who spoke about Southeast Asia as a "warm" and "heartful" place, a reflection of South Korea's lost past as they imagined it. Kim Boram, a twenty-one-year-old university student, recalled participating in a volunteer trip to Nepal at a time when she was "burned out" from competition and tensions with classmates from the first few years of college, and "wanted healing." The two weeks she spent working with schoolchildren in Nepal were refreshing in that regard: "Honestly, in South Korea, people judge according to their appearance a lot. But there, people don't judge by the surface, and I really like that. . . . After I came back, those two weeks felt very relaxing, and it made me feel like life can be like this."

Such narratives about Southeast and South Asia as a place of intimate human connections as opposed to "dry" and "judgmental" South Korea reflect the degree of fatigue that these South Korean youth felt in their daily lives. They also reflect South Korea's newly earned global standing, which enabled its young members to draw on the romanticized trope that was once used to represent the East as opposed to the West, only now using it to represent Southeast and South Asia in relation to South Korea. After her "healing" experience in Indonesia, Hyesin quit her corporate job and returned to Indonesia as a volunteer teaching the Korean language, before her current job of teaching Korean to migrant wives in South Korea, a contract position that needs to be renewed every year without job security and pays less than half of her former corporate job. Hyesin's long-term plan was to establish an NGO in Southeast Asia. Likewise, Boram was still in college and volunteering to help with migrant children's schoolwork as she pursued her goal of working at an international organization like the United Nations.

For other young South Koreans, transnational migrant labor activism exemplified possibilities of resistance, with "overseas" portrayed as a place of revolutionary potential to mount resistance against global capitalism. Koo Hojoon, a thirty-four-year-old activist with a student movement background, first became involved in migrant advocacy as a documentary filmmaker because he saw migrant workers as a symbolic case of the exploitation inherent in neoliberal globalization. He argued that in the era following the Asian financial crisis, a neoliberal impulse took hold of the South Korean economy and society, but since the global financial crisis of 2008, a growing movement in the country advocated for an alternative to global capitalism. For Hojoon, Nepal, Bangladesh, and the Philippines constituted a transnational sphere of solidarity where migrant worker activists who were deported from South Korea continued their activism. "Through the lens of returned migrant workers," Hojoon said, "I would like to make the documentary to report the resistance and alternate visions of globalization that is not top down." It was at the intersection of their personal desires for fun and intimacy and their pursuit of an alternate vision of global interconnectedness that young South Korean men and women entered migrant encounters.

ON HUMAN DIGNITY

Pastor Bong Kyungsoo and Seol Yuna could not have been more different. Pastor Bong was a married father of two, an evangelical Christian missionary in his mid-fifties with conservative political views who became a pastor in a church serving Chinese migrants in South Korea after a mission trip to China. Yuna was a single woman with shorter hair even than Pastor Bong, a free-spirited filmmaker and cultural activist in her late thirties supporting migrants' cultural activities, such as photography and videography. Pastor Bong was based in an industrial town full of migrant workers on the outskirts of Seoul, and socialized mostly with other evangelical Christians and missionaries; Yuna was based in a hip, bohemian neighborhood in Seoul where she spent her time having "fun" with young feminists, queers, anarchists, and artists. Neither found himself or herself entirely at home in the migrant advocacy movement in South Korea, predominantly led by social-justice-oriented pastors such as Pastor Choi and Pastor Kim of Peace Center, but for very different reasons. Pastor Bong found the movement "too political" and "too confrontational," and Yuna thought it was "too serious" and "too conservative."

Despite their many differences, Pastor Bong and Yuna shared a similar emotional connection with migrants in South Korea:

> Pastor Bong: Some migrants I met broke my heart—some South Koreans don't see migrant workers as people but as machines. There was an employer who made migrant workers work eighteen hours a day. When I first heard, I could not believe it, so I went there myself to see it, and it was true! One migrant worker got injured, developed disc problems in his lower back, and became unable to work. His contract was for two years, and three months were left in his contract, but when he couldn't work, the employer tried to send him back to his country. So this person was twenty-three years old. Can you imagine, being a twenty-three-year-old man with a messed-up lower back and sent back home? I don't know what to make of it. Shouldn't there be some basic human decency, a bare minimum?

> Yuna: We as human beings all have thoughts, desires, and a need for rest, and we all get sick time to time. It's not like these people are disposable machines, and you throw them away when they are used up, like "You should just return to your own country." When we go somewhere, we want to plant our roots, and express our own desires—that's what people do as human beings. But there is no institutional support or social recognition of this in South Korea. . . . Because many still don't think of migrant workers as people with lives but as temporary beings we use, and they are just earning money. But if you put yourself in their shoes, that's not how we live when we go anywhere.

Pastor Bong and Yuna both raised fundamental questions about the dignity of migrants in South Korea. It may be legal to use migrant workers' labor and send them back when they cannot work anymore, but does that meet the standard of "basic human decency"? Is it acceptable to treat people like "machines" and "throw [them] away" when convenient because they are not South Koreans but migrants? What does it mean to treat people like human beings? Asking these questions led people as different as Pastor Bong and Yuna beyond their respective comfort zones of religion and artistic expression to unexpected sites of migrant activism, including protests against immigration crackdowns and the labor office where they advocated for migrant workers against their South Korean employers.

Despite differences in their life trajectories based on generation and gender, South Korean men and women were united in their migrant encounters through their persistent claims for the respect of human decency and dignity. Minseok, a migrant activist in his late twenties, recalled the moment he first learned the English word *dignity* from a migrant worker activist from the Philippines: "It meant a lot to me—that we are working for the dignity of people. And that people who think like that have kept this space of activism alive. . . . I am indebted to that legacy."

South Koreans often phrased their particular claims for human dignity in terms that mirrored their own life narratives: men who came of age in the labor movement emphasized workers' rights for migrants; women who experienced gender-based subordination in their marital families demanded respect for migrant women from their husbands, in-laws, and the broader society; and youth like Yuna who pursued personal freedom argued that migrants too should be supported to pursue their desires. In spite of their different narratives, these South Korean men and women together made the radical claim that migrants are "human beings" with dignity and that they need to be respected as such. Their demands for migrant dignity against legal, social, and cultural exclusion in South Korea were also a claim for their own belonging in the South Korean polity. Their advocacy projects for migrants were also projects of their own citizenship.

FOUR

Everyday Politics of Immigration Raids in the Shadow of Citizenship

"Look—It's that house over there." Florence pointed to the rooftop patio three buildings away from the slipper factory. Though our view was blurred by smoke and steam against the gray sky, we could make out laundry waving in the wind. The laundry was left behind by the Filipino couple who had lived there, Florence told me, after they were arrested during an immigration raid two nights earlier in front of a small outlet mall right across the street from the factory complex. That Friday night, an unmarked van from the immigration office had been hiding in the parking lot, waiting for migrant workers entering the mall. Five undocumented migrants from the Philippines and Bangladesh were detained that night, including the couple who had washed their dust-filled pants and T-shirts and left them hanging to dry under the sun.

"It's so frightening," Florence murmured. "You could be gone just like that. I don't think you met Alfred, but you've probably seen Monette at the church. They lived in that house for a long time—eight years?" She stared at the house for a few seconds, and abruptly turned around. Shaking her head and shoulders as if getting rid of a bad omen, she said:

I am really afraid. Last night, I woke up in the middle of the night, think-ing: What would happen to us? If I get caught, what should Rob do? What if he gets caught? We talked about it; if either of us gets caught and goes back to the Philippines, one of us will just stay, keep working and sending money home. But I don't want that to happen. I don't want to be separated from him. I am really afraid.

This was Florence Ocampo's first encounter with an immigration raid. Florence was a newcomer to South Korea, and her three-month tour-ist visa had expired only a few days earlier. After graduating from col-lege in the Philippines, she married a classmate, Rob Ocampo, and they had two boys together. Money was tight for their family, so she sought overseas work. Her first attempt—domestic work in Taiwan—failed mis-erably when she found out that her "maniac" boss had installed a secu-rity camera in the shower. She returned to the Philippines after only two months. Because her contract was not completed, she had to pay back her placement fee along with a penalty. Then her husband's second cousin in Factorytown invited them to South Korea. Excited by the prospect of a combined income of more than $2,500 per month, they migrated together, leaving their children with Rob's parents. Unlike in Taiwan, Florence lacked a legal working visa in South Korea. For the first time in her life, she was facing the reality of being an undocumented migrant, and she felt reluctant and fearful.

Like many other migrants in Factorytown, Florence and Rob worked to build a life in South Korea against the forces of exclusion from the South Korean state, in this case embodied by its migrant nonsettlement policy. Lacking a legal status to reside and work, a core dimension of citizenship, they were under the constant threat of immigration raids that could uproot their lives on any unlucky day.

The lives of Florence and other undocumented migrants have been a key subject of migration scholarship globally, as scholars have demonstrated the significance of legal status as a social and political condition that affects the everyday lives of migrants, reporting a high degree of disadvantage for undocumented migrants. Without state authorization for their pres-ence, these migrants must operate in what Susan Coutin called a "space of nonexistence," with increased vulnerability to exploitation and rights violations.[1] Increasingly criminalized as "illegal," undocumented migrants across the globe are also subject to heightened forms of policing, which induces tension and anxiety as well as fear and stigma that operate as barriers to claims-making.[2]

At the heart of the production of "illegality," critical migration scholars argue, lies the state's production of disposable and vulnerable workers.[3] As Kitty Calavita shows in her analysis of immigration law and policies in Spain, the state utilizes restrictive immigration laws to create a flexible and contingent workforce for a post-Fordist economy.[4] Similarly, Nicholas De Genova argues that "undocumented migrations are constituted in order not to physically exclude them but instead, to socially include them under imposed conditions of enforced and protracted vulnerability," which serves as a "disciplinary apprenticeship in the subordination of their labor."[5] Through ethnographic research of immigration raids on the ground, this chapter brings to the fore the dual operation of exclusion and inclusion, demonstrating how the state's enforcement against "illegality" creates a condition of containment for migrants.

In Factorytown and Basetown, immigration raids functioned not only as a method of enforcing immigration control and regulating legal statuses but also as a disciplinary mechanism for migrants, both documented and undocumented. Undocumented migrants like Florence faced particular vulnerabilities due to the threat of deportation, but immigration raids did not just target migrants without a legal status. The enactment of immigration control in South Korea disproportionately targeted certain areas—the borders of migrant-segregated neighborhoods—and the migrants who "stood out" as racial others, as political activists, or as violating the implicit rules of community conduct. Thus immigration raids contained migrants within geographic and social boundaries in the shadows of citizenship, actively producing and reinforcing systems of exclusion through physical and social boundaries in migrant communities, reminding migrants of the risk of potential transgressions. The state governed the border through explicit force and implicit rules that restricted migrants' mobility and actions.

In South Korea, immigration control occupied a central place in the daily lives of migrants, but it did not leave them helpless. Instead, it led to vibrant contestation and negotiation among the state, migrant advocacy NGOs, and migrant communities. News—and rumors—of immigration raids traveled quickly throughout the community; strategies to avoid immigration officials were shared widely; and tales of migrants escaping and surviving the raids were told and retold with pride. Closely following the practice of immigration control on the ground—when and where the immigration officers patrolled, whom they targeted, and when and how migrants navigated these patrols—this chapter shows how immigration raids acted as a spatial and social measure of discipline and containment for migrants with and without legal status, and how migrants and South Korean advocates bargained with and challenged this form of control.

GOVERNING THROUGH FEAR

Fear—*takot* in Tagalog—was one of the words I heard most often from Florence in Factorytown. There were many things that she was afraid to do. When her friend asked her to join them at McDonald's on the weekend or at the downtown market after work, she was tempted, but she always refused for fear of exposing herself to the risk of immigration raids. "No need for that!" Karen Tomás, her Filipina neighbor complained. "Whatever will happen will happen. It's all God's will." For Karen and others who had spent more than ten years in South Korea without legal documents, the fear of immigration raids was no longer as salient as it was for newcomers like Florence. "I was like that at first," Karen added. "She will get used to it just in a couple of months. You can't live like that."

Factorytown was home to over seven hundred undocumented migrants, though it was hard to get an accurate count because migrants were constantly moving in and out or experiencing changes in legal status. Migrants went from legal to undocumented through multiple routes. Some like Florence came to South Korea on a tourist visa and overstayed; others came on a legal work visa and overstayed their contract period or left their assigned workplaces. In Factorytown, most undocumented migrants were previously industrial trainees or EPS workers (short-term guest workers), but in other towns near US military bases, there were a small minority of women who left hostess work. Among undocumented migrant women, some initially migrated as spouses of South Korean men, but left their marriages or had engaged in a "marriage of convenience," before they secured permanent residency or legal citizenship. In the company of these undocumented migrants, Karen believed that Florence would soon find a way to live comfortably with her status, or lack thereof.

Karen was quickly proven wrong. Florence's first winter in South Korea was a harsh one, and it intensified the ever-present fear in Factorytown. One cold day in November 2008, only five months after Florence's arrival, a large-scale immigration raid swept through the factory complex, leading to the arrest and deportation of more than a hundred people, almost 10 percent of Factorytown's migrant population.

This raid was an example of what De Genova calls "the Border Spectacle," a highly visible scene of *ex*clusion and display of state power that masks the more routine *in*clusion of migrants as subjugated labor.[6] I was on a bus to Seoul that morning when I received a phone call from a staff member of Peace Center telling me about the massive immigration raid. I hurried back to Factorytown, and as I made my way to the factory complex, I saw four full-size immigration buses blocking the entrance. Pastor Kim Wonsik—the leader of Peace Center—was standing helplessly to the side with the rest of the staff and volunteers. Immigration officers in black vests were still running through the alleys of Factorytown, but they were already on their way out. The windows of the immigration buses were too dark to see inside, but Pastor Kim told me that the buses were almost full with migrant workers.

Seonwu Eunmi, a South Korean woman in a common-law relationship with a Bangladeshi man, was standing near the buses, tearfully begging immigration officers: "This is our son, and the marriage paperwork is just taking time! Please release the father of our son!" When they refused and told her to come to the immigration office, she fell to the ground, sobbing. When the buses started their engines to leave, a few people made a futile attempt to lie down in their path, shouting, "How can you do this to us?" and "You can't take them away!" But more than two hundred uniformed police and immigration officers were there to enforce the raid, and it was unimaginable that the migrants or the advocates could do anything to stop them. The battle was already lost.

As the buses left one by one, it felt as if the whole factory complex stopped breathing. Except for about twenty of us standing defeated at the entrance of the factory complex, there was no one on the street. The usual hustle and bustle of the lunch hour and the noise of machines operating in the factories were replaced by eerie silence. As the last immigration bus drove out of sight, the whole town seemed frozen.

Commotion returned to the complex at a dizzying pace. Pastor Kim hurried to the Peace Center office to write a press statement against the immigration crackdown, while staff members busied themselves calling reporters and other migrant advocacy organizations around the country. Others called the migrant workers they knew to find out who had been arrested. Florence and her friends were hiding together behind a locked door, frantically calling their husbands, boyfriends, and family members to see if they were safe. Karen was angry and scared. She exclaimed, "Why do they treat us like criminals, when all we do is work hard? I want to tell them: don't call us illegals!"

In the midst of intense emotions, we soon learned that during the immigration raids, some immigration officers had chased migrant workers into the nearby mountains and arrested them there. Others broke into homes where migrants were hiding behind locked doors. Detaining as many migrants as they could, the officers did not bother to check documents before handcuffing them and putting them in a bus; instead, they released those with legal visas one by one. Under pressure to make the raid go as quickly as possible, the officers passed over migrants who looked phenotypically Korean, such as Mongolians and Chinese, and focused their actions on migrants with darker skins who appeared "foreign," such as those from Bangladesh, Sri Lanka, and the Philippines.

Within a few hours, migrant activists from the Seoul Capital Area started to gather in Factorytown, along with several journalists from the progressive media. The Peace Center staff members guided them to migrant homes with broken doors, to hospitals where migrant workers who were injured during the chase were treated, and to individuals with newsworthy stories of heartache, like Eunmi, the South Korean woman whose Bangladeshi common-law partner was arrested despite his being the father of a South Korean child. The activists prepared for a series of protests against the immigration crackdown, starting with a rally that evening in front of the National Human Rights Commission of Korea in downtown Seoul.

In the days following the crackdown, migrants in Factorytown had nowhere to feel safe. Some told me that when immigration officers left in a hurry, they yelled, "We will be back!" Migrants were cautious about leaving home, but they also felt insecure in their apartments. Florence's husband, Rob, added three locks to their door, hoping that if the immigration officers struggled to break through the door, they might give up and try another home. Some factory owners, afraid of an immigration ambush during work hours, put steel chains on their main gate, which made the factory appear closed from the outside. Florence's factory was one of these. Workers now entered through a small hidden entrance in the first floor that might prove dangerous in the case of a fire or other emergency.

Practically speaking, the chained gate did little to hide the presence of migrants—the noise of cutting wood and moving furniture coming from the factory betrayed the people working inside. Symbolically, however, the chains served as a reminder of a lesson that Florence and other migrants were learning the hard way: being undocumented in South Korea meant living in fear and hiding in plain sight.

CONTESTING IMMIGRATION RAIDS

The state exercises the exclusive power to grant or deny legal status and to enforce immigration control, but this does not mean that other actors simply comply with the state's decisions. In particular, the mobilization of migrant communities and migrant advocacy groups in many major industrial towns across the nation complicated the South Korean state's strategy of immigration raids and deportation. In Factorytown, multiple migrant advocacy organizations struggled against the immigration raids, including the Migrants' Trade Union and faith-based migrant advocacy NGOs. Because of these groups' mobilization efforts, migrant communities as well as the employers of migrant workers—who could not operate the factories without migrant labor—protested against immigration enforcement. Within a few hours after the massive immigrant raid in Factorytown, Peace Center organized a public protest in front of the human rights commission office and sent out press releases that brought national media attention to their cause.

Director Baek Kwangsu, a government official at the Seoul immigration office, was explicit in his disapproval of the migrant advocates' actions. The day of the protest, I visited the Seoul immigration office with Lee Mikyung, a staff member of Peace Center. We had a task to accomplish: to persuade the immigration office to release Lilyan Castillo, a Filipina woman arrested that morning who was the mother of Elizabeth, a three-year-old girl born in South Korea. Mikyung told me that the immigration office sometimes grants a temporary release for a mother of a baby in need of care. However, persuading Director Baek to release Lilyan was far from an easy task. We began to present our case, but he interrupted. "Your organization is helping illegals, right?" He looked at us with disdain and launched into a long tirade.

"What did you people call the immigration raid this morning, a lawful enforcement of our country's immigration law?" He picked up papers from his desk—printouts of the Peace Center's press statement—and slammed them down: "What is this? A rabbit chase, you said? Ridiculous! And what? Human rights abuse? You guys really don't have any respect for the law!" What made him most angry, he said, was migrant advocacy NGOs' claim that the government was committing an injustice against migrant workers. "You see, we have to make this very clear. We are treating migrant workers very well. We only have problems with the illegals, and what we do is the government's business, but the NGOs are saying we persecute migrant workers! Ha!"

Director Baek's appeal to "the government's business" referred to the South Korea nonsettlement policy. In his mind, as in the law, a clear boundary existed between undocumented migrants and other "lawful" migrants. On this basis, he felt that the immigration crackdown against undocumented migrants was entirely justified. He continued, "We South Koreans need to learn from Japan. In Japan, I heard that the NGOs for migrant workers don't offer any help to illegals. They are lawbreakers: they are breaking the law of our country, and we shouldn't have any dealings with them."

Because we needed his authorization for our request, Mikyung and I sat through this speech with awkward smiles plastered on our faces. By our side, Lilyan's baby, Elizabeth, was crying her lungs out, calling ceaselessly for her mother. After patiently listening to Director Baek, Mikyung made her request, but he was adamant in his refusal. He would not believe that Lilyan was the only adult caring for Elizabeth. He claimed that our request was a ruse to get him to release Lilyan so that she could relocate to work somewhere else in South Korea. "If you are telling the truth and if there is no one who can look after her," suggested Director Baek, "just bring the baby here! That solves the problem, doesn't it? She can stay here with the mother and they can return to the Philippines together—how about that?" After a few more futile attempts, we left the immigration office with baby Elizabeth, defeated.

Director Baek presented the official understanding of the immigration raid as a tool to separate from regular migrants a distinct group of migrants without a legal permit to work or stay in the country, commonly referred to as "illegal," "undocumented," or "non-status" migrants. Yet migrant advocacy NGOs like Peace Center contested the supposed division between migrants and "illegals," and advocated for the regularization of undocumented migrants through legal and policy reforms. Even more important, migrant advocacy NGOs in Factorytown routinely took direct action at the local level to stop immigration officers from arresting workers within the factory complex boundaries. When migrant factory workers spotted a suspected immigration van, they called a migrant advocacy NGO. The advocates would then jump in their cars and chase the immigration van in an attempt to release the migrant workers. These actions produced a long-standing conflict between NGOs and immigration officers that under-girded Director Baek's resentment of Peace Center.

Mikyung and I had taken part in the same actions that Director Baek railed against in his speech. For example, one chilly Friday evening in November 2008, I sat in the passenger seat of Mikyung's van, bracing myself as we took a hard right turn into a dark alley. "Where did you say the immigration van was?" she shouted into the phone. "Fresh Mart? Okay, we'll be there right now." But when we reached the store, the immigration van was nowhere in sight. The owner came out of the store and reported that immigration officers had grabbed four migrant workers. "Shoot! We must have just missed them. How dare they come in here and take our people like this?!" Mikyung exclaimed as she sped into the maze of Factorytown roads in search of the van. After driving around the factory complex for fifteen minutes, she finally gave up. When I asked Mikyung what she would have done if we had found the van, she replied, "We'd block the van and beg and plead. Like, 'Can you please release them? Don't you feel sorry for them? They are only working hard.'" "Does that work?" I asked doubtfully. "Well, mostly not. They have their quotas to make. If that fails, then we try, 'Please let just the woman go; she has a little baby.' It used to work before sometimes, but these days it doesn't anymore. But we have to try, right? We can't just give up without putting up a fight."

This was one of many van chases that migrant advocates from Peace Center and other NGOs participated in to protect the migrants they thought of as "our people." In contrast, advocates saw the immigration officers as interlopers who "dared to come in" to the space of Factorytown people—migrants, employers, and migrant advocates. Their sense of

ownership and belonging in this space was rooted in a history of contestation and victory that was passed down to newer migrants and advocates
and kept alive in people's memories.

Jenny Mendoza, a Filipina woman in her late thirties, was an eighteen-
year resident of Factorytown, living proof of the success of collective
mobilization against immigration crackdowns. Whenever the topic of
immigration raids came up, she never failed to tell her story of surviving an
immigration crackdown in 2005. "October 17, Tuesday!" she recalled, was
the "happiest moment of my life in South Korea." In 1996, when she first
came to South Korea, Jenny worked as an industrial trainee at an electronics company in Seoul for eight months until she ran away from her factory
and worked without a legal permit in Factorytown. She met her "husband"
Rey, another Filipino migrant worker, and they had a son together, but they
did not legally marry in South Korea. Her life was ordinary until that raid
on October 17, 2005. During her lunch break, Jenny said, she was at home
with Rey when they heard a knock on the door. Thinking that it was a
cable installer, Rey opened the door, and two immigration officers pushed
their way in and demanded to see visas. Jenny and Rey were handcuffed
and put into a van. As they waited in the van for more than an hour, it
quickly filled with people: "There was everyone! Like thirty people, Nige-
rian, Filipino, Chinese, everyone!"

But when the immigration van was about to leave the factory complex,
something unusual happened. People from Peace Center and South Korean
factory owners in Factorytown—who were angered that the immigration
office was taking away their workers—surrounded the van with their own
cars and trucks and blocked the exit. They sat on the ground in front of
the immigration van and started to rally, demanding the release of the
migrant workers. Then the television news crews came to cover the protest.
To Jenny, who was watching from inside, it felt "like being in the movie,
so unreal." The standoff between protesters and immigration control lasted
for more than seven hours, and it was broadcast live on the news. When
darkness set in, Pastor Kim made a deal with the immigration officials that
they would let the immigration van go, but in return, the immigration
office would release all the arrested undocumented migrants, except those
with forged passports. Finally, at around 9:30 p.m., the exit was unblocked,
and Jenny and the other migrants in the van were taken to the immigration office, given bread and milk, and interrogated. After three days, they

were brought back to Factorytown and set free. Jenny fondly remembered, "There were cameramen, and people gave us flowers and welcomed us! We came back home! It was the happiest moment in Korea."

Experiences of collective victory like these, though few and far between, enabled migrants in Factorytown to maintain a sense of home and solidarity in South Korea, even in the face of fear. Despite occasional successes, actions against the immigration office did not mean that migrants felt unlimited freedom and mobility in South Korea. Instead, what emerged from the on-the-ground interactions between the immigration office, migrant communities, and NGOs was a delicately scripted code of conduct that contained migrants in South Korea spatially and socially.

THE POLITICS OF CONTAINMENT: LESSONS FROM THE DETENTION CENTER

Located in the city of Hwaseong, almost three hours from downtown Seoul by subway and buses, was the immigration detention center I visited most during my fieldwork. In Korean, the detention center was ironically called "Foreigner Protection Center" (*oigukin bohoso*), but the migrants who were detained and soon to be deported did not feel at all protected in this space. I dreaded this place, and my research participants felt the same way. On one occasion, I made the trip to visit Virgie Andrada, who had been arrested in Factorytown two nights earlier by immigration officers and detained until her deportation back to the Philippines. Visitors came for different reasons: to deliver money and passports, to help with an asylum claim, or simply to say good-bye. The atmosphere in the waiting area was heavy as the visitors sat alone with their thoughts, not looking at others or revealing even a hint of a smile.

Inside the visiting booth, the air felt even heavier. Each visitor was given thirty minutes and no more. It had been only two days, but Virgie looked as though she had lost weight. The uniform of a pink crewneck T-shirt and loose training pants made her look pale. Past the right side of the booth's partition, a middle-aged South Korean factory owner was on the verge of tears as he delivered passports and luggage to arrested migrant workers from his factory. On the left, I could hear a Chinese woman sobbing while she visited a man who seemed to be her husband or a close family member.

She soon began wailing and banging her hands against the glass panel. A security guard rushed over to issue the stern warning: "No touching!"

"Why me? I really don't understand," Virgie mumbled through the microphone. A thick glass panel separated us. Through the smears and handprints, I saw the wrinkles on her forehead deepen as she stared up at the ceiling, deep in thought. At first, I thought her question was rhetorical, the kind of question that people often ask when they face circumstances beyond their control, like cancer or a traffic accident. But soon I realized that she wasn't lamenting her misfortune, but seriously inquiring. She directed the question to me: "Why did they come after me? I didn't do anything special. I was just at *home, factory, home, church* all the time!"

Virgie had spent the past nine years in South Korea as an undocumented migrant, a status known in the Filipino community as "TNT," a Tagalog acronym for *Tago-ng-Tago,* or "always hiding." The constant fear of immigration raids was an uncomfortable yet familiar part of her reality. If she had been caught during a random raid, she would have felt devastated— having just celebrated her fortieth birthday, she did not want her life in South Korea to end just yet. But she also would have felt less confused. On the day of her arrest, she was working in the auto accessories factory as usual when two immigration officers entered. The workers all froze— like many factories in the complex, this one was filled with many undocumented migrants from the Philippines, Bangladesh, Nepal, and Pakistan. But to the relief of all others and the shock of Virgie, she was the only one arrested. This narrow focus indicated that someone had reported her. This kept Virgie awake at night, seriously contemplating the reason for her arrest.

Yes, Virgie admitted, she had a passport under a fake name and had overstayed her visa, but she was far from the only one. Her life in South Korea was ordinary: working at a factory from 8:30 a.m. to 6:00 p.m., coming home for dinner and rest, and attending church on Sundays. "Why would anyone bother to report me?" She shrugged her shoulders and again repeated, "It's not like I did anything special. I didn't do business. I don't have any enemies. I never went out of my path! Then why me?"

Her question echoed back in Factorytown, where Filipino migrants were busy debating the reason for Virgie's arrest and offering different theories. Karen, who went to church with Virgie, jokingly said that someone might have laid eyes on Virgie's handsome Filipino boyfriend and wanted to get rid of the competition. Others pointed fingers at a fellow migrant worker who had borrowed money from Virgie and would no longer have to pay her back. But no one had a good answer, and Virgie never learned why she was deported.

Her arrest was so puzzling because it ran against a widely shared assumption in Factorytown. Most undocumented migrants followed a code of conduct to protect themselves from deportation: migrants must stay within the confines of the factory complex—a space of "home, factory, and church"—and remain invisible to the South Korean public so that the immigration office will turn a blind eye to their presence. Virgie's arrest came as a shock; it seemed to rupture the hidden contract between the immigration office and the people of Factorytown.

Migrants' belief in this contract was not entirely accurate—as the major crackdown of November 2008 attests—but it was empirically grounded. Historically, the earlier phase of migrant labor in South Korea began in the late 1980s with migrants from Southeast Asia who overstayed tourist visas in the absence of a formal system for migrant labor. Even after the institution of the guest-worker system, undocumented migrants constituted two-thirds of the total migrant workforce between 1994 and 2002 in South Korea,[7] and the immigration office had no choice but to tolerate their presence. Although immigration raids had intensified since the reform of the guest-worker system in 2003, South Korea still hosted about two hundred thousand undocumented migrants within its borders in 2008 at the time of Virgie's arrest,[8] mostly workers who were hiding in plain sight.

Given the high concentration of undocumented migrants in major industrial towns such as Factorytown across South Korea, if the immigration officers wanted to deport them, it was an open secret where to find them. But the demand for migrant labor in labor-intensive manufacturing remained, particularly for the skilled labor of long-term migrants who were indispensable to small-scale factories and central to the local economy. Thus the choice of targets for immigration enforcement was rarely random but instead selective: it was contingent on who "stood out" among the undocumented, which served the function of keeping migrants in line. Immigration arrest was the price migrants paid when they went "out of [the] path," as Virgie called it, outside the spatial and social borders governing their lives.

BORDERS OF CONTAINMENT:
POLICING MIGRANTS

Immigration officers occasionally entered factories during the day or broke into migrants' homes when they were asleep. However, it was far more common for immigration officers to spot and arrest migrants outside the factory complex—beyond the realm of "home, factory, and church"— for example, in a pub or marketplace downtown, where they would be easily noticed. Immigration officers participated in the open secret of undocumented migrants' segregation by targeting migrants who entered public spaces beyond the borders of migrant neighborhoods. Undocumented migrants minimized their chances of detention and deportation by limiting how often they left the factory complex. They exited this physical space only after carefully assessing the risk, and often used a door-to-door taxi service instead of a bus when they had to leave—for example, to go to the post office, pharmacy, or hospital.

Immigration raids frequently targeted industrial towns with a high number of migrants, such as Factorytown, as opposed to upper-class or middle-class neighborhoods or tourist destinations. Sheila Salazar, a live-in domestic worker and nanny in Chôngdamdong, one of the most affluent neighborhoods in Seoul, came back to Factorytown every weekend to attend Filipino church and see her partner and friends. In South Korea, unlike Hong Kong or Taiwan, the carework sector was not open to migrant labor except *chosônjok* (coethnic Chinese), and Sheila was working without legal authorization, going back and forth between work in factories and live-in carework. Some South Korean employers preferred undocumented Filipina domestic workers for child care to *chosônjok* women with working visas because they wanted their children to learn English. When I asked whether she worried about immigration raids at her employer's place, Sheila said: "No, not really. It's all rich people there where my employers live. Why would immigration ever come there? I go to the department store with the family, and I never see any foreigners." It was only on Saturday afternoons, when she traveled from Chôngdamdong to Factorytown on public transportation, that she felt nervous. In particular, when she neared the vicinity of Factorytown, she was afraid that she might run into immigration officers patrolling the area. Once she entered the factory complex, she felt relatively at ease, but she was most tense when she "crossed the border": on the bus from Seoul to Factorytown and during the five-minute walk from the bus stop to the entrance of the factory complex.

The immigration raids were also racially based, targeting those who looked phenotypically different from ethnic Koreans, those with darker skin tones from South Asia, Africa, and Southeast Asia. Because these migrants stood out among South Koreans in public spaces, some South Korean local residents called the immigration office to report them. Even authorized migrants with legal work documents were not free from this targeting in the border areas. For example, Nam Joohyun had come from Vietnam seven years earlier to marry her husband, a factory worker in Factorytown. For the first few years she was in South Korea, Joohyun had a spousal visa, and after giving birth to her son, she naturalized as a South Korean citizen, changed her Vietnamese first name to a Korean one, and took her husband's last name against the common custom in South Korea in which women maintain their last name even after marriage. Legally, she did not have to fear immigration officers, but whenever she went to the open market at the center of Factorytown, or any other place outside the factory complex, she felt uneasy.

Joohyun's Korean proficiency was limited to fragmented everyday words like the names of food. She spent most of her time working with her sister and other migrants in her factory, and her husband was the only one with whom she spoke Korean on a daily basis. He was her bridge to a life in South Korea outside of home and factory. "My husband understands everything I say!" she said in fragmented Korean, slowly enunciating every word. "When I go to the bank, my husband needs to translate everything I say to the person there." When I asked whether her husband spoke Vietnamese, Joohyun said, "No, he translates my [nonfluent] Korean into Korean. I don't know why, but he is the only one who understands me."

Whenever her husband did not accompany her, she felt awkward and alienated outside the factory complex. Joohyun recalled an evening, only a few years after her arrival in South Korea, when she was buying vegetables at the open market, and a man wearing a beige jacket and workpants suddenly grabbed her arms from behind. Startled, she thought she was being robbed or, worse, kidnapped. The man said something in Korean, but she could not understand him, and he pushed her to the corner of the market. She cried out for help in Korean and Vietnamese, but the people in the market just walked by. The man repeated, *"Ajumma, bisa issô*? [Lady, do you have a visa?]" Recognizing the word for "visa," she showed him her foreigner registration card. It turned out that he was an undercover immigration officer who was hiding in the market to spot and arrest undocumented migrants, and her "foreign" look made her a target. She was not pushed into the immigration van, but that day left a scar of fear. Since then, whenever she could, Joohyun avoided public places beyond her home and the factory complex unless she was with her husband.

On their face, the purpose of the immigration raids was to deport undocumented migrants. But on the ground, it appeared that these raids had a second purpose as well: to contain migrants—undocumented or otherwise—in segregated spaces out of public sight. Although officially the immigration raids targeted only "illegals," the mingling of legal statuses and interpersonal and kinship ties within the migrant community meant that immigration control affected the daily practices and emotions of both documented and undocumented migrants in South Korea. Undocumented migrants were often the husbands, wives, brothers, and daughters of documented migrants who worried about their safety. Migrants with an unexpired work permit under the guest-worker system or with a spousal visa knew that their legal status could easily be lost because these documents came with conditions that restricted migrant workers' mobility or required a citizen spouse's continued sponsorship. In the face of such constraints, immigration raids against undocumented migrants represented a constant threat even to documented migrants, who were haunted by warnings of their possible fate if they ever lost their status.

Legal status and rights on the books did not provide documented migrants like Joohyun with perfect security from immigration raids on the streets of Factorytown. But a lack of legal documents did not necessarily render migrants in a state of constant fear either. Rather, the immigration raids structured the lives of undocumented migrants within a particular zone of containment. Although the unspoken rule that migrants were safe inside the factory complex was broken from time to time, as in the case of the massive crackdown in Factorytown in 2008, it still held significant power. In fact, migrants' and advocates' outrage over the immigration raid into the factory complex revealed their deep sense of betrayal stemming from the breaking of this unspoken rule. The first Sunday after the crackdown, Pastor Kim at Peace Center was barely able to contain his emotions as he stood before his Filipino congregation during the workshop service:

"I am sorry, I am so sorry that I couldn't protect you. I am the sinner. I failed to do my work. This is a complete injustice." Pastor Kim's strong expression may sound extreme, but it reflected his sense of responsibility to protect migrants in what he assumed to be a safe space. After worship, the church members gathered in the houses of those who had been arrested to pack their belongings, still awestruck by what had happened. They collected money to purchase airline tickets to the Philippines for migrants held in detention centers. South Korean pastors and staff members drove back and forth to bring arrested migrants their luggage, passports, and money.

After the initial shock subsided, Pastor Kim's worship service two weeks later told a different story. He consoled migrants, telling them that he had met with high officials and parliament members to protest the violent crackdown. Kim reassured the migrant congregation: "It should be okay now. I can't say that immigration will not come, but such a massive crackdown will not happen again for a while. So stay inside this area, and don't go out, and you should be okay." Pastor Kim meant that if migrants stayed inside the factory complex, within the spatial boundaries implicitly imposed on migrants, their presence would be more or less tolerated by the local community and immigration officials. In this sense, the regime of containment was not exclusively enforced by immigration control but also reiterated by migrant advocacy NGOs and migrants through their narratives of safe and risky spaces and codes of conduct.

DISCIPLINING MIGRANTS: GOVERNING SOCIAL BOUNDARIES

Migrants were not only physically contained within "home, factory, and church"; they also avoided overstepping social boundaries by engaging in low-wage work and not participating in political activism or doing—in Virgie's words—"anything *special*." Unlike in Virgie's case, migrants and migrant advocates in Factorytown were not at all surprised when the immigration officers arrested and deported Shakil Ahmed, a Migrants' Trade Union (MTU) member and an active leader of the local Bangladeshi community. "I knew it!" Pastor Kim said, "I knew he would be caught from the moment he started going back and forth to Seoul like that." Immigration raids often targeted politically active migrants, such as leaders and active members of the MTU, for deportation. In fact, whenever the MTU staged a public protest, activists routinely watched out for immigration officers who were taking pictures of migrant participants, which acted as a significant deterrent to political activism. Since the MTU's inception, all of the organization's leaders had been targeted by immigration raids and deported, and the organization also routinely lost rank-and-file members to targeted immigration raids. Despite a 2015 Supreme Court ruling granting the MTU official legal status—only after ten years of refusal—such targeted crackdowns reveal that migrant workers have been denied the full right of association, key to workers' collective action in South Korea and beyond.

One evening, Sung Junho, a South Korean MTU activist, was fuming as he walked into the union office in a rush and asked if any of us could help pack the belongings of five Indonesian MTU members to bring to the detention center. These undocumented migrant workers had made a labor claim to receive their severance pay, which is granted to workers regardless of their visa status under South Korean law. In response, the factory owner refused to pay them and threatened to report them to the immigration office. All five workers were arrested at home earlier that day and were now in the detention center awaiting deportation. Did their arrest have something to do with their involvement with the MTU, or was it simply because they had claimed labor rights? Junho was not sure, but either way, immigration raids operated to discipline and punish migrants who trespassed their socially accepted boundaries.

As stories of targeted immigration raids spread throughout the migrant communities, people talked about the need to avoid "making trouble" because upsetting a neighbor, employer, or friend could result in a call to the immigration office. In Basetown, Amy Samiento, a Filipina migrant hostess, told other migrant women her stories of barely escaping immigration raids as cautionary tales. Amy fell in love and left the club to move in with her American GI boyfriend Tom, but even after she was pregnant and gave birth to their son, Tom kept seeing other women. When their son was barely two months old, Tom married another Filipina hostess and stopped financially supporting the baby. Amy took active measures to secure child support, contacting Tom's commanding officer and even protesting in front of the American embassy. When Tom threatened to report Amy to immigration—her visa was voided when she left the club, and her status was not regularized because Tom did not marry her—Amy called his bluff, thinking he would not harm the mother of his child. But one day, Tom's friend and fellow American GI called Amy to meet for lunch at the Filipino restaurant in Basetown. That morning, she was late because the baby had thrown a tantrum. On her way to meet him almost forty-five minutes late, she overheard others saying that there had been an immigration raid in the restaurant. She quickly turned back and ran home as fast as she could: "I knew then it was Tom's setup. Now I am a burden to him, and he wants to get rid of me!" Afterward, she lived with the fear that Tom would somehow find a way to deport her, and ultimately gave up her efforts to seek child support.

Even as immigration control was imposed on migrants who trespassed social boundaries by engaging in political action and claiming rights, the migrant community—with its own factions, hierarchies, and disputes—utilized immigration control to discipline its own members. The threat of "reporting to the immigration office" operated as a mechanism to expel people who broke the social code of conduct. In the Nepalese community, even those who were the most vocal about the immigration raids admitted that when they learned of a Nepali scamming other Nepalese community members or getting into fights and becoming a "troublemaker," they strategically used the immigration office to deport that individual. "Well, we just send them away," said Ashok Gurung with an awkward smile. Likewise, within the Filipino community, even Pastor Paul, who was enraged by the massive immigration crackdown in Factorytown, and Jenny Mendoza, who proudly told the story of surviving the immigration raid, did not hesitate to make such threats. When Jenny became aware that her husband, Rey, was having an affair with Cheryl, a younger Filipina member of Pastor Paul's church, she reported it to Pastor Paul and announced it to the congregation. She pleaded that she and Rey had a son together, alleged that Cheryl had betrayed her and the church community, and threatened to call the immigration office if Cheryl continued to see Rey. Pastor Paul concurred, and Cheryl moved out of Factorytown.

Unequal power relations within the coethnic community shaped how migrants practiced internal surveillance and mutual policing of their boundary of containment. Admittedly, immigration enforcement was at times used to prevent harm to the community by removing a select few who committed fraud or violence in a situation where victims were unable to report to the police due to their undocumented legal status. Yet it also enforced a moral code of conduct devised by more powerful members of the community, and offered less protection for marginalized members, such as single women like Cheryl.

In particular, the power differentials between those with a stable status—mostly through marriage to South Korean citizens—and those without were salient. At times, antagonism surfaced between marriage migrants and undocumented migrants. In Factorytown, Martin Torres, a Filipino man in a de facto marriage to a South Korean woman, owned a grocery store that sold Filipino and other Asian goods. Because he was a married man in the Philippines, he was not able to regularize his status through official marriage. But their business was doing well, and when winter came in 2009, they started selling fish cake (*odeng*) in hot anchovy broth, a popular Korean street food. The story had it that one day, a friend of Martin, a Filipina woman who was legally married to a South Korean man, came to their stand and asked for a free fish cake. Martin refused and demanded that she pay for it. Becky Garcia, who was telling the story, raised her voice: "And she got upset! They have known each other for a long time, but that's how Filipina women married to South Koreans are. She went home and reported him to the immigration, and she's been boasting it to people! That one piece of fish cake got him deported. He should have just given it to her." Whether or not this particular story was entirely factual, such stories of marriage migrants exploiting the vulnerability of undocumented migrants traveled widely within the migrant community as cautionary tales for migrants to monitor their own actions and the actions of others.

HIDING IN PLAIN SIGHT: THE POLITICS OF CONTAINMENT

The policy of nonsettlement for migrant workers was almost impossible to implement for the South Korean state, which hosted two hundred thousand undocumented migrants within its borders. As this chapter has shown, many of these migrants built homes in South Korea, living and working in segregated neighborhoods in industrial towns across the country as members of tightly organized ethnic and religious communities, yet doing so under a threat of immigration raids.

This chapter has taken a close, personal look at immigration crackdowns to show that immigration raids were less about enforcing the state's non-settlement policy than about containing migrants in the spheres of "home, factory, and church" out of the South Korean public eye. Immigration officers participated in the open secret that undocumented migrants were concentrated in such neighborhoods by policing their boundaries and targeting migrants who entered public spaces on the borders of migrant towns. In doing so, they engaged with the collective mobilization of migrant communities and migrant advocates who defended the migrant space from the immigration raids.

Even though migrant wives and documented migrant workers were not subject to deportation, some became hesitant to enter these public spaces due to their experiences of being arrested and released based on their racial conspicuousness. In addition, immigration raids targeted politically active migrants and those who "made trouble" by claiming their rights, including leaders of the Migrants' Trade Union, denying their on-the-books rights of association and labor. The borders of containment were decided not only by the immigrant officers but also by South Korean locals who spotted migrants who looked "different" and called the immigration office, advocates who fought against and bargained with immigration authorities, and migrants reporting other migrants. Immigration crackdowns thus operated as a strategy to contain and discipline migrants—with or without legal status—in the shadows of citizenship and to enforce social and spatial boundaries for migrants' practice of rights and belonging.

FIVE

The Making of Migrant Workers and Migrant Women

On a hot summer day in 2010, forty-two solemn-faced women gathered in front of the office of the National Human Rights Commission of Korea in downtown Seoul. Amid the skyscrapers and busy passers-by, the women held a black banner that read: "I Too Could Be That Vietnamese Migrant Woman." The women immigrated to South Korea via cross-border marriages with South Korean men; their demonstration was held in protest of the tragic death of a twenty-year-old Vietnamese woman. She had been killed only seven days after her arrival by her South Korean husband, who had a history of mental illness. The women publicly mourning her death were not only from Vietnam but also from the Philippines, China, and Cambodia; together, they held a press conference in front of the commission as migrant women (*iju yŏsŏng*) married to South Korean men. One Chinese migrant woman took the microphone and made a desperate plea to South Koreans: "Please be kind to us; be a good neighbor to us. If only one person in her town cared and protected her, she would still be alive today."

The migrant women's call for benevolence and protection differed from the usual South Korean mode of protest—accusing the wrongdoer and demanding that the state take action—though another speaker did touch on the failure of the South Korean state to regulate the matchmaking business, including through the full disclosure of South Korean potential husbands' medical histories. One South Korean activist who came to support the press conference expressed her discomfort to other South Korean activists in attendance: "Why not strongly demand things from the government, like their official apology?" The South Korean staff of the migrant women's advocacy NGOs who helped organize the conference did not stand under the banner and make speeches but instead stood to the side, deliberately avoiding the spotlight. "I hear you," one said in response, "but this is what the migrant women prepared themselves. Isn't that what counts?"

Two years earlier, in the very same spot, a different group of migrants and migrant advocates—fifty-three men and women from migrant advocacy NGOs and trade unions—had come together to protest the immigration crackdown against undocumented migrants. Several activists condemned the South Korean government for its human rights violations. Speakers detailed the events of the immigration raid. "This morning, we witnessed so much inhumane and unlawful violence and injustice committed by the immigration officers," a South Korean activist from the Migrants' Trade Union (MTU) shouted. "Migrant workers [*iju nodongja*] were chased down by immigration officers like rabbits, and their homes were broken into. There was one Filipina woman who was pregnant. Although she had a legal work visa, she was so frightened by the raid and she had a miscarriage!" These advocates narrated the stories of migrant workers, yet migrant workers themselves were noticeably absent from the protest. Only one migrant worker activist joined the protest, and he was not given an opportunity to make a speech. At the end of the rally, protesters raised their fists in unison, chanting in Korean, "Legalize migrant workers! Stop the crackdowns!"

These scenes of protest illustrate two distinct modes of political mobilization by and for migrants and offer a lens into the collective subject-making of migrants in South Korea. In these events, migrants in South Korea—women and men of diverse racial, ethnic, and national origins and legal statuses—were represented in the public sphere as two separate groups of *migrant workers* and *migrant women*—or marriage migrants (*gyŏlhon iminja*)—with distinctive demands, voices, and degrees of self-representation.

On the surface, the differences between the two groups might seem self-evident, stemming from their legal categories and statuses. Marriage migrants, who had spousal visas and were eligible for naturalization, might claim political membership more easily than labor migrants, who were in South Korea as temporary workers and often had a precarious legal status if they stayed beyond the five years of their labor contract. This explanation privileges the status conferred by the state as the key status, presupposing that migrant wives and migrant workers naturally fell into two distinct categories upon the moment of their arrival in South Korea.

This chapter decenters the state and the state's bestowal of legal status in the production of migrant subjects by showing that the seemingly solid division between migrant workers and migrant women in their collective representations did not emerge naturally but instead is situated in ethnic and religion-based migrant communities and in encounters with South Korean civil society. In particular, the chapter examines how labor and marriage migrants in South Korea emerged in the public sphere as divergent cross-ethnic subjects—migrant workers and migrant women—through the interaction of multiple groups of South Korean civil society actors, including migrant advocacy NGOs, social welfare centers, and trade unions. Their day-to-day encounters, each with distinct terms of engagement, shaped migrants as subjects in the public sphere, and even excluded certain groups of migrants from political subjecthood when they did not easily fit the categories of migrant workers or migrant women. A problematic discourse common in South Korean media and popular debates conflated "migrant women" with "marriage migrants," rendering invisible women labor migrants—migrant women factory workers and hostesses—as well as migrant men who marry South Korean women and settle in South Korea.

ETHNIC AND RELIGIOUS COMMUNITY MOBILIZATIONS

Daisy Sulit, a thirty-five-year-old Filipina woman, met her South Korean husband ten years earlier in a furniture factory in Factorytown, when she was working at a sanding job as an undocumented worker and he was a spray man. The couple now had a five-year-old son and lived in one of the makeshift stacked-container units populated almost entirely by Filipino migrants. Because her husband now worked at a water purifier sales job and was rarely home, Daisy's social interactions almost exclusively involved

Filipino neighbors, co-workers, and church members. She had gained a work permit and later South Korean legal citizenship via marriage, but this did not bring any concrete changes to her daily life: she received the same pay as before—the "migrant" wage, lower than South Korean workers'— and when immigration officers raided her factory, she hid in the storage room with her co-workers, pretending the factory was closed. The official category of "marriage migrant" or "migrant woman" was foreign to Daisy, even though she now belonged to this group. She knew some other Filipina women in Factorytown who had married South Koreans, but she did not socialize with migrant wives from any other country, and she did not imagine a shared bond with such women as migrant wives.

Similarly, Irene Viray, a twenty-five-year-old Filipina woman, met and married a South Korean factory worker through a matchmaking agency. Only a few weeks after she arrived in 2008, she began working from 9:00 a.m. to 6:00 p.m. at a plastic injection factory in Factorytown alongside other Filipino migrant workers. When she found this job, she dropped out of her Korean language classes, which were offered weekday mornings as part of an immigrant integration program for migrant wives. She would have liked to learn some Korean, but sending remittances to her natal family in the Philippines took higher priority. Through her co-workers in the factory, Irene became part of the local Filipino Catholic community led by Father Thomas, although her South Korean husband disapproved of her spending too much time with other Filipinos.

For migrant women like Daisy and Irene, the boundary between marriage migrant and labor migrant was a fluid one, challenging the dichotomy of "wife or worker."[1] Migrant women in South Korea like Daisy and Irene transcended these categories and lived as part of an integrated Filipino ethnic community. They attended Filipino church services, shopped at ethnic grocery stores selling rice noodles and egg pies, worked in factories with other migrants, and participated in social and religious activities such as baptisms and birthday celebrations. The reach of the Philippine state was strongly felt in South Korea, reminding them of the country they had left behind, temporarily or permanently. As sociologist Robyn Rodriguez reminds us, immigrants' transnational experiences are shaped by nationalist projects in their sending countries that extend beyond territorial borders.[2] This is particularly salient in the Philippine case, where the nation-state has deployed a discourse of "new national heroes" to incorporate migrant contract workers overseas into the national imagery.

In South Korea, the Philippine embassy, located in the capital city of Seoul, and the Catholic Church worked to cultivate and maintain Filipino national and ethnic identity among migrants. The center of the Filipino community in South Korea was Hyehwa Catholic Church in Seoul, where Filipino priests offered Tagalog mass every Sunday in a church filled with more than two thousand Filipinos who had come to South Korea as migrant workers, marriage migrants, professionals, and international students. Jokingly called the "Filipino takeover," the streets surrounding the church were filled with over seventy vendors selling Filipino food, cosmetics, and phone cards. As Lyn Mata, a regular churchgoer and a migrant domestic worker in a foreign embassy, said: "As soon as you leave the subway station, you see only Filipinos. You feel like you are back in the Philippines!"

During my visits to Hyehwa Church in the winter of 2009, the Philippine ambassador took the front pew, and the priest publicly thanked him for his presence and encouraged the church members to bring any problems to him. Various events and services that the Philippine embassy provided were also announced during mass, including an event commemorating fifty years of South Korea–Philippines diplomatic relations, in addition to church-organized activities, such as a field trip to Catholic memorial sites and a beauty pageant.

Beyond Hyehwa Church, multiple Filipino priests were deployed in various cities of South Korea with significant Filipino migrant populations to offer a Tagalog mass as part of the mission to care for the spiritual lives of overseas Filipinos. Father Thomas, who was stationed in Factorytown, traveled to offer Tagalog mass services in five different cities in the province, organized bowling leagues, and provided labor counseling for Filipino factory workers. In the Catholic church in Factorytown, Father Thomas and visitors from the Philippines often reminded the congregation, "Each of you is an ambassador in South Korea. How you behave reflects on our nation." The church encouraged a strong work ethic and monetary remittances to families in the Philippines and discouraged migrants from wasting money on gambling or other vices. "Filipino pride," the national uplift of the Philippines, and the role of overseas migrants as "ambassadors" were common topics of conversation in the space of the church.

In addition to their religious membership, labor and marriage migrants were interconnected through kinship ties because Filipino migrants who came to South Korea as workers or wives often invited relatives and hometown neighbors to migrate. Thus both migrant wives and migrant workers were embedded in the same tight familial, cultural, and religious networks and activities within ethnic communities. Such was the case not only for Filipinos but also for other ethnic groups, including Nepalese, Bangladeshis, Vietnamese, and Burmese, who within their respective coethnic communities invited a famous singer from Nepal, set up a prayer room during Ramadan, celebrated Easter in a Vietnamese Catholic congregation, and mobilized in support of a democratic government in Burma. So how did the distinct groups of migrant workers and migrant women emerge from such intertwined ethnic communities of marriage and labor migrants? The answer lies in their encounters with various South Korean civil society actors.

MOMENTS OF CROSS-ETHNIC SUBJECT-MAKING

Roselle Reyes, a forty-seven-year-old Filipina woman who had spent sixteen years in Factorytown as an undocumented worker, firmly believed that she had earned the right to claim a legal status to live and work in South Korea through her hard work. When I asked whether the government should provide a working visa for all migrant workers, she replied, "Definitely for all Filipinos! Because we are hardworking people. Others are lazy." At that moment, Florence Ocampo, a twenty-eight-year-old Filipina neighbor who was busy peeling and eating apples next to us, intervened: "*Ate* [older sister], but that's discrimination! You can't say that only we Filipinos get the working visa and not others. We are all the same here." Roselle resisted at first, saying, "But I am just saying what I know! These Bangla[deshis], I've worked with them many times, and they stop working as soon as the boss leaves the factory. But we Filipinos are not like that. We work whether or not anyone is watching!" But Florence was persistent. When she again claimed that it was impossible to give working visas only to Filipinos, Roselle paused for a few seconds before conceding: "Okay, okay! Working visa for everyone!" Although Roselle initially identified with Filipino ethnic

identity as a primary boundary, echoing the Philippine state's representation of Filipino workers as particularly diligent and hardworking, in the
course of the dialogue, she reached a moment in which she agreed that—as
migrant workers in South Korea—Filipino and Bangladeshi workers were
"all the same here."

Such dialogues did not take place in a vacuum; migrant factory workers in Factorytown were regular participants in activities hosted by Peace
Center and other migrant advocacy NGOs that brought together multiple
ethnic groups of migrants for social and political events. They went on
summer hiking trips, attended protests against immigration crackdowns,
and competed in basketball and volleyball leagues together with migrants
from other countries. These NGO-sponsored encounters created a sense
of collectivity among migrants beyond their ethnic and national communities, enabling the formation of migrant workers as subjects of rights in
South Korea.

Whereas social and political gatherings organized by South Korean
advocacy NGOs enabled the collective subject-formation among migrant
workers, for migrant women in cross-border marriages, the various educational programs specifically targeted toward their integration played a
critical role. Women of diverse ethnic and national backgrounds met in
education programs, which operated as a space to form a collective identity
while acculturating their ethnic identities. When they enrolled in Korean
language programs at Peace Center, migrant wives were often given Kore-
anized names—a version of their given name that was easy for Koreans
to pronounce—or even a new Korean name. These women learned the
Korean language from a textbook produced specifically for migrant wives
by the Ministry of Gender Equality and Family. From the textbook and
through instruction from teachers, migrant women learned that the term
multicultural family referred to "families like yours, in which husbands and
wives are from different countries"; they also learned about various services
targeted toward migrant women. They learned that "marriage migrants,"
"migrant women," and "multicultural families" were recognized categories
in South Korea that referred to them, and the classroom became a site that
gave meaning to these newly acquired group identities.

The classrooms offered spaces for conversations and sympathy among
migrant women that produced a sense of collectivity. One morning in
the intermediate Korean class, some students started complaining about

possessive South Korean husbands who did not let migrant wives go out. "My friend's husband is just like that," said Kelsey Ng from the Philippines. "She can't even come to church, or to the Center to learn Korean. He hates when she meets with other Filipinos, thinking that she would cheat. Even when I call her at home, her husband gets mad." In response to Kelsey, Cho Hayoung from Vietnam said with a deep sigh, "What do they think we foreign women are? That we would run away if they don't keep us in the house? How come they don't know, women run away because they act like that?"

A few weeks later, the lesson plan according to the Korean language textbook included a reading exercise with simplified guidelines for the naturalization process for marriage migrants: information about eligibility, cost, and required documents, including the application, passport, naturalization statement, financial documents, and marriage certificate. In addition to these official documents, it listed items that could establish "proof of the marriage," including "photos, supporting letters from people around you, letters exchanged before marriage, etc." Yong Minji from the Philippines, who was about to start the application process, asked the instructor what other documents she needed. When Hong Youngjoo, a South Korean volunteer teacher, replied that she was not familiar with the process, the migrant women who had already been naturalized chimed in: "What they want to see is whether you are really married to your husband, and that it is not fake. So you can bring letters from your common friends who have seen you dating, letters from your neighbors saying that you've been living together for how many years, and oh, I also brought printouts of the emails we sent to each other from long time ago." Other women used their friends' experiences as a cautionary tale: "My friend told me that the interviews at the immigration office can be really embarrassing. Like the interviewer asking about whether you had boyfriends before, and about you and your husband at night, things like that because they want to know whether you are really married. So be prepared."

By sharing common experiences and concerns during and after class— topics including the immigration process, husbands, in-laws, and child rearing—migrant women created a collective identity as "we foreign women" and "marriage migrants," through a structured curriculum set by the South Korean state and administered by civil society organizations. This identity offered a potential basis to make claims in the public sphere.

SOUTH KOREAN CIVIL SOCIETY AND MIGRANT SUBJECT-MAKING

The separate subjects of migrant workers and migrant women emerged from their intertwined space of ethnic and religious communities through migrants' interactions with South Korean civil society actors, such as migrant advocacy NGOs, trade unions, and social welfare centers. These South Korean actors were embedded in the sociohistorical context of the formation of South Korean civil society. The flow of labor and marriage migration that began in the late 1980s and increased in the 1990s coincided with the nascent democratization of South Korea that occurred after 1987. Since that time, South Korean civil society has undergone a significant transformation from a pro-democracy force in opposition to military dictatorship to a body supporting diverse types of civic and political participation. The civil society actors in Factorytown and beyond—Peace Center, the MTU, and City Hall Center—reflected multiple coexisting modes of civic engagement in South Korea. The relationships that South Korean civil society actors reproduced in their interactions with migrants as paternal authorities, maternal educators, and comrades shaped the divergent migrant subject-making in the South Korean public sphere.

Contesting Visions in the Making of Migrant Workers

Protestant pastor Kim Wonsik started Peace Center in the early 1990s in Factorytown with the mission of serving the weak and downtrodden at the margins of society. In the ensuing years, migrants from the Philippines, Nepal, and other Asian countries moved into his parish. Influenced by social justice ideals, Pastor Kim was motivated by his religious faith and his commitment to selfless devotion to people in need; he explained, "There are people who need help, and God sent me to serve. They call me Father. How could I turn my eyes away from them?" In addition to leading church services for the Filipino congregation on Sundays, Peace Center brought together multiple ethnic communities of Factorytown migrant workers by offering direct, concrete assistance, such as medical care, help retrieving unpaid salaries, and labor law education. In the mid-1990s, faith-based groups advocating for migrant workers united as a coalition to demand that the South Korean state adopt legal and policy reforms to ensure migrant workers' human rights. The coalition drew on the labor of clergy and semi-narians committed to faith-based carework to provide homes for the elderly, shelters for runaway girls and the homeless, welfare centers for the disabled, and migrant worker centers. Peace Center was a part of this coalition.

Although faith-based migrant advocacy NGOs like Peace Center were the predominant actors in migrant advocacy in South Korea, a smaller segment of the migrant workforce also came into contact with South Korean labor activists. In 2001 in Factorytown, several migrant workers joined these direct organizing efforts under the Equality Trade Union; in 2005, this organization became the Migrants' Trade Union (MTU). Because the MTU emphasized migrant workers' self-representation and organization, migrant workers formed the leadership, and South Korean activists took a supporting role. The South Korean activists involved with the MTU were secular, younger, and more politically driven than the staff of faith-based migrant advocacy NGOs. Woo Yuseon, a thirty-three-year-old South Korean MTU activist, had a background in student activism during her university years. She had never met a migrant before she started working for the MTU, but, she explained, "I wanted to get involved because I thought the issue of migrant labor was at the root of global capitalism." From Yuseon's perspective, her work was part of a larger struggle for marginalized workers' rights and democracy, rather than specifically focused on helping migrant workers. These activists also supported struggles of evictees, irregular factory workers, and farmers who faced losing their land because of military base expansion.

Despite significant differences between Peace Center and the MTU in their ideological leanings and modes of engagement, these organizations showed a high level of convergence in their political activities as an alliance for migrant workers. At the day-to-day level, these organizations engaged in similar activities, such as labor counseling, and regularly joined the same protests against immigration crackdowns. Yet their modes of everyday interaction with migrants distinguished these organizations from one another, setting boundaries between migrants and South Korean advocates that influenced migrants' political participation and subject formation.

Paternalism at Peace Center

Peace Center's organizational structure was based in a paternalistic hierarchy in which the pastor had authority over other staff members and over migrant workers—the target group for the center's advocacy and services and the group construed as beneficiaries of help.[3] Even though Peace Center adopted the secular language of labor and human rights in its advocacy work, the religious authority structure governed the norms of interaction in daily activities. This was reflected by the South Korean pastors and staff members' use of *banmal*—the informal mode of speech that also reflects a social hierarchy—in their interactions with migrant workers. *Banmal* can be used as an expression of intimacy, and at times migrants accepted it as such, especially when it was used by Pastor Kim, who had established fatherly relationships with migrants in town. But when younger or new pastors, seminarians, and other staff members used *banmal* to speak to migrants, they often met resistance or withdrawal. The conversational norm in which staff used *banmal* when speaking to migrants reinforced the hierarchy between South Koreans and migrants.

As a native speaker of the Korean language and having grown up in Korean culture, in which age, even a few years of difference, matters in shaping speech patterns and interpersonal hierarchies, I found myself deeply troubled when South Korean staff members in their thirties and forties spoke *banmal* to older migrant workers. Migrant workers in Factorytown ranged in age from their twenties to their fifties, yet to the South Korean advocates at Peace Center, all migrants seemed to blur together as a group of young men and women who did not merit age-appropriate respect. This practice at times came from a false assumption about migrants' Korean proficiency; while some migrants indeed could not distinguish *banmal* from *jondaemal* and thus did not take offense at being talked down to, those who had been in South Korea for some time spoke Korean with fluency and took this as a sign of disrespect.

Certainly, not all faith-based migrant advocacy organizations in South Korea practiced hierarchical interaction styles, but this was not unique to Peace Center. The practice of using *banmal* to address migrants was often a source of contention between older and younger generations of advocates. Hyun Youngjung, a thirty-four-year-old migrant advocate introduced in Chapter 3, said that in the two faith-based migrant advocacy organizations where she worked after college, the pastors mostly used *banmal,* but she thought this was acceptable because the pastors were older (in their fifties and sixties), had a long history with migrants, and were generally respectful in their interactions. However, she and other young activists grew more concerned when South Koreans volunteering or working on a short-term basis treated migrants as if they were children. The problem, as she and other activists I spoke to understood it, was that older volunteers, seminarians, and junior pastors were often sent to the organization for practicum without much training about migrant issues or general human rights awareness. Yet the problem was difficult to address because people saw them as "meaning well" and "working hard" in a spirit of religious self-sacrifice.

Moreover, the problem of language and interaction norms was not one of individual behavior but, rather, resulted from the structural condition of migrant workers' dependency and vulnerability in South Korea. Especially for undocumented migrant workers who faced the risk of immigration raids, South Korean pastors and advocates assumed the role of benevolent protectors. They not only organized on behalf of migrant workers in their political advocacy work but also, on the day-to-day level, accompanied migrant workers when they left the zone of containment—for example, to go to the labor office, embassy, or hospitals outside the factory complex. For example, Rosalie Doromal, a thirty-five-year-old Filipina migrant worker in Factorytown, was hesitant to ask a Peace Center staff member to take her and her husband to a hospital. She said, "I just hope they don't think I ask too many favors." Because migrant workers viewed requesting assistance from a migrant advocacy NGO such as Peace Center as asking for a personal "favor," they were expected to—and many indeed did—feel a sense of gratitude and debt to South Korean migrant advocates, who were willingly available when migrant workers needed assistance, in contrast to other South Koreans who were hostile or indifferent. Thus South Korean immigration law and policy, which rendered migrant workers less than full members in South Korea, also fostered paternalistic relations and structural inequities between South Korean advocates and migrants, even as the goal of advocacy purported to challenge those inequities.

The tension between the everyday paternalism and the projects of migrant rights and justice became salient one day when I accompanied Lee Mikyung, a staff member at Peace Center in her forties, on a visit to Vidu Sarkar, a Bangladeshi worker who had been injured during the immigration crackdown and hospitalized for a month. Mikyung had negotiated with the owner of Vidu's factory, who was initially reluctant to cover Vidu's medical expenses and salary during his recovery as required by the workers' compensation program, and we were delivering the good news that the owner had finally agreed to submit the application. Vidu and I knew each other from Peace Center activities, and I called him *bhai* (a term for older brother) because he was fifteen years older than I. Not knowing we were acquainted, Mikyung introduced me to Vidu in *banmal,* saying, "This is a kind older sister [*yŏgi jo'eun nuna*]." I was taken aback by the title "older sister," and clearly so was he, as he immediately responded from his hospital bed in *jondaemal* (a respectful mode of speech): "Why is she my older sister? She's definitely a younger sister [*dongseng*] to me." Mikyung did not take his correction seriously, replying, "Whatever—it's the same," and she started to talk about the workers' compensation.

The interaction among Vidu, Mikyung, and myself exemplified the paradoxical nature of faith-based migrant advocacy organizations' assistance to migrant workers. On behalf of Peace Center, Mikyung helped Vidu access workers' compensation, his right as a worker according to South Korean labor law. Had Peace Center not intervened, the factory owner may very well have decided to forego the application altogether, and Vidu would not have had equal protection under the law, having to pay for his surgery and hospitalization himself without receiving any pay during his recovery time, even though the law mandated compensation for injured workers. Yet such encounters also reproduced a hierarchical relationship between South Korean migrant advocates and the migrant workers.

When advocacy work was offered in a way that reinforced a hierarchy in which South Korean advocates gave help and received gratitude, recipients were forced to choose between material help and social respect. Ali Faruk from Bangladesh chose respect and distanced himself from Peace Center. After several years of working in Factorytown as an undocumented worker, he had settled in South Korea with his South Korean wife and their children. When he came to visit Vidu in the hospital room, he said:

> When I went back to Peace Center after a while, I met this new pastor who started talking in *banmal* to me. He wasn't even old. And he doesn't know me. It's not like we are close friends, or I am a young man. Before, listening to *banmal* was okay. I let it go. But now I am a grown man, the father of two children.

Ali continued to admonish, "They say that they are working for human rights. If they themselves don't respect the human rights of migrant workers, then what kind of human rights are they talking about?" Distancing himself from Peace Center was not an easy decision for Ali because he greatly appreciated all the help he had received from Peace Center and from Pastor Kim; he still remembered how the pastor had helped recover his friends' unpaid salary, which was part of the reason he initially "let it go" when staff members spoke to him in *banmal*. Ali also fondly recalled how he had gathered together with his Bangladeshi friends and with Filipino and Nepalese migrants in the Peace Center common room. But for Ali, there was more to having human rights and labor rights than recovering an unpaid salary; it also meant being recognized and respected as "a grown man" with an equal and full personhood, which he felt was denied at Peace Center.

That both of the migrant workers who openly expressed their discomfort with paternalistic relationships in South Korean migrant advocacy NGOs were from Bangladesh rather than the Philippines was not coincidental. Whereas the Filipino migrant community was predominantly church based, with a clergyperson as its leader, Bangladeshi and Nepalese workers organized more autonomously in relation to South Korean advocates. Bangladeshi migrants were overrepresented in the MTU movement, which distinguished itself from faith-based migrant advocacy. For instance, when asked about the lack of engagement from Filipinos with the MTU, Ali said in a disapproving tone, "They just listen to the priest and think that's all there is." Although the MTU actively engaged in outreach to the Filipino community and became more successful at recruiting Filipino members over time, for the majority of Filipino migrant workers in Factorytown, faith-based advocacy NGOs and the church-based community were much more prominent in their lives. In this context, the paternalistic relationships that spilled over from the space of the migrant church to other realms of interaction with migrant advocates were received more seamlessly by Filipino church members in Factorytown than by their Bangladeshi and Nepalese co-workers. For migrant workers who had a strong sense of debt to South Korean advocates, challenging hierarchies and claiming their own voice as equals came with significant costs. The prevalence of faith-based migrant advocacy in migrant worker mobilization partly explains why migrant workers' direct voices were largely absent from the migrant worker protest in the chapter-opening vignette, an issue that critical voices began to emerge to address.

Risky Comradeship at the Migrants' Trade Union

In contrast to South Korean–centered, largely faith-based advocacy, the Migrants' Trade Union (MTU) emphasized the collective empowerment of migrant workers through the use of migrants' direct voices and through equal comradeship between migrant and South Korean activists. Consciously distancing itself from the paternalistic helper role employed in faith-based care work, the MTU embraced nonhierarchical relationships of mutual comradeship among workers united in a common struggle. The leadership of the MTU, headed by Michel Catuira from the Philippines in 2009–2010, consisted of migrant workers; in everyday interactions, migrant members and South Korean activists and volunteers, mostly in their twenties and thirties, called each other "comrade" (*dongji*), a gender-neutral and nonhierarchical form of address common in trade unions, and used English or *jondaemal,* the respectful form of speech in Korean. Although it was not always feasible, the MTU tried to have translators present at events, educational programs, and counseling sessions, so that migrants who did not speak Korean or English could participate.

Whereas many faith-based migrant advocacy NGOs received funds from the local and central governments for migrant assistance activities, the MTU struggled to achieve registered trade union status in South Korea, but the Ministry of Labor refused to grant trade union status to the MTU because of the involvement of undocumented migrants. Tension between faith-based groups and the MTU declined after 2007, when a more conservative government came to power and led an aggressive immigration crackdown against undocumented migrant workers, making the internal differences within the migrant advocacy movement less significant.

The MTU's activities were similar to those of faith-based migrant advocacy NGOs. Most of their daily work involved labor counseling regarding unpaid salary and severance pay. Although they used the title "trade union," their lack of legal union status and low rate of mobilization among migrant workers meant that the MTU was unable to engage in collective bargaining. South Korean advocates and activists instead assisted migrant workers by negotiating with factory owners, accompanying migrant workers to the labor office, and filing legal cases. MTU activists actively used such interactions as an opportunity for migrant workers to express themselves in their own voices.

On one occasion, I accompanied a Filipina migrant worker, Rusiell Elizalde, and an MTU activist, Kyoung Eunjin, to the labor office as a volunteer interpreter. Rusiell's factory refused to provide severance pay after she had worked there for two years. South Korean law stipulated that an employer with fewer than five workers did not have to pay severance pay, and Rusiell's factory owner manipulated this provision by dividing his factory into smaller units on paper. The South Korean official in charge at the labor office barely talked to or even looked at Rusiell, the claimant, and instead talked to Eunjin and to me. This pattern was very common—when migrant workers were accompanied by South Korean advocates, other South Koreans routinely ignored the migrants and talked almost exclusively to the advocates. But Eunjin's actions were distinct from those of other NGO staff members: instead of answering every question directed to her, she kept repeating, "Ask Rusiell. She's right here." On our way out, the factory owner, a man in his fifties, grabbed Eunjin's arm and made his plea: "Let's not act like this among us South Koreans. You understand how nicely I treated them! With my personal money, I bought them snacks, drinks, and meat! Why is she acting so ungrateful now after everything I've done?" "But sir," Eunjin adamantly replied, "favors are favors, and law is law. And you should talk to Rusiell, not me." In less than a week, the factory owner gave in and paid Rusiell her severance pay.

The MTU made a deliberate effort to enable migrant workers to speak for themselves in negotiations with South Korean employers and state actors, and they were keenly aware that this effort differentiated them from faith-based migrant advocates. Sung Junho, a South Korean MTU activist in his thirties, emphasized the value of migrant workers' autonomy in the MTU's daily activities, saying, "We can't just do it for them." He elaborated:

> Let's say South Korean activists go together with migrant workers to fight with a factory owner. Of course, we have to fight, too, but we can't do it in their stead. It really is a fine line. . . . We have to find a way through continuous discussion with migrant workers, and there are no right answers. At the MTU, I struggled because if I don't pick up certain tasks, the union activities don't function, but if I do pick them up, then am I delaying the empowerment of migrant worker activist leaders? Should we choose a slow

and difficult route but one where migrants move forward on their own? To what extent? Those questions were constantly on my mind.

Another confounding factor was that for migrant workers, involvement in MTU activism entailed significant risk. MTU activists suspected that during their public events, immigration officers took pictures of migrant worker participants to target for later arrest. At the outset of my research, Factorytown was home to several MTU members and leaders, but one by one, by crossing the social boundaries of containment, most became targets of immigration crackdowns and were deported. Michel Catuira, the leader of MTU, had a legal working visa, but the immigration office canceled it, claiming that his employment was simply a front for his full-time activism. The MTU presented a petition in court against the state's denial of Mr. Catuira's entry, which eventually failed despite wide support from various South Korean civil society organizations and Amnesty International.

The risks of comradeship under such political conditions posed a significant barrier to migrant workers' mobilization and raised the question of the MTU's viability. Bharat Tharu, a Nepalese worker in Factorytown whose involvement with the MTU fluctuated, described his feeling of ambivalence. He identified strongly with the MTU's emphasis on the autonomous organizing of migrant workers, as compared to "following South Koreans all the time," because "fighting for our rights ourselves is important." He continued:

> But it is not like the MTU is free from South Koreans' initiatives either. They are not out in the front, but they are there. At first, many of us didn't know that. We heard that now we, migrant workers, fight for ourselves, and we got all excited, and look what happened to them now? Many of my friends were arrested by immigration soon afterwards, and they had no idea that would happen. Would they have gotten involved if they knew it was coming? I don't know, maybe or maybe not. But our South Korean comrades didn't tell us anything like that when they encouraged us to participate.

Bharat did not suspect that South Korean activists deliberately hid the risk from migrant workers, nor did he blame them for his friends' deportations. He remained a firm believer in the ideals of camaraderie and equality. He did question, however, whether such a model was appropriate for migrant activism in South Korea, given that the levels of risk assumed by South Korean and migrant "comrades" were so starkly divergent within the legal apparatus that clearly differentiates citizens and noncitizens. This dynamic echoes the historical precedent in the South Korean *minjung* movement in the 1980s, during which university students and intellectuals chose to work in the factories for political organizing and labor activism, side by side with factory workers without higher education. Historian Namhee Lee describes the discrepancy in the risks to their livelihood experienced by factory workers involved in labor activism and by the student activists who could return to their studies if they lost their jobs or if the movement failed.[4] Indeed, this is a question that the MTU or any movement that emphasizes solidarity and coalition building across differentials of power and risk must take seriously in order for an actual state of comradeship to emerge and continue.

In opposition to paternalistic interactions at Peace Center, the MTU actively promoted and pursued a model of equal camaraderie across different migrant groups and between migrants and South Koreans, yet, as already noted, the mobilization of migrants through the MTU was severely constrained by migrants' precarious legal and political condition in South Korea. Despite such constraints, the MTU survived and maintained a transnational network of key migrant worker activists who were deported to the Philippines, Nepal, and Bangladesh but stayed connected to each other and to labor movements in their home countries. In some cases, South Korean activists raised funds to support returnees' continuing activism in their home countries. Former leader Michel Catuira became active in the Philippines in Migrante International, an international organization for Filipino migrant workers, and was elected as the deputy secretary general in December 2014. Yet even among the MTU members, few migrant workers in South Korea were willing to risk becoming highly visible activists for fear of losing their path to mobility and security for themselves and their families. In contrast to faith-based migrant advocacy organizations that were locally grounded in most major industrial towns in South Korea and could mobilize large numbers of migrant workers, the MTU incorporated only a small minority of such workers. However, the MTU offered an alternate vision of migrant activism based on solidarity, a vision that entered into a productive tension with the faith-based carework model of migrant advocacy.

MATERNAL CONVERGENCE IN THE MAKING
OF MIGRANT WOMEN

"The problem of migrants in South Korea is because of the hypocrisy of our government," said Pastor Kim of Peace Center. "They keep talking about so-called multiculturalism, but they only care about marriage-migrant women. And look how they inhumanely treat migrant workers who've been in our country longer and in larger numbers." In 2006, the South Korean state shifted its policy to emphasize marriage migrants' integration, while its exclusionary policies toward migrant workers remained in place. This shift, and the increase in government and private funding for the projects of "so-called multiculturalism" gave rise to the cross-ethnic subject of migrant women that was distinct from that of migrant workers.

The Ministries of Health and Welfare, Education, and Gender Equality and Family, as well as many local governments, implemented immigrant integration programs for migrant wives under the category of "multicultural families." In 2007, the national government contracted with the social welfare department of a university near Factorytown to run a local Multicultural Family Support Center; by 2014, there were 30 such centers in the province and 218 in the nation. Because of its location in City Hall, the center near Factorytown was referred to as "City Hall Center." City Hall Center used national government funding to hire professional social workers and educators to run classes in the Korean language, computer training, cooking, and vocational training for migrant wives.

Also in 2007, Peace Center, along with many other migrant advocacy NGOs nationwide, expanded their work to include migrant wives. Pastor Kim's critical stance against the narrow focus of multiculturalism in South Korea did not stop Peace Center from actively seeking funding from the local government and corporate and religious organizations to offer educational programs for migrant wives in and near Factorytown. In the process, Peace Center instituted a division between the migrant women team, whose staff members were in charge of counseling and education for migrant wives, and the migrant worker team, whose staff members offered labor counseling and medical assistance to migrant workers. Peace Center and City Hall Center were aware that they were competing with each other to serve the same group of migrant wives; indeed, many women attended both centers' programs.[5]

The migrant women who participated in educational programs at Peace Center and City Hall Center were a highly diverse group, coming from many countries in East and Southeast Asia, with ages ranging from early twenties to late forties. The women came to the educational programs for various reasons. Some wanted to help their children with their home-work; others came for temporary refuge from their mothers-in-law, to meet coethnic friends, or to learn conversational Korean so that they could talk to their husbands, in-laws, and employers. But the need for immigrant integration programs was most often legitimated in reference to the effects mothers would have on children. As Bae Yoonsook, a volunteer Korean language teacher also quoted in Chapter 3, stated, "Our second [future] generation is in their hands." This maternal rhetoric was at the heart of these educational programs for migrant wives.

Competing and Converging Maternal Care

Despite a high degree of heterogeneity among migrant wives in terms of class, ethnicity, and living conditions, they were constructed as a single group with common needs. The metaphor of *newborn babies* was com-monly used in reference to this group of women by both migrant women and center staff members. Jenny Gomez, a woman from the Philippines who spent more than twelve years in South Korea, explained: "If a woman comes to South Korea to marry, and let's say she's been here for three years, it means that she's like a three-year-old. Culturally, that's how it is, because everything is new. People around her, the in-laws, have to be patient and help them to grow, and take care of them." In an extension of this meta-phor, the in-laws, especially mothers-in-law, were portrayed as responsible for providing the nurturance and care necessary for a marriage migrant's growth. Yet migrant wives and South Korean volunteer teachers and staff members often talked about in-laws as lacking a cultural understanding of what it is like to learn a foreign language and as hastily imposing their own standards on migrant wives. Jenny expressed her frustration that many of her friends' in-laws became impatient when their daughters-in-law could not speak Korean fluently after several months: "Would a baby learn to speak just like that? No, it takes time, but they don't understand that."

At Peace Center, Mikyung worked on both the migrant worker team and the migrant women team. In a speech she gave to volunteer teachers on the migrant women team, she highlighted the role of Peace Center as a maternal educator:

> Our Center has to become like their [migrant women's] natal home, so that they can come to us and talk about anything on their mind. We should be like their mothers in their natal family [*chinjŏng ŏmma*], always standing by their side when they face problems with their husbands and in-laws, and teaching them patiently and slowly, one step at a time.

This portrayal of migrant women as newborns recognized their potential to grow and become full members in South Korea with the help of support and education. Centers such as Peace Center and City Hall Center adopted the maternal role of taking care of these women, determined to support their growth in the new surroundings of South Korea through education programs and community building. As An Juhee, a Chinese woman who changed her name to a Korean one, wrote in her essay for Peace Center's monthly newsletter, "The center has become my natal home with teachers just like my own mother."

Peace Center and City Hall Center each operated under a distinct mode of civic engagement as a faith-based advocacy organization and a professional social service organization, respectively. These organizations competed to provide "maternal care" to migrant women. At Peace Center, a heightened sense of competition led to internal tensions regarding the degree of professionalization within the migrant women team. Moving away from its previous model of selfless devotion based on religious faith, Peace Center hired licensed social workers who were not religiously motivated, including Park Hani, a woman in her thirties with a social worker's license and a certificate to teach Korean as a second language. After her arrival as program director, the volunteer teachers of Korean language classes felt a push toward greater professionalization through the introduction of quizzes, midterms, finals, and grade reports.

One concrete change that volunteer teachers often complained about revolved around the institution of a class roster. Every Friday afternoon, all Korean language teachers at Peace Center were asked to submit an attendance report. Almost ritualistically, volunteer teachers never failed to complain about this duty, which many felt was unnecessarily complicated. Each day, teachers were asked to take attendance at the beginning of class and to record statistics at the bottom of the roster—how many students attended, were late, or were absent, overall and by country of origin—in addition to the lesson plan and assignment for the day. At the end of each week and again at the end of each month, attendance statistics by country of origin were compiled by hand.

One week at Peace Center, Hong Youngjoo, a volunteer teacher, began the familiar tirade, "What is this for? Who cares about how many students are from Vietnam or China? Why do we have to calculate all this every time?" That particular Friday, she was especially upset because she had found multiple errors in her own calculations for the monthly report. "Exactly!" Han Misook chimed in. "I'd much rather spend this precious time listening to our students instead of calculating these numbers." The discontent expressed by Youngjoo and Misook was generated not only by tedious and time-consuming work but also by work that was impersonal, distinct from the more intimate tasks that volunteer teachers took pride in, such as correcting students' writing, preparing for teaching, or visiting migrant women at home.

Despite these recurring complaints, volunteer teachers never received a firm answer from administrators as to the purpose of the reports. Hani, the program director, was adamant that the information was necessary to show funders (such as the city government, corporations, religious organizations, and individual sponsors) exactly how the programs operated. When pushed, however, she reluctantly admitted that such statistics were not a reporting requirement for any particular agency. As program director, however, she firmly believed that it was her job to ensure that the report was ready in case any sponsors demanded to see it, especially government officials who had the power to discontinue the funding. As volunteers, teachers did not feel as though they had the power to refuse this tedious accounting, but they were vocal in their disapproval, especially to Mikyung, who was also unhappy about Hani and her interventions.

Mikyung insisted on continuing the faith-based care work model and did not approve of Hani's initiatives. She thought that their work should not focus on language education in a narrow sense but should instead offer a space where migrant women could come to rely on one another. "Is it that important that the migrant women know a bit more Korean vocabulary? No, that's not the point!" Mikyung told all volunteer teachers at a weekly teacher's meeting, as a tacit protest against Hani:

> There are other centers with more money, and they might have better
> language programs, but that's not the most important thing. They hire

teachers, but our teachers come out of genuine heart. If these women were looking for the best class, they would have gone to the university. They come to us because they know we care. Many students come and miss quite a bit of classes because they get pregnant, their babies are sick, or they have to go to work, but they come back. And we have to understand that.

By "other centers with more money," Mikyung distinguished Peace Center from City Hall Center, which she saw as an impersonal bureaucracy filled with paid employees motivated by money instead of genuine care.[6]

City Hall Center was not run solely by professional social workers, however. Indeed, this organization was also undergoing a transformation. Just as Peace Center was becoming more *professionalized,* City Hall Center was becoming *volunteerized.* Although City Hall Center's Korean language classes were taught by paid Korean language teachers with certificates, the Center mobilized many volunteers for the migrant wives' educational program, and its specialty was home-visit Korean classes and mentoring programs run almost entirely by South Korean women volunteers. Ryu Hyungsook, a retired schoolteacher who had participated in the home visits for two years, reported the importance of the intimate care she provided: "We go to their houses to teach Korean, but because we are right there, we do more than just teaching language. I do lots of counseling for them, for the couples, for child rearing, because I see firsthand how they are raising their children. And the whole family thanks me."

The two centers converged in claiming that migrant women were more than recipients of services and education as active participants in the program. Both organizations promoted self-help and community building. Nationwide, social welfare centers and migrant advocacy NGOs working with marriage migrants increasingly hired migrant wives as peer counselors and educators, center staff members, and translators, and actively encouraged them to volunteer to help other migrant women or to represent migrant women publicly. In Factorytown, people involved with Peace Center and City Hall Center were proud of Subin Kim, a twenty-six-year-old woman from Vietnam whose determination and high aspirations were readily apparent. Even though Subin had arrived in South Korea only three years earlier, thanks to her extensive efforts, she was fluent in Korean. What impressed Peace Center teachers most was her desire to help other migrant women. She volunteered as a teacher's aide for the beginner-level Korean class for Vietnamese women, she said, "because I learned so much here; I would like to give back as much as I can." Subin also volunteered at City Hall Center as a peer counselor who made home visits, and later became a paid staff member of City Hall Center and worked to organize migrant wives' self-help communities. In the eyes of the maternal South Korean educators, migrant women like Subin exemplified a transformation from "newborn babies" into full members of South Korean civil society through the educators' successful nurturing and care.

MIGRANTS AND COMPETING MODELS OF CIVIC ENGAGEMENT IN SOUTH KOREA

The ethnically and religiously organized migrant community in South Korea emerged as two separate and distinct groups of migrant workers and migrant women in the South Korean public sphere through interactions with various groups of civil society actors that served as mediators of rights and agents of integration. The ways in which migrants were formed and represented as collective subjects show as much about South Korean civil society as about the migrant communities, revealing how the distinct modes of civic engagement in South Korea—faith-based advocacy, labor activism, and professional social work—contested and competed with one another.

As discourses of citizenship and equality, both paternalistic and maternal approaches toward migrant workers and migrant wives revealed their own limitations based in the hierarchical relationship they established and reinforced between South Koreans and migrants. Mobilizing efforts in the MTU movement seemed to resolve this inequality through the discourse of comradeship, but because of state repression, migrants faced substantively higher risks than their South Korean "comrades."

Unlike migrant advocates who formed paternalistic relations in which migrant workers remained on the receiving end of help, maternal educators were determined to nurture and empower their students via participation, voice, and community building. In fact, the maternal approach showed higher levels of success in incorporating migrant wives into the role of educators. Migrant wives also entered formal politics as representatives of migrants in South Korea. In the June 2010 local election, the ruling Grand National Party (GNP) appointed two migrant women, naturalized Korean citizens who immigrated via cross-border marriages, as candidates for the proportional representative election, highlighting the need to represent the significant number of "multicultural families" in the area. Among them was Jasmine Lee from the Philippines, who became a candidate for the Seoul Metropolitan City Council.

Jasmine Lee's candidacy involved a concerted effort by South Korean civil society actors. She participated in a project called Marriage Migrant Women as Politicians, led by the Center for Korean Women and Politics, and was supported by the Ministry of Gender Equality in the 2010 local election. In a newspaper interview, Jasmine Lee said that before participating in the project, she used to think that politics was just "a difficult thing." She said, "Before, I just voted for the candidate picked by my [South Korean] father-in-law, without looking carefully at their platforms. But as I learned about politics, I began to see which candidates are for *our benefit*."[7] Lee's statement revealed a shift from following the patriarchal authority of her father-in-law to seeking collective representation for migrants. Two years later, in June 2012, Jasmine Lee became the first migrant to be appointed member of the National Assembly of South Korea.

Which goals migrant women like Lee will pursue "for our benefit" in South Korean society remain to be seen. Their advocacy may lead to various forms of coalition building with nonmigrant South Koreans, or they may represent only migrants and frame their issues as separate and distinct. The meaning of "migrants" as a political category also remains an open question. Will it be limited to migrant wives and their children as members of "multicultural families," or will it include migrant workers with and without a legal status in South Korea? One thing is certain: the collective migrant subjects in the South Korean public sphere did not emerge naturally from their state-conferred legal status. Instead, their cross-ethnic migrant subjectivity was produced through encounters between migrant groups and South Korean civil society actors, which will continue to shape the struggles around migrant rights and belonging in South Korea.

Workers and Working Girls

Gendering the Worker-Citizen

Katherine and Rachel never met each other, but I always wished they had. Both were thirty-seven-year-old optimists with loud laughs and high energy that drew people in. Their lives in the Philippines before migrating to South Korea were similar as well: both fell in love with their high school sweethearts, neither attended college, and both later became single mothers. When they heard about migrant work in South Korea, each saw it as an opportunity to be a good mother and support her family. Yet when I met them in 2009 in two different migrant neighborhoods in South Korea, Katherine's and Rachel's lives had sharply diverged. They occupied distinct labor market sectors as migrant workers in South Korea, which shaped their access to labor and social rights.

Katherine Bautista entered South Korea in 1999 with an "industrial trainee" visa and was assigned to a thread factory. She lived in a stacked-container unit in the factory backyard, her salary was frequently paid late, and the factory owner maintained control by withholding migrant workers' passports. After a year of working under these conditions, Katherine heard about a better job opportunity and ran away, leaving her passport and unpaid salary behind. Along with many of her co-workers, Katherine moved to Factorytown near Seoul, where she lived for the next nine years, working at a furniture factory and becoming actively involved in the local Filipino community, where she knew almost everyone by name. While organizing the Filipino basketball league in town, she met her husband, who was also a Filipino factory worker. Even though she was afraid of being caught and deported whenever she stepped outside of her migrant neighborhood, Katherine felt at home in South Korea. She said, "I'd like to immigrate if they let me. I'd like to work and live here, and just take vacations in the Philippines." Even though she no longer had a legal work visa or a written labor contract, Katherine was proud to have hired a labor lawyer who successfully obtained her unpaid salary and severance pay from the owner of the thread factory. Katherine could recite details of South Korean labor law, had access to health care, and participated in a protest demanding the legalization of undocumented migrant workers.

Rachel Cruz came to South Korea with an "entertainer" visa in 2008 and was assigned to work as a hostess in a club serving American GIs in the military camptown of Basetown. Rachel's club owner withheld her passport and ignored her labor contract, which promised decent wages, one day off per week, and health insurance. However, unlike Katherine, Rachel felt she had no recourse. For eight months, she watched in frustration as some of her co-workers were involuntarily sent away to other clubs or back to the Philippines. Rachel wanted to run away, but she did not know where to go or how to find work. Despite unfavorable working conditions, Rachel prayed that the club owner would extend her contract for another year so that she could continue to work in the club. Worried about the precariousness of her life in South Korea, she told me, "Pray for me. I really hope the mommy [the club owner] keeps me here." Rachel was careful to take care of herself while in South Korea and never missed her morning workout routine at the gym, even after working—which often involved heavy drinking—until 2:00 a.m. the night before. She saved the tips and gifts she received from customers and made plans to save at least $200 per month in a separate bank account. Yet her prayers went unanswered: a few weeks after our last meeting and three months before her contract ended, Rachel's promoter escorted her to the airport and put her on a plane back to the Philippines.

Katherine was an undocumented migrant worker—rendered "illegal" by the laws on the books. Yet she was able to claim her labor rights, participate in protests, and build a life in South Korea, in spite of her legal vulnerability. In contrast, Rachel was a documented guest worker, yet her position in South Korea was almost entirely subject to the whim of her employer. Katherine and Rachel, similar in so many ways, experienced a divergent practice of rights. How can we make sense of this difference?

The discrepancy between these two groups of migrant women workers is particularly intriguing because the labor rights violations and mobility experienced by migrant hostesses like Rachel in the late 2000s were remarkably similar to the conditions faced by many migrant factory workers in the 1990s. In both cases, South Korean employers regularly engaged in abusive practices, such as withholding passports, reneging on the fair pay stipulated in the labor contract, and denying access to workers' compensation or health care—practices that propelled Katherine to leave her thread factory. Yet in the mid-1990s, stories of the abuse of migrant workers galvanized mostly faith-based migrant advocacy groups nationwide, which alongside the successful mobilization of migrant ethnic communities, led to significant gains in the expansion of rights and citizenship for migrant workers.

This chapter examines the extent to which the progress made through advocacy for "migrant workers' rights" was realized by two distinct groups of migrant women workers: factory workers and camptown club hostesses. Women like Katherine and Rachel labored in organizations with distinct gendered labor regimes and were mobilized by distinct civil society actors that produced entirely different sets of migrant rights.

GENDER AT WORK IN FACTORIES AND HOSTESS CLUBS

Migrant factory workers and hostesses were bounded by the parameters of the segregated migrant districts where their workplaces were located—the factory complex in Factorytown and the club districts in Basetown. Beyond the characteristics of particular workplaces, the labor process in these sectors of work shaped the formation of the migrant community in each town and had important implications for migrant women's ability to claim rights. Migrant women in the factories labored in the company of working men on the shop floor, which enabled the recognition of their skills and the formation of a migrant community for mutual support. In contrast, migrant hostesses were isolated and set into competition with one another in service of American GI customers.

Women Workers in Factorytown

In Factorytown, Filipina women were part of a multinational and mixed-gender workforce from many countries across Asia and Africa. These women worked alongside men in small and medium-size factories owned by South Koreans, producing furniture, slippers, shoes, car accessories, and noodles. Within the factories, there was often a clear division of men's and women's work, even as workers from different countries worked side by side on the same task. For example, in one furniture factory, Filipino and Bangladeshi men cut wood and assembled furniture, while Nepalese and Filipino women did the sanding and polishing. In a slipper factory, men operated the machine to produce slippers, and women packaged them. A small number of factories hired men or women workers almost exclusively—for example, beaded jewelry making for women and refrigerator assembly for men. On average, women's monthly incomes ($900–$1,200) were lower than men's ($1,100–$1,800), both because the classification of women's work as "lighter" and "low-skilled" was used to justify a lower base salary and because men worked significantly more overtime with extra pay. Most women worked from 8:30 a.m. to 6:00 p.m. six days a week, sometimes shorter on Saturdays; during my fieldwork, we often cooked and ate dinner together while their husbands and boyfriends were still at work, earning overtime pay.

Although women's work was considered less skilled than men's, migrant women in the manufacturing sector benefited from the structure of factory work, which valued experience and seniority as assets. As women workers accumulated time in a factory, they developed skills that improved their status and made them potentially competitive in the labor market. These skills and resources served as a basis for long-term employment and a sense of job security, even in the absence of a legal visa or written contract. Many migrant factory workers in Factorytown had a long tenure in one factory, which became a source of pride. Roselle Reyes, a Filipina woman in her late forties, proudly declared, "I am an expert in sanding. They would not be able to find someone else like me because I've been doing this for fifteen years." She pointed to her right hand where she had held the sanding tool in a furniture factory for years and said, "Look at my hands. The bone here on my thumb has moved to over here. Don't I deserve something for this?" She argued that, at the very least, the South Korean government owed her a working visa and amnesty for all the hard work that she put into the factory; her hands were her witness.

The immigration crackdown put in place by the South Korean government against undocumented workers like Roselle suggests that officials did not agree; however, South Korean employers recognized the value of the skilled workforce and demonstrated their respect for the experience of women migrant workers through continued employment and regular pay raises, albeit with a persistent gender pay gap. Despite the risk of fines for immigration law violations, many employers in Factorytown preferred long-term undocumented workers like Roselle because their work skills and Korean language proficiency were superior to those of legal workers who entered South Korea under the EPS, a short-term guest-worker system. About 60 percent of workers in Factorytown were undocumented, and it was common for factories that hired migrant workers for legal minimum wage under the EPS to also hire undocumented workers at a higher pay grade because of their experience.

In addition to the pride she felt in her work, Roselle also gained a sense of honor from providing for her three children and her parents in the Philippines throughout her twenty-seven years of migrant labor and from helping her siblings and extended family migrate to South Korea, Hong Kong, and Taiwan by paying their placement fees. Leveraging her and her husband's lengthy tenure with their employer, she was able to obtain jobs for relatives in her factory. One worker who had been helped by Roselle was Florence Ocampo, introduced in earlier chapters, a twenty-eight-year-old Filipina woman from the same hometown. At first, Florence struggled in her job as a sander—having worked as a domestic worker in Taiwan and in the service sector in the Philippines before migrating to South Korea, she did not have the necessary skills for factory work. Roselle promised the factory owner that she would train Florence until she caught up with the speed of the line. After seven months of work, Florence told me, "Now, I have skills. You know, I can go anywhere to another factory and find work." Despite this confidence, Florence did not move because she felt comfortable working with Roselle and her other co-workers, and she was able to negotiate with her manager to receive a raise according to her skill level.

Such referrals and instances of mutual help within the coethnic networks were common in Factorytown; migrant factory workers helped family members, relatives, church members, and co-workers out of a sense of solidarity, which strengthened their sense of coethnic community across gender lines. The coethnic social networks among migrant workers provided resources necessary for migrant workers' entry into the labor market and gave employers a steady flow of workers bound by kinship, who are less likely to leave. For migrant women, the coethnic community offered the opportunity to mobilize not only other women's networks and resources but also those of migrant men with whom they had close ties as wives, girlfriends, sisters, mothers, relatives, and neighbors. The strong coethnic community in Factorytown included both documented and undocumented workers and offered resources to address their particular vulnerabilities: for "legal" workers bound to an abusive employer, the migrant network provided opportunities for new jobs and evidence that undocumented life was feasible. For undocumented migrant workers vulnerable to labor abuses based on the lack of a formal contract, the community acted collectively in negotiations with employers, even in the absence of organized trade unions in Factorytown.

To a certain degree, migrant women workers in Factorytown also benefited from symbolically sharing the male-centered camaraderie that Korean employers had with migrant male workers, though they were not necessarily included in such bonding. Many South Korean factory owners and managers in Factorytown, who were mostly working-class men, formed affective bonds with migrant men through many hours of working together on the shop floor and male-only socializing after work. For example, Chang Byungho, a South Korean manager in his forties, spoke at length about his "debt" to migrant workers while we were having drinks and grilled pork after work in the makeshift stacked-container apartment on the second floor of the factory where Florence and her husband lived:

> If we stumble here and die, it's not like my blood and their blood is a different color. When I had my own factory, these people, Filipinos (pointing fingers to three Filipino men in the room), built it up with me. When the company was going through difficulty, they said, "It's okay, let's do it together," and waited for two or three months without pay when other South Korean workers left me. I told the workers, we are not Koreans, Banglas, Filipinos, but we are all our company people.

Byungho's gratitude to migrant workers in his factory for their selfless hard work led him to cultivate a sense of solidarity that transcended national and racial boundaries. It is noteworthy, however, that he did not point to any migrant women in the same room in his acknowledgment, including Roselle, who had worked together with her husband in the factory for the same time period. For Byungho and other South Korean employers, migrant women in the factory belonged to "our company people" only partially—less as full workers themselves but more as the wives, sisters, and cousins of male workers, migrant or South Korean.

To be sure, such sentiments of team spirit among migrant workers and their employers should not be overstated—despite his positive feelings, Byungho acknowledged that he paid migrant workers less than South Koreans for the same work, because "that's a lot of money in their home countries." There were also cases of exploitative working conditions, schemes to underpay workers, discriminatory treatment against migrants, physical and verbal abuse, and sexual harassment. Although I was privy to factories with unfavorable conditions and moments of antagonism, I also witnessed genuine bonding between South Korean factory owners and migrant factory workers based on what Michéle Lamont calls "the dignity of working men,"[1] such as a middle-aged South Korean man sobbing and hugging migrant male workers at the detention center when they were being deported, or a South Korean manager asking for matchmaking for himself and the sister of a close migrant worker "younger brother." Because many of the factories in Factorytown were small, with fewer than ten workers, and because the South Korean owners and managers had often started out as factory workers, the boundary between migrant workers and South Korean owners was less rigid than one might expect. The factory owners were highly aware that without migrant workers, their factories would not be able to sustain themselves.

In an unusual yet telling case of male bonding between South Korean and migrant men, one Nepalese migrant in his late thirties who had worked in a garment factory in South Korea for many years, Anil Pande, became a factory owner with the support of the owner / "older brother" (hyông) at his former workplace. Anil hired mostly South Korean middle-aged women workers for a few years before the immigration crackdown intensified in 2003 and he began to get involved with migrant activism. Other migrant advocates jokingly called him "migrant capitalist," and he would blush, but his close friendship with South Korean men, previously his factory owners, managers, and co-workers, was remarkable, and they even visited him in Nepal after he was deported.

Migrant women workers were excluded from male-centered bonding and social networks, but they were able to benefit from these networks through relationships with coethnic migrant men who protected them from disrespect and abuse as wives, girlfriends, sisters, cousins, and so on. Single women, married women whose husbands were in the Philippines, and women in relationships with women faced workplace challenges that married women whose husbands were present did not have to confront, such as fighting off sexual advances from South Korean managers and factory owners. This was one of the reasons, I was told, that some Filipina women entered into a "couple" (read: extramarital) relationship in South Korea: to have male protection. Often the Filipino community members would point out to me which heterosexual romantic pairs were "really married" and which were "couples," but with little moral judgment because they acknowledged that "it is a long time to be away."

The women workers in Factorytown had resources to deal with labor rights or other violations in the workplace: the organization of factory work that valued experience, and a coethnic community that provided a sense of collective solidarity in the company of working men, especially through intimate connections with migrant men. These resources provided Factorytown women with the ability to claim rights vis-à-vis their employers; the same was not true of migrant hostesses in Basetown clubs.

"Working Girls" in Basetown

In Basetown, Filipina women constituted the overwhelming majority of hostesses working in the clubs surrounding the US military base. All the hostesses were women, and less than 10 percent of hostesses were South Korean or from the former Soviet Union. Club owners and managers were both men and women, and most were South Korean. The camptown clubs catered to American GI customers almost exclusively, though a small number of clubs selectively opened their doors to migrant workers from South and Southeast Asia after curfew at the US military base. The clubs served GIs stationed in South Korea, selling them intimacy, fun, comfort, and, in some cases, sex. Hostess services consisted of largely two categories: "Juice" sales and "bar fines." When a customer paid $10 to buy a hostess a glass of Juice—a mixed drink made of juice and liquor—he also purchased the woman's company for fifteen to twenty minutes as they chatted or played pool and darts. Some clubs also had a system of "bar fines," in which a customer paid $200–$300 to take a woman out for a whole night. Other clubs also had "VIP rooms," where more explicit sex-for-money exchanges took place in a private setting.

Unlike the pay structure in the factories where workers received a monthly income for forty to forty-four hours of work per week plus overtime pay, hostesses' income was dependent on individual performance and fluctuated from less than $500 to more than $1,500 per month. Although most hostesses had a written labor contract that stipulated a minimum wage of about $850 per month for forty-four hours of work and one holiday per week, no one I met received her minimum pay or a weekly day off. Instead, migrant hostesses commonly worked in the clubs from 5:00 p.m. to 12:00 a.m. during the weekdays and from 12:00 p.m. to 2:00 a.m. (and later, until the last customer left) on the weekend, with one day off per month, if any.

Migrant hostesses received approximately $400 as monthly base pay, which was commonly withheld by the promoter who brought them to South Korea, to be paid as a single lump-sum payment only when they returned to the Philippines—a practice at the heart of the "indentured mobility" of migrant hostesses that Rhacel Parreñas observed in Japan.[2] The rest of their income comprised tips, commissions on Juice sales, and, for workers who participated, commissions on bar fines. This meant that if hostesses did not earn enough in tips and commission—10–20 percent of Juice sales and 30–50 percent of the bar fine—their daily livelihood was at risk because they would not have money to buy food and toiletries. Many club owners also instituted quota systems under which each hostess was required to sell a certain amount, ranging from two hundred to four hundred Juices per month. If a hostess failed to meet this quota, she might receive a reduced commission, pay a penalty, be transferred to another club, or even be sent back to her home country. To guarantee a certain level of Juice sales, hostesses needed to cultivate regular customers, or "boyfriends," who would frequent the club to buy them multiple drinks and take them out on a bar fine. With these men, many women developed romantic and sexual relationships that sometimes led to cohabitation and marriage.

The organization of work in camptown clubs put migrant hostesses under the paternalistic control of employers. Although hostesses ranged in age from late teens to mid-forties, they were often called "girls," and sometimes "juicy girls" or "drinkie girls," derogatory names referring to their Juice sales, rather than being respected as workers. They were expected to call their employers "mommy" or "daddy" and were subject to personal control by employers, who punished workers for infractions. The parent-like nature of these relationships was used, in the minds of the employers, to justify employers' control over women's mobility and intimate lives. Some clubs had managers escort women back and forth between their residences and the club, and when a hostess was caught leaving her house unsupervised, she was fined a large sum of money.

The Phoenix Club, where Riza Lacson worked, employed a fine system in order to constrain hostesses' mobility and behavior. Riza explained, "Once I had to call my mom, and my phone card ran out. So I went to the store to get a new card. And they fined me $100! Everything is one hundred. Late for work, one hundred. Crying in front of a customer, one hundred." Many women ran away from these clubs; Riza herself had run away two weeks before I met her. The high rate of running away leads to an even higher level of surveillance of the women left behind, reinforcing a vicious cycle causing even more women to run away. However, this practice of restricting women's mobility also occurred in milder forms in other clubs, such as "grounding" migrant hostesses like children for the early months of their work to make clear that they were under club owners' authority and surveillance. Although these practices served the interests of club owners, both owners and managers argued that their paternalistic actions were necessary to protect naïve hostesses.

Like the male bonding that connected South Korean factory owners and managers to migrant male workers, South Korean female club owners and managers sometimes bonded with migrant hostesses. Whereas some club owners and managers controlled migrant hostesses through excessive and arbitrary fines, physical and verbal abuse, and threats of deportation, others were caring and formed an intimate bond with migrant hostesses. Amy Flores, a migrant hostess who had worked in Japan prior to coming to South Korea, felt very close to her club owner, whom she saw as a "big sister." Her club owner was a South Korean woman in her forties who wore a short hairstyle and baggy men's clothing, dropped the "f-word" every other second, and was quite protective of her "girls," habitually saying, "If anyone does any harm to our girls, I'll break his knee."

Some South Korean club owners and managers connected with migrant hostesses by drawing on their own past experiences as hostesses. Sa Mijin, a club manager in her fifties, told me about the pelvic exam at the state-run public clinic (bogônso) that was mandatory for women working in the camptown clubs since the 1970s, mandated in the name of preventing the spread of sexually transmitted diseases. She recalled that back in the 1970s, if anyone failed the test, she was denied the approval stamp to work in the club and locked in a separate house until she was deemed "clean."[3] Mijin expressed her anger at the clinic staff members who abused their power by coming to the clubs at night and demanding to have sex for free in exchange for the approval stamp. Now working as a manager at a club with five Filipina hostesses, Mijin escorted the workers to the public clinic for their exams. On one trip a few months earlier, a Filipina woman who had just arrived in South Korea refused the exam. Mijin said, "I really felt sorry for her, because, you know, who would want to go up there and spread your legs like that? I went through it myself so many times, and I know how terrible it is."

The sympathy and protective attitudes of the owners and managers did not necessarily translate into respect for labor rights. "These girls don't know what's good for them," asserted Hwang Jinsook, a South Korean club owner who used to be a club hostess in the 1980s; Jinsook reported that she forbade migrant women in her club from going out at night by themselves, "because it hurts them." She explained,

> When these girls have a boyfriend, they feel bad making him pay $200 for one night [on a bar fine], and they think, I am going out with this guy and why is the club owner getting a 50 percent cut? And they start sneaking out at night and give themselves for free, thinking that he will marry them. Or they run away with him. But that's stupid. . . . Men never appreciate you if you are doing that. Instead, they take you for granted and leave.

Jinsook understood her actions as looking after the women rather than as controlling them. She believed that the hostesses should follow her advice to "test" men's commitment through the bar fine system. Under such paternalistic relations, migrant hostesses were not considered as adult workers who could make their own informed decisions but rather as working "girls" who needed direction and guidance. Many hostesses disagreed with this interpretation, but they either complied with club rules or ran away instead of challenging employers, because they had limited resources to do so.

Unlike factory work, in which workers gained security by improving their skill set over time, work experience as a hostess did not necessarily provide migrant hostesses similar benefits. Although intricate skills were involved in the intimate labor of hostess work, including flirtation and emotional labor that hostesses cultivated over time,[4] other factors attracted American GI customers to the clubs, such as youth and "freshness." Many club owners preferred to hire young women rather than older, more experienced hostesses, and they frequently sent women away to other clubs to bring in "new girls." In Basetown clubs, the arrival of new hostesses was news among the American GIs, and they visited the clubs to "check out" the new women. The club manager would point out that "this is a new girl" and ask the GIs to buy welcome drinks. The men obliged without exception, benefiting the club.

Clients' preference for novelty set the stage for a short-term rotation among clubs, which made migrant hostesses' lives precarious. Under the subcontracting system, in which hostesses belonged to a promoter who contracted with multiple clubs, women were rotated—both voluntarily and involuntarily—among different clubs in various camptowns in South Korea. If a woman's performance was not considered adequate after several moves, promoters would send her back to the Philippines without prior notice, regardless of her contract period. Due to employers' power to place and relocate hostesses, migrant hostesses had limited capacity to make demands and claim their rights vis-à-vis club owners and promoters. In addition, although a small number of runaway hostesses made their way into the manufacturing sector, most migrant hostesses lacked the knowledge and social networks in South Korea to enable such a move.

Unlike migrant factory workers who were grounded in a local site and able to form a tight coethnic community based on workers' pride and kinship that became a significant resource, migrant hostesses in Basetown faced isolation.[5] For some women, hostess work carried a stigma based in sexual morality that made them feel ashamed and caused them to hide from others, and other members of the Filipino community also expressed their disapproval. Maria Albano, a thirty-eight-year-old Filipina woman who worked in Basetown clubs, was ashamed and angry to be in a situation where she felt she had to work as a hostess. She exclaimed, "I didn't go to college to be a whore!" She migrated to South Korea without knowing the sexual nature of her work and was dismayed to discover that she would not be working as a singer but as a "juicy girl." For Maria, selling Juice and companionship to American GIs compromised her honor. She said, "I swallowed my pride. I sold more Juice than the quota. My boyfriend came to see me every day and bought me lots of Juice. He took me out on a bar fine every week, so I earned lots of money for them!"

During seven months of swallowing her pride, Maria kept to herself and avoided others outside of the clubs. Although she was a devout Catholic and regular churchgoer in the Philippines, Maria never attended the Tagalog mass in Basetown because she was too ashamed to take part in communion. Because the church was at the heart of the Filipino ethnic community in South Korea, alienation from religious activities exacerbated the isolation of migrant hostesses.

Beyond sexual morality as a source of isolation, the structure of commissions and tips, along with intense pressure to sell Juice in the clubs, encouraged competition for GI customers rather than solidarity among migrant hostesses. In Basetown, most Filipina women had only a few friends who worked in the same club, and these friendships were fragile. When a GI who used to buy drinks exclusively for one hostess began courting another woman in the same club, the relationship between the two women became tense and often soured. Because many women were serious about their romantic relationships, they took it personally when another hostess flirted with their regular customers to sell Juice. For some women, this sense of fierce competition continued even after they ran away from the clubs to live with their GI boyfriends. "You can never trust a Filipina," Arlene Rivera, a thirty-five-year-old Filipina woman declared bitterly as she told a story about a woman whom she had treated like a younger sister, but who, in her words, "stole my fiancé," after Arlene ran away from the club to live with him. Her American GI fiancé married the younger woman and moved back to the United States with her, leaving Arlene, a single mother of a three-year-old boy, alone and undocumented in South Korea. Although some hostesses did form strong bonds against the odds, the structure of hostess work—based on a short-term rotation and individual connections with customers rather than team work—was rarely conducive to fostering a tight coethnic community or worker solidarity that hostesses could rely on to claim rights as migrant workers.

The gendered organization of work in these two labor market sectors partly explains why Katherine and Rachel, two Filipina migrants with similar backgrounds, experienced their rights as migrant workers in very different ways in South Korea. But the workplace was only part of the story; another key factor in migrant women's rights was the distinctive civil society mobilization in South Korea that brought the rights of migrant workers to the national stage.

CIVIL SOCIETY MOBILIZATION FOR MIGRANT RIGHTS

By tracing the on-the-ground struggles for migrant rights, I highlight how the national social movement context of South Korea shapes the gendered forms of civil society mobilization for migrant factory workers and hostesses. While stigma related to sexual morality is linked with the lack of rights for migrant hostesses as compared to migrant factory workers, the hostesses' exclusion from the dignity of workers played a more significant role.

Fighting for Workers' Rights in Factorytown

Pastor Paul was legendary in Factorytown. A Korean man in his mid-fifties who had been involved in antipoverty student activism during college, Pastor Paul led Jesus Church, a small, predominantly Filipino congregation of dedicated evangelical believers, and for more than a decade had devoted his life to the mission of aiding migrant workers. "God, he is a man of action," said Katherine with admiration. Katherine often made fun of the evangelical zeal of the congregation of Jesus Church and jokingly called them "too holy," but her respect for the pastor was apparent. Recounting Pastor Paul's story, she said:

> See, once upon a time, Boyet [a member of Jesus Church] didn't get his salary for several months. And the factory owner refused to pay and said to him, "Go away. I will report you to the immigration if you bug me." So Boyet went to Pastor Paul for help. And he got very upset! "How dare the owner treat my church member like this?!" So he went to the factory and waited and waited. And finally the factory owner showed up, and they got into a huge fistfight! And he won! That's how he got the salary.

When I asked Pastor Paul whether the story about Boyet was true, he laughed and said, "Fistfight is a big exaggeration, but back then, I was young and became angry easily. These people worked so hard, and how could he not give them their pay? It is the fruit of their hard work! Now I have grown old, and I just go to the factory, pray to God out loud, 'please change this person's heart.'"

Until the mid-1990s, migrant workers like Boyet were excluded from legal protection under South Korean labor law. Even after workers became entitled to legal protection—a significant gain for migrant activism—power differentials between migrant workers and employers, language barriers, and insecurity based on their precarious legal status made them vulnerable to labor rights violations. When migrant factory workers did not receive the money they worked for, they regularly sought the assistance of coethnic community members and South Korean advocates like Pastor Paul to file cases at the labor office or negotiate directly with factory owners to enforce their rights. Explaining his motivation for migrant advocacy despite facing contention with other South Koreans, Pastor Paul said,

> When I see how migrant workers carry on with their lives, I have the deepest respect and sympathy. . . . I always tell them, you are all breadwinners. You are fulfilling responsibility for your families. You might be illegal, but wherever you are, you are under God. You are supporting your families with your sweat and tears, so you are honorable breadwinners who deserve blessings from God.

Advocacy for migrant workers based on their dignity as "breadwinners" was firmly grounded in the legacy of South Korean civil society mobilization for the dignity of workers, which included both male and female factory workers. Specifically, the *minjung* (common people's) movement rose against the military authoritarian regimes and mobilized South Korean workers in the 1970s and 1980s to improve substandard working conditions and exercise labor rights, as well as to regain their dignity as workers.[6] In particular, women factory workers were at the forefront of such struggles, especially in the 1970s, in their efforts to build democratic unions and to gain recognition as legitimate workers with rights, against the notion that they were temporary workers—not breadwinners—who would quit after getting married.[7] It was not until later, in the 1980s, that male workers in the heavy manufacturing sector became dominant in labor activism.[8] All major industrial cities in South Korea had locally active migrant worker advocacy organizations; the overwhelming majority of these organizations were Protestant and Catholic church-based NGOs with a legacy of labor activism in the 1970s and 1980s.[9] Beginning in 2001, a more radical wing of migrant activism mobilized migrant workers under a separate trade union, forming the Migrants' Trade Union (MTU) in 2005.[10]

Since the mid-1990s, a vibrant migrant advocacy movement in South Korea facilitated the expansion of labor rights for migrant workers, achieving significant gains, including compensation for workplace injuries in 1994, the expansion of the Labor Standards Act to industrial trainees in 1995, and the right to severance pay regardless of legal status in 1997.

Ultimately, the Industrial Trainee System was reformed in 2003, and the Employment Permit System (EPS) was instituted to provide—at least nominally—migrant workers the labor rights accorded to Korean citizens, such as health insurance, workers' compensation, severance pay, minimum wage, and the right of association.[11] After that point, migrant advocacy groups pushed two major agendas in order to claim rights and belonging for migrant workers in South Korea. The first was freedom for migrant workers to choose their employer, because the EPS bound migrant workers to a particular workplace and limited workplace changes. The second was the legalization of undocumented migrant workers—who made up 24 percent of the migrant workforce—and the halt of immigration crackdowns.[12] Advocacy groups also organized the Migrant Workers' Mutual Aid for Health Care to provide health insurance to undocumented migrants.

In addition to advocating for formal rights at the national level, these groups were highly effective at the local level in the fight to ensure that migrant workers were able to access their labor and social rights on the ground. Faith-based South Korean advocacy groups were at the heart of community life for migrant factory workers in Factorytown. In addition to Pastor Paul's Jesus Church, there were three other Catholic and Protestant church-affiliated migrant advocacy organizations in town. Their religious activities, such as Sunday mass and Bible study, were attended predominantly by Filipinos as well as a handful of Christian migrants from Africa, but all migrant workers—regardless of their affiliation with the church or their ethnicity—sought assistance from these advocacy organizations to resolve labor, medical, and other issues. These organizations sustained the community against the constant threat of immigration crackdowns and created the conditions for the de facto long-term settlement of migrants in spite of government policy. Under the leadership of migrant advocacy

NGOs, migrant workers in Factorytown of various coethnic communities and legal statuses were able to collectively mobilize to advance migrants' rights.

A critical discursive tool deployed by migrant advocacy NGOs and trade unions was the discussion of migrants' contributions to South Korea through their standing as workers. In November 2008, about 150 people, including activists from the MTU and migrant advocacy NGOs, migrant workers, and factory owners in Factorytown, all gathered for a candlelight vigil, a popular form of protest in South Korea that signals nonviolent activism, against the immigration crackdown. Father Won Jinheon, the director of a national migrant worker advocacy network, asserted during the protest: "These people are not criminals. They are workers, and thanks to them, the economy in this town, and also in this country, has developed. They are not paper cups that we can use and then throw away!" Protesters also stressed that the factory jobs occupied by migrants were undesirable to most South Korean workers and that their work was necessary for South Korea and should be recognized as such. In so doing, they were using workers' dignity as a significant discursive resource to extend rights to migrants as deserving members of society based on the long-standing connection between work and citizenship.[13]

Furthermore, South Korean faith-based migrant advocacy groups portrayed migrant workers as deserving people with an ethic of sacrifice for the family. One Sunday in the autumn of 2008, Filipino members of Justice Church in Factorytown traveled to a prominent Protestant church in Seoul to perform a skit titled "Migrant Workers and Simchông." This church in Seoul was central to pro-democracy and women factory workers' struggles during the military dictatorship in the 1970s and 1980s and had become a source of support for migrant factory workers in recent years.

Written by Pastor Seol Younghyun, the skit adapted a popular Korean folktale of filial piety, in which the female protagonist Simchông sacrifices her life for her blind father, is miraculously saved by a god, and returns as the wife of a king. The skit opened with a scene in which a Filipina woman leaves her country after her father dies and her family is in dire poverty. Her mother cries in despair, "Now he's gone, and there's nothing to eat in the house. How will I feed my four children?" The daughter replies, "Don't worry, Mother. South Korea is recruiting migrant workers. I will go." The daughter then travels to South Korea, but with her meager salary as an industrial trainee, she cannot support her family; she then runs away from the factory and earns more money as an undocumented worker. The skit ends as this Filipina woman meets Simchông face-to-face. "You are just like me," Simchông says, "because we were both willing to make a sacrifice for our families." After the performance, Pastor Seol delivered a clear message: "I hope you now understand why migrant workers are here. Even without visas, they need to work to help their poor families." Many congregation members responded "Amen" out loud, while some cried in the audience.

On the basis of the previous struggles of South Korean women to claim dignity for women factory workers as family breadwinners, migrant women in Factorytown were able to claim and benefit from labor and social rights alongside male workers, as in the case of Katherine, who successfully brought a legal case against a factory owner who had withheld her salary and severance pay. However, because labor and social rights for migrant workers in the manufacturing industry were still configured under a masculine model that was then extended to women workers, advocates often missed women's gender-specific claims to such issues as maternity rights and maternal health.

When women workers became pregnant, they were often fired and then asked to return to work after the birth without any paid leave. When Liezel Villaflor, a Filipina woman in her early forties, discovered that she was pregnant, she did not tell her factory owner and managers until she was five months along: "Because if I had told them two months ago, they would be like, 'You're stupid. Go to a doctor [for an abortion].' Many people still said, 'Why don't you just abort the baby? Here in Korea, it's legal.' And I told them, 'Why? This is God-given life.'" Liezel believed that the South Korean factory owner and managers did not respect her as a mother but instead viewed her only as a worker. She said,

> We didn't plan this baby, but my husband is happy that we are having a baby. They [the factory owner and managers] don't think about me; they only think about themselves and the work. If I leave, it's difficult for the factory, but what about what I want and my personal life?

When she entered her seventh month of pregnancy, she quit the factory as the managers expected her to, and later gave a birth to a son. A few months later, she found a job at another factory that paid less than her previous job but with fewer hours, and worked there until she sent her baby to the

Philippines to be raised by her mother. She handled the costs of pregnancy and childbirth in terms of time away from work and a change of workplace as a personal matter rather than a collective issue. The cost of pregnancy was even higher for documented migrant workers who were bound by contract to a particular factory. Gemma Huanita, another Filipina woman in Factorytown, originally had a working visa but became undocumented when her factory refused to renew her contract in the middle of her pregnancy and she could not find another factory to hire her within the two-month job search period.

Although South Korean labor law stipulated ninety days of paid maternity leave and documented migrant workers were eligible for this benefit, I did not observe the practice of this legal provision or any efforts on the part of migrant advocacy groups to mobilize for this maternity-related labor right. Such maternity provisions were difficult for South Korean women workers to obtain in practice, and feminist organizations and women's unions in South Korea continued to advocate for their enforcement. These organizations challenged male dominance in the labor movement by putting women's issues such as maternity leave, sexual harassment, and employment discrimination on the agenda of labor activism,[14] but their efforts had not yet been extended to include migrant women workers.

The discrepancy between advocacy for the issues common to both men and women and activism addressing issues particular to women workers was evident in the case of workers' compensation. For most workplace injuries, South Korean migrant advocacy groups were very effective in fighting to extend benefits to undocumented workers and in ensuring that both documented and undocumented workers could claim their rightful compensation, to the extent that even local South Korean workers with all the privileges of citizenship would sometimes seek their help as well. When a machine operator cut his fingers or a furniture assemblyman hurt his lower back, local migrant advocates helped him file paperwork to receive benefits and sometimes fought with factory owners who asserted that the injuries were not work related. When women factory workers suffered similar injuries, they received similar attention from migrant advocacy groups. However, when a woman worker had a miscarriage, advocacy groups treated this as an individual misfortune rather than as an issue of workplace safety. The coethnic migrant community did not let the individual woman suffer alone, as other Filipina women cried with the woman who lost the baby, cooked food for her, and took care of her. Migrant women workers also made an explicit connection between miscarriages and the workplace. "It's that damn plastic," said Roselle. "Everyone knows that's the problem. Why would so many women in the slipper factory lose their babies like that?"

However, the issues of maternal rights and health were not part of the labor and social rights discourse among migrant advocacy groups in South Korea. Mobilization based on worker's rights and dignity provided both men and women migrant workers with expanded rights, yet the lack of gender-specific demands in the ways that workers' rights were conceptualized and claimed affected the practice of rights for migrant women in the manufacturing sector.

Protecting Women-as-Victims in Basetown

"Things just don't change here in the camptowns. The same things that happened with South Korean women twenty years ago are now happening with Filipina women—violence, prostitution, abandonment. But our country [South Korea] still does not view these foreign women as victims of human trafficking," sighed Chun Aeran, a director of Sisterhood Center. Sisterhood Center had been working with women in the camptown clubs for more than two decades and was one of the key South Korean feminist NGOs that successfully achieved antiprostitution reforms in 2004, including the Protection of Victims of Sexual Trafficking Act. As part of this legal reform, Sisterhood Center was able to receive government funding to assist women in the camptown clubs as "victims of sexual trafficking." Despite these policy changes and the financial support for her work, Chun still felt lonely and frustrated: "We are the only organization that helps these foreign women. We are doing this work now, but if we dissolve, there would be no one these women could rely on. The labor office, the immigration office, the Ministry of Gender Equality, the police—they all don't care about these women."

Chun was correct that Sisterhood Center was one of very few South Korean organizations that advocated on behalf of migrant hostesses or offered them assistance. Being "the only" such organization took a toll on the three social workers at Sisterhood Center, who had to balance multiple tasks and case files and travel to camptowns near and far for counseling sessions and outreach work. The staff members told me that about 60 percent of their cases were located in Basetown, and the rest were spread across different camptowns surrounding Seoul and in the southern parts of South Korea. Despite the Center's outreach efforts, only a few migrant hostesses were aware of its work, but even with such limited publicity, the staff members' hands were more than full. On any given day, a social worker might help an elderly South Korean former camptown hostess fill out an application for social welfare benefits; help a Filipina hostess who ran away from the club find shelter and retrieve her passport from the promoter so that she could marry an American GI and be issued a spousal visa; and perhaps end the day by helping a Russian hostess file for divorce from the American GI husband who abandoned her and cut off all communication after he left South Korea. In most cases, migrant hostesses contacted Sisterhood Center for assistance after they ran away from the club, but in rare cases, the Center intervened to help a migrant woman who called for help from the club where she was confined, or offered medical or legal assistance to women still working in the clubs.

Whereas rights claims for migrant factory workers were modeled on the conception of migrant workers as contributors to South Korea, claims made by feminist organizations for hostesses focused on migrant hostesses as women victims in need of protection who were deceived into prostitution. A 2007 report by Sisterhood Center stated:

> Among the foreign women who enter South Korea, including those who enter with an E-6 [entertainer] visa and end up working as prostitutes, no one has voluntarily entered the country for the purpose of prostitution. Thus, we must recognize that the prostitution of foreign women, particularly those with E-6 visas, is due to the brokering of the South Korean agency and the camptown club owner, and in these cases, foreign women need to be protected as victims.

During my fieldwork in 2009, Sisterhood Center and other organizations for camptown hostesses were active leaders in coalition work with mainstream feminist groups in antiprostitution campaigns and rallies. As exemplified by the statement that "no one has voluntarily entered the country for the purpose of prostitution," it is clear that the Center approached the camptown club industry not as legitimate workplaces needing labor rights advocacy but as sites of criminal activity. US-led international antitrafficking directives influenced antiprostitution law and policy reforms in South Korea to redefine women engaged in sexual commerce—who were previously considered

criminals—as "victims of prostitution" and to include protections for trafficking victims.[15] Yet the discourse of women's victimhood was also firmly
grounded in the South Korean feminist movement's approach to the issue
of prostitution, which was rooted in the legacy of "comfort women," or the
forced military prostitution of South Korean women under Japanese colonial
occupation.[16] Advocacy on behalf of "comfort women" and South Korean
camptown hostesses both began with a basis in Christian social justice, feminism, and antimilitarism. Although the pathways of these two forms of advocacy diverged in the 1990s,[17] they converged again in the early 2000s under
the global discourse of "victims of sex trafficking." At the time of my fieldwork, there was a nascent movement of sex worker activism at the margins of
mainstream feminism in South Korea, but it had not extended to mobilization efforts or advocacy for migrant hostesses.

Sisterhood Center advocated for protective measures and provisions for
migrant hostesses, including legal and medical support and shelter services.
It was not a typical "rescue industry"[18] organization, whose primary mission
is to rescue women from the sex industry. While they certainly took an antiprostitution position and employed a transnational discourse of victimhood,
Sisterhood Center's daily practices more closely resembled a harm-reduction
approach. Support from the Center was not limited to self-identified victims,
and it did not require the women to leave the clubs in order to receive assistance. Yet instead of framing the services it offered as the collective rights
of migrant hostesses, those services were offered under a casework model
of social work to individual women who demonstrated need. For example,
when Ela Navarro, a Filipina hostess in Basetown, had an appendix rupture
that required immediate surgery, her co-worker Arlene called Sisterhood
Center to take her to the hospital and cover the medical expenses. Ela was
immensely grateful for this help because the cost of the surgery—more than
double her typical monthly income—was unaffordable to her. Ela, and many
others like her, were entitled to health benefits under her labor contract, but
they never received these benefits. Despite the prevalence of this problem, Sisterhood Center addressed medical needs on a case-by-case basis and did not
demand the enforcement of Ela's or other migrant hostesses' contracts. Given
Sisterhood Center's excessive workload, it was difficult to imagine that they
could take on such a task, even if they had tried to do so.

Making demands for rights would require a high level of collective mobilization on the part of migrant hostesses, an action thwarted by the organization of work in the club industry, as examined in the previous section. In

addition, organizations like Sisterhood Center received little support from other sectors of South Korean civil society, notably the migrant advocacy groups, such as churches, trade unions, and other migrant advocacy NGOs, that were at the forefront of advocacy for the rights of migrant workers. Unlike migrant factory workers, migrant hostesses in the camptowns were not seen as "workers" whose rights and dignity need to be respected.

The actions of Father Thomas, a Catholic priest and migrant advocate introduced in Chapter 5, exemplified this difference. In Factorytown, Father Thomas was actively involved with Filipino community mobilization through social activities and labor counseling. Like Pastor Paul, Father Thomas spent countless hours with Filipino and other migrant factory workers, organizing bowling and basketball leagues, accompanying them to the labor office, and managing a charity mobile clinic. In contrast, in Basetown, he offered only a weekly mass and had not planned any other efforts to mobilize the migrant hostesses. When I asked whether he intended to begin programs like those in Factorytown, Father Thomas said no, explaining, "Nobody will come. They are busy sleeping and meeting their boyfriends, and some can't go out because their clubs don't let them." Although he was aware that some women faced conditions of restricted mobility, he did not think of the hostesses as real workers in the way that factory workers were. He said:

> Some [migrant hostesses] run away and work in the factories, but many stay because they know factory work is difficult. . . . They have to carry heavy stuff, risk having their fingers cut, and they have to dress like *ajumma* [middle-aged women]. At clubs, it's easy work, you dress sexy, and drink, sing, dance, and you can sleep the whole day the next day. And they think marrying an American soldier is their way out.

Father Thomas's hostess workers were not real workers in the way factory workers were—characterized by physical demand, risk of injury, and desexualization. Rather, he perceived hostess work as "easy work," selling women's sexual appeal, eliding the long working hours and high degree of physical and emotional labor involved in hostess work. It was noteworthy that he, a Catholic priest, mentioned hostess work as "easy" rather than morally questionable work in the eyes of the church. This perception of the hostesses' work affected his willingness to participate in advocacy work on their behalf. Other South Korean migrant advocates and activists were less explicit about why they did not include migrant hostesses in their advocacy for migrant factory workers and, more recently, farm workers as well. When asked about migrant hostesses, many migrant advocates said they did not know much about hostesses, but they thought that these workers' needs were a better match for feminist organizations than for their own.

Although stigma related to sexual morality no doubt played a role in Father Thomas's and other advocates' hesitation to advocate for migrant hostesses, what truly limited advocacy on their behalf was their exclusion from the dignity of workers, leaving the Sisterhood Center isolated in its efforts. Unlike migrant factory workers, migrant hostesses did not fit the model of workers with rights and dignity in the eyes of South Korean civil society.

Most of the migrant hostesses I met thought of themselves primarily as workers. Hostesses were "breadwinners" who put in hard work in a labor sector that required long working hours and a blurred boundary between work and nonwork hours. Yet unlike migrant factory workers in Factory-town, migrant hostesses in Basetown did not have Pastor Pauls who would engage in a fistfight with their employer to claim the "fruits of their hard work," nor a coethnic community to offer mutual support. Instead, migrant hostesses in the camptown clubs had access only to the language of victim-hood and to social provisions for their protection, while the precarious-ness of the rotation system made their mobilization even more challenging. The services offered by Sisterhood Center were indispensable to migrant hostesses, especially to those who wished to leave the clubs. However, for migrant hostesses who wanted to stay and work in the camptowns, there was great need for protection of their labor and social rights, protection that was unlikely to materialize as long as they were narrowly framed as vulnerable women-as-victims.

GENDERING THE WORKER-CITIZEN

At the beginning of this chapter, I offered the stories of Katherine, a migrant factory worker who had the ability to claim labor rights, and of Rachel, a migrant hostess who did not. I asked how we can understand this divergence in the practice of rights for migrant factory workers and host-esses, despite their shared conditions as women migrant workers in South Korea. Delving into the process of producing gendered rights, I showed that Filipina migrant women experienced distinct workplace organizations in the factories and hostess clubs. Women factory workers like Katherine shared a skill-based wage structure and had access to respect and resources as workers through their relationships with Filipino men in the coethnic community. In contrast, migrant hostesses like Rachel faced precarious working conditions under the paternalistic control of employers and in competition with other hostesses.

Civil society mobilization embedded in South Korean social movement legacies also influenced migrant rights for migrant factory workers and hostesses. On the shoulders of strong labor activism within the *minjung* movement in South Korea, the discourse of the worker-citizen was highly effective in expanding migrant rights and citizenship. However, not all sectors of work offer societal and moral standing that can serve as grounds for rights claims, and gender is salient in determining who is deemed worthy of the dignity of workers. For migrant factory workers, South Korean civil society mobilized on their behalf for the expansion of social and labor rights without attention to their gender-specific needs as women. For migrant hostesses, although feminist NGOs advocated for more protective measures for victims of trafficking, without the involvement of other migrant advocacy groups or trade unions, this effort rendered the women invisible as migrant workers who might want to keep and improve their jobs, and weakened their standing as the subjects of rights and citizenship claims in South Korea.

SEVEN

Between Women Victims and Mother-Citizens

Carrie Perez was afraid to open the door when she heard her husband's footsteps on their apartment stairs each night. Too often, he came home from work drunk and angry. When he did, she walked on eggshells to avoid setting off his temper. When he was in a rage, Carrie's husband became physically abusive, pushing or even choking her. One terrifying night, he threw a kitchen knife at Carrie that landed only inches from their baby. When he was angry, he would yell, "Get out! Go back home to the Philippines!" This was not the marriage Carrie had hoped for when she traveled to Factorytown on a spousal visa.

Sixty miles away, in the club district of Basetown, Michelle Ramos, another Filipina migrant woman, was also struggling with false promises, though of a different kind than Carrie's. Michelle had entered South Korea not on a spousal visa but to work as an entertainer. When she migrated, she was told she had been hired by Club Mirage to sing. Upon arrival, Michelle learned that she had in fact been hired to serve drinks and entertain American GIs as a "juicy girl," a name she detested. The club owner withheld her passport, restricted her mobility, and pressured her to spend the night with customers on bar fines. When she refused, the owner yelled at her, "I will send you back! Why do I need to keep you if you are not bringing in the money?"

Although their particular predicaments are unique, migrant women like Carrie and Michelle share a situation of gendered precarity in South Korea. Feminist advocates in support of women's global human rights and in opposition to violence against women regard these migrants' situation with great concern. Feminist organizations in South Korea utilized UN treaties and transnational advocacy networks to advocate for policies to protect the human rights of migrant wives and hostesses under the common discourse of victimization and trafficking, demanding that the state acknowledge migrant women's particular vulnerability in the absence of legal citizenship and assume accountability for their protection as vulnerable victims.[1] In response, the South Korean state instituted some protective legal and policy measures. However, the majority of migrant women I met during my fieldwork who experienced conditions of violence and coercion—including Carrie and Michelle—did not claim these human rights–based provisions even though they were aware of them and had even considered doing so. In this chapter, I delve into the social worlds of migrant women to understand how they negotiated the discourse of victimhood and mobilized other pathways to dignity and security.

By discussing the limits of victimhood as a basis for claims of citizenship, I do not mean to undermine the significance of advocating for and providing protective measures for migrant women subjected to violence, confinement, and other forms of abuse. For some migrant wives and hostesses facing conditions of structural vulnerability, human rights–based measures are necessary and even lifesaving. However, it is critical to pay attention to the women who do not respond to such measures, and to understand their decisions in relation to their moral worlds. Under the discourse of victimhood, these women face the predicament of having to choose between rights and dignity. The feminist discourse of human rights for women victims exists not in isolation but in tandem with other discourses based on women's standing within heteronormative families and as the subjects of upward mobility.

This chapter highlights the dilemmas migrant women faced as they considered taking up victimhood as a basis to claim membership, and shows that migrant wives and migrant hostesses chose divergent paths to rights and dignity. Whereas migrant wives relied on the moral status of motherhood to assert their membership and deservingness to the South Korean nation, migrant hostesses rejected the status of either prostitute or victim to continue their path to mobility, which offered limited basis for citizenship in South Korea, yet was more aligned with their gendered pursuit of moral respect and recognition.

FEMINIST ADVOCACY AND THE PROTECTION OF WOMEN VICTIMS

The South Korean feminist movement mobilized a human rights discourse to advocate for migrant women, a discourse based on a long legacy of organizing around violence against women.[2] By focusing on bodily and psychological harm in their mobilization efforts related to domestic violence against migrant wives and trafficking in camptown clubs, South Korean feminist groups argued that migrant women were vulnerable and required the protection of the South Korean state. Human rights reports on the issues facing migrant wives and hostesses in South Korea typically focused on two sources of victimization. First, these reports pointed to the practice of South Korean club owners and husbands or in-laws of withholding women's passports and restricting their interpersonal interactions. These actions constrained migrant women's ability to leave in the case of abuse. Second, they discussed migrant women's vulnerability to deception and fraud as a condition of trafficking; migrant hostesses were falsely informed about the working conditions at the clubs (regarding pay, working hours, holidays, benefits, and, in some cases, the sexual nature of the work), and migrant wives were misinformed about important details regarding their husbands' economic or health condition.

Feminist discourses blamed migrant women's victimization on multiple actors: matchmaking agencies who controlled migrant wives, South Korean husbands and families-in-law who treated migrant wives as if they were "commodities," club owners and promotion agencies that brought migrant hostesses over on false promises, and, most of all, the South Korean state, which failed to regulate cross-border marriages and camptown clubs to protect the human rights of migrant women.

Feminist advocates in South Korea used the discourse of trafficked victims as a device to hold the state accountable. Treating the two groups of migrant women as interrelated cases, they called attention to state culpability in the plights of migrant hostesses and migrant wives. As discussed in Chapter 6, South Korean feminist organizations such as Sisterhood Center considered migrant hostesses as trafficking victims based on their understanding of sexual commerce as harmful to the women whose bodies and sexualities it commodified. They treated marriages stemming from club encounters as questionable; as Sa Soohyun, a staff member of Sisterhood Center, stated, "I have seen too many GIs desert their Filipina wives. Because they started as clients, how can the marriage be just fine?"[3]

Regarding marriage migration, feminist advocates were careful not to treat all cross-border marriages as trafficking, while also highlighting the strong risk of trafficking involved in such marriages. For example, the Ministry of Gender Equality commissioned a 2003 report on migrant women in South Korea from key migration experts and feminist scholars. The report included policy suggestions regarding migrant wives and migrant hostesses. In particular, it warned that cross-border marriages through brokers could be used for the purposes of trafficking:

> Even though brokering international marriages is legal under domestic law, the international marriages that are taking place in Southeast Asia, including the Philippines and Vietnam, China, Mongolia, and Russia, are difficult to perceive as *marriages based on pure love* [*sunsuhan sarang*]. These Korean agencies recruit those who want to enter international marriages to join three-night, four-day or four-night, five-day international marriage tours. International marriages happening in such a rushed manner entail the risk of turning foreign women into victims of trafficking [emphasis added].[4]

By advancing the ideal of marriage based on "pure love" as opposed to brokered "international marriages," this statement drew on a problematic dichotomy between heteronormative marriages based on love and marriages devoid of love fraught with "risk," and between agents capable of love and victims of trafficking. Such dichotomies leave little room for the complexity of migrant women's desires, in that it is possible that women wish to marry for reasons based on *both* love *and* economic stability or that some view economic support from a husband as proof of his love.[5]

Invoking the language of human rights that referred to involvement in sexual commerce and cross-border marriages as risky for migrant women, feminist advocates affirmed that the proper place of sexuality was within the institution of romance-based marriage. Feminist concerns about ending the exploitation of migrant women in the camptown club industry or halting domestic violence against migrant wives were thus conflated with stopping the migrant flow into the clubs and cross-border marriages altogether. In the case of migrant hostesses, feminist groups took the explicit stance of claiming migrant hostesses as trafficking victims and advocated under a moral imperative to stop trafficking. Regarding marriage migration, feminist groups argued that these marriages were prone to abuse and should therefore be tightly regulated, if not avoided altogether. At a forum on migrant women's human rights, Dan Bohee, a Korean feminist activist, referred to her work as a counselor at a domestic violence hotline for migrant wives as "cleaning up guys' messes." The audience applauded when she exclaimed, "How long should we continue doing this? I suggest that we go to the sending countries and stop this problem at its roots."

Feminist advocacy challenged the conditions of migrant women's vulnerability and won from the South Korean state important protective measures for migrant women as a matter of human rights. These measures included a multilingual hotline for migrant women in thirteen languages, legal assistance and counseling services, shelters, and, in the case of domestic violence, alternate pathways to permanent residency for migrant wives. However, the particular configuration of human rights for migrant women that centered on victimhood provided only a limited basis for women's membership in South Korea, presenting them as subjects in need of protection. Feminist advocacy centered on women's victimhood also ran up against challenges because the migrant women they intended to support were uneasily located as "boundary markers"[6] between the conflicting state projects of "protecting women" and "protecting borders" from noncitizens.[7] The discourses of victimhood and trafficking foreclosed alternate discourses as a basis for claiming rights and effectively advocated for border protection as a way to protect women.[8]

MIGRANT WIVES: CONTESTING VICTIMHOOD AS EMERGING CITIZEN-MOTHERS

Despite the physical abuse she faced at home with her husband, Carrie could not easily pursue the human rights–based provisions meant to protect her as a victim, including counseling, police protection, and divorce. For her, divorce represented personal failure as a woman and confirmed the stigma assigned to migrant women suspected of pursuing marriages only to secure permanent residency. She felt that migrant women carried an extra burden to affirm their commitment to marriage and family in order to refute the suspicion that they were "fake wives." As Carrie and other Filipina women jokingly said during an afternoon cooking gathering, "If we were South Korean women, we would have divorced even before the end of the first month of our marriage!"

The pressure Carrie felt to make a special effort to prove the legitimacy of her marriage began at the moment of her arrival. She remembered how deeply hurt she was when she first met her in-laws.

> My mother-in-law was not happy that I am from the Philippines. Why?
> Because she thinks the Philippines is poor. I am from a poor country.
> You can't blame her because that's the only thing they show on TV. Poor.
> So they think if you are from the Philippines, you would send money to
> the Philippines. That's why I never send money. When I came to marry,
> I brought her a golden bracelet and necklaces, and I never received any-
> thing. Not from her, not from my husband. No jewelry, no flowers.

To challenge her in-laws' perception that she had married for financial reasons, Carrie decided to prove her sincerity by cutting off financial support to her natal family, to "follow the Korean way." Carrie still felt bitter about the jewelry and flowers that she never received from her husband or his family—not because of their financial value but because they were a sign of respect.

But she hoped that if she tried hard, she could "earn their respect" by becoming a good wife to her husband. Her husband worked long hours in the factory, and after work, he drank heavily with his male friends. Carrie worked at a few factories before giving birth to two children, and later taught English at a neighborhood kindergarten while taking full responsibility for the household work. Although Carrie thought men's treatment of women in South Korea was unfair, she tried to adapt to it as part of "Korean culture." She said, "South Korea is way too much male-centered. They say things like, 'Men are heaven; women are earth.' I didn't even understand what it meant when I first heard that, but that's what my husband and the in-laws talk about, that I have to follow what my husband says. We have no such saying in the Philippines."

When migrant wives perceived their husband's controlling behavior as the "Korean way," certain oppressive practices were normalized, and perseverance was valorized. To confront the suspicion that they entered "fake marriages" only to pursue material gain and legal citizenship, migrant wives attempted to prove their faithfulness even when their husbands engaged in controlling behaviors such as hiding the women's passports or not allowing them to meet other coethnic migrants. In a media literacy class for migrant wives at Peace Center, we watched a short autobiographical documentary written and produced by an ethnically Korean migrant woman from Uzbekistan who married a South Korean man. She told the story of her arranged marriage and described her acute homesickness in rural South Korea. Although she wanted to divorce her husband and return home, she was unable to leave because her in-laws and husband hid her passport. After a few years of struggle, she gave birth to a child who became an anchor for her life in South Korea. The documentary ended with her calm narration that one day when she was cleaning the house, she found her passport, but she decided not to leave home. She had accepted that "it was my choice to come here."

After showing the documentary, the instructor asked migrant wives for their thoughts. Jang Gayun, a Filipina woman who had lived in Korea for ten years, expressed little sympathy for the woman: "I don't understand why she wanted a divorce—it's not like there was any big problem in the family. Her husband seems nice, not beating her up or anything." Others chimed in: "That's true that her family looked nice, but their village seemed really rural, and she feels lonely away from her family. That must have been hard for her. I can understand. But it's good that she's now happy with her baby." The women continued to debate whether her wish to divorce was justified, centering their discussion on her motives and choices rather than on her husband and in-laws' decision to withhold her passport to control her mobility.

Migrant wives did not agree with feminist NGOs' stance that crossborder marriages treated women as "commodities" and that the women were "victims of trafficking." "We are a normal family, just like any other. I don't know why people want to single us out. We have struggles, but don't all families?" Linda asked. For women who daily negotiated their place in South Korea under suspicion from in-laws, neighbors, and other South Koreans, a discourse that labeled their family formation as a form of trafficking was not appealing. Establishing their legitimate status within the institution of marriage was very important to many of the women. To counter the assumption that their marriages were illegitimate because they lacked a romantic basis, many migrant wives actively emphasized spousal love and intimacy. Linda recalled the moment she met her husband as "love at first sight":

> When I opened the office door, there he was. He was fair-skinned, tall, and handsome, and I instantly liked him. Thankfully, he okayed me, and we got married. . . . When I saw him again at the airport in Korea, I had a feeling, "Wow. He's so attractive." Since we were apart for several months, I really wanted to see him and wanted to hug him right there, but my mind wasn't ready yet. I was too shy. But when we went to the parking lot, I had another feeling. My heart was trembling and beating so fast. It was the first time I felt that way. I have never felt like that in my life.

In addition to emphasizing romantic love, some women who married South Korean men through the Unification Church also talked about a higher level of connection and commitment to family. For example, Ruth Namoc recalled how she met her husband in 1980 after experiencing firsthand the futility of romantic love:

> In 1979, my boyfriend left me. He went to become a seaman, went abroad, but married another woman. I decided to kill myself and got myself poison. When I tried to drink it, suddenly I became numb and couldn't move. Later that day, I saw a flyer. It said, "Where do people go after they die? Come to this lecture to find an answer." There I found the [Unification] Church, and true love.

In the Unification Church—as well as in the culture of the Catholic Church in which the majority of Filipina women were raised—the sanctity of marriage was highly prized. The Unification Church distinguished "true love" from romantic love as a deeper, lasting connection. For migrant wives like Ruth, the "true love" represented by marriage offered her a sense of fulfillment and moral respectability.

Carrie's faith was one of the major reasons she wanted to stay in her marriage. She said, "I have two faiths—Catholic and Unification Church. For me, it's the same—same God, same principles, the importance of family. . . . Without the Church's teaching, I would not have survived in South Korea. Even if I didn't understand Korean, *samonim* (the pastor's wife) told me I should read the scripture, and I still do every day." Some women, especially those who arrived only recently, were isolated and unaware of the protective measures available in South Korea. Yet thanks to a far-reaching public awareness campaign on violence against migrant women mobilized by feminist organizations, most of the migrant wives I met knew of human rights–based measures they could use to seek protection, especially in the case of physical violence. Carrie was also aware of these measures, but even though she wanted the abuse to stop, she did not take advantage of them because she wanted to maintain moral respectability as a full member of her family and community.

Migrant wives like Carrie had access to an alternate discourse that enabled them to make direct claims on the South Korean state and society to seek an end to their abuse: maternalism. Because motherhood is glorified by both the Catholic Church and the Unification Church and affirmed by the South Korean state, social workers, and migrant advocates, the rhetoric of motherhood constitutes a powerful discourse with which to claim rights. The discourse of motherhood has offered South Korean women an avenue to exercise agency in a patriarchal society, though according to anthropologist Haejoang Cho, doing so also paradoxically sustains Confucian norms.[9]

Carrie said that instead of reporting her husband to the police or filing for divorce, after the birth of her children, she used her status as a mother to demand dignity from her husband. Whenever he became violent or yelled, "Go back to the Philippines!" she yelled back, "No, I will not! This is my children's house. This is my house. You get out!" The claim "This is my children's house" allowed Carrie to assert her status as a mother of South Korean citizens, entitled to her place in the country. Carrie also moved these words into action, locking her husband out of the house when he was drunk so that he was forced to sleep in the public bathhouse. Carrie went on a personal strike and stopped cooking for her husband for almost two weeks, and she recruited the help of her pastor to teach her husband about the damage excessive drinking does to family life. Carrie said her husband finally apologized and began to change his violent behavior.

The moral status of motherhood enabled migrant wives to claim a right of belonging to Korea independent from their husbands, not only on a personal level but also on a collective level in negotiation with the state. One morning during Korean language class, Yeo Sojung, a migrant wife who had arrived from the Philippines only a few years ago and changed her name to a Korean one, complained that the immigration office required the physical attendance of the Korean spouse for the renewal of a spousal visa. "It is ridiculous," she argued. "My husband is busy and has to go to work, so it's extremely difficult to make time. Why can't I just go there by myself and file it?" Claiming the ability to represent herself based on motherhood, she continued, "I think mothers should be exempt from that requirement. They are afraid of foreign wives running away, but where would we mothers go, leaving our children behind? I have two children, and there's no way I would go anywhere." Although her statement reflected the patriarchal understanding that children belong to their father, so that mothers would have to "leave [them] behind," Sojung also drew on the belief that mothers are inseparable from their children to claim migrant wives' place in South Korea. Indeed, in practice, the immigration office often allowed married migrant women to extend their visas without being accompanied by their husbands if they had Korean-born children.

The rhetoric of motherhood was also used by migrant wives to make political demands. Nguyen Thi Hong Hanh, a migrant woman from Vietnam, spoke as a representative of migrant wives at an NGO-sponsored panel discussion on proposed changes to immigration law that would affect migrant wives. Speaking of migrant women's vulnerability as noncitizens, she said:

> Even now, we migrant women become illegal over-stayers if our husbands do not confirm our status through their sponsorship once every year. That's why it is so urgent to enable us to live in South Korea without the husbands' sponsorship. Because there are too many people who are unable to escape painful lives, even though they cry every day because of violence, disrespect, and mental torment from husbands and the in-laws and their eyes are never dry, but they have to return to their home countries when they divorce. If they cannot stand it anymore and run away from home, they become undocumented. In South Korea, the undocumented do not have any rights, and many migrant women enter into a status where they keep on living, but not like full human beings.

After highlighting the plight of migrant women—of pain and tears due to their precarious legal status—she continued to make her demands of the South Korean state and society based on maternal rhetoric:

> I heard from many that in rural areas in South Korea, the only young people there are migrant women who married older South Korean rural bachelors, and that the only children born in rural areas are the ones these

migrant women gave birth to. If this is the case, *doesn't South Korean society need migrant women very much?* Isn't that why international marriage is so easily authorized? I do not understand why South Korea makes it difficult for the people they need to naturalize.

Hong Hanh's claim invoked migrant women's contribution to the nation through motherhood, which established their status within the Korean moral landscape and provided a solid basis for rights claims. By pointing to the "need" of the South Korean nation-state for the reproductive labor of migrant women, she argued that the needs of migrant wives—as mother-citizens, rather than as abstract holders of human rights—should be taken into account in South Korean policy.

The emphasis on motherhood is rightly criticized by feminist scholars and activists as limiting women's pathways to citizenship through reproduction[10] and excluding women who are not mothers. Claims for citizenship based on motherhood had a clear limitation—if the legitimacy of one's standing is achieved through motherhood, the discourse of motherhood can also be used to weaken women's belonging and rights claims. This was the case when, during the election of the National Assembly in 2008, Judith A. Hernandez, a thirty-eight-year-old naturalized South Korean citizen who immigrated from the Philippines via cross-border marriage, was for the first time appointed as a proportional candidate of the minor Creative Korea Party as part of the attempt to give voice to "the multicultural citizens." Although she failed to win the seat, she attracted significant media attention and brought to the fore the question of migrant citizenship in South Korea. Hernandez's candidacy became controversial because her South Korean husband had passed away four years earlier, and she had married a Bangladeshi migrant worker. Her two children from the previous marriage were not living with her in South Korea but were instead being raised in the Philippines by her natal family, which made her a target for criticism among other migrant women. "She's not even raising her children herself," said Linda. "Of course, raising a child is hard, but that's why we are mothers. Would her children even speak Korean properly, after spending most of their time in the Philippines? How can she say she would run for politics for her South Korean children?"

Despite its apparent constraints, the discourse of motherhood, more than the discourse of human rights based on victimhood, resonated with migrant wives and the South Korean public. It offered migrant wives a respectful status through which to claim membership in the polity, which the universal and thus unspecified terms of human rights claims did not. This discourse was effective because it conferred an elevated moral status that migrant wives could use to assert membership both within their families and in the state and civil society at large. Through discursive claims-making, migrant wives emerged as a collective subject of rights and belonging as mother-citizens.

MIGRANT HOSTESSES: COMPLICATING VICTIMHOOD AND MOTHERHOOD

Many South Koreans I met in Basetown dismissed the idea that migrant hostesses' rights were violated, claiming that "they all come knowingly," as if the decision to work as a hostess implied consent to exploitation. A club owner, Dan Hyunok, said, "It is total nonsense, this whole business about human rights. What do they say? 'Foreign women's human rights?' Those people don't know anything about these girls. They say that we force these girls into prostitution! What they don't know is that they were already prostitutes back home in the Philippines."

Sitting in a dimly lit corner of a Basetown club filled with cigarette smoke, I listened as Hyunok delivered a lengthy lecture on outsiders' misconceptions of camptown clubs, especially those who "ranted" about human rights abuse of migrant hostesses. As a former hostess who married and divorced an American GI before purchasing Club Sky over ten years earlier, Hyunok was a self-proclaimed "expert" on the camptown clubs.

What was intriguing about Hyunok's statement was not the veracity of her assertion about migrant women's prior involvement in prostitution, which in my experience with hostesses was generally false, but how she used this assertion to dismiss claims for their human rights. Granted, Hyunok's statement was rhetorical, and she was also speaking from a defensive position—as a club owner, she was targeted as one of the main abusers of migrant hostesses. But Hyunok was not alone in using an assessment of migrant women's moral worth to dismiss claims for their human rights. In fact, migrant women's position in the broader moral landscape regulated their sexuality and determined whether their claims for rights and dignity were respected or disregarded.

Migrant hostesses entered a space that was outside the institution of marriage. They were segregated and contained in several red-light districts surrounding US military base camptowns, space marked by the stigma of transactional and interracial sex. Contrary to feminist advocates who considered them victims of trafficking, many South Koreans and Filipino migrants considered migrant hostesses "prostitutes" or "fallen women" who might damage society's morals. "It's a matter of principle, doing that kind of work. Doesn't matter how poor you are," exclaimed Pauline Pacpaco, a Filipina woman who married an American civilian working for the US military in the Philippines and who moved to Basetown temporarily. She expressed a strong dislike of Basetown: "Here there are so many Filipinas wearing panties and bras, courting people on the street. What kind of a woman does that?" Pauline spent most of her time at home, except when she traveled with her husband by car. She said that the Filipina women working in the clubs were there because they came "from broken families, with no discipline, no morals, like a single-parent household where there's no parent to care for the children." In her mind, women who grow up in a "normal household" would not do this type of work, nor would their parents allow them to.

In the face of such stigma, the status of trafficked victim offered migrant hostesses a certain moral status, which was especially redeeming for the minority of women who were deceived about the sexual nature of the work prior to their arrival in South Korea. For these women, working as a hostess, and especially being pressured to go out with customers at night on a bar fine, put them in a personal and moral predicament. Michelle Ramos was one of these women, and she firmly announced, "I am a victim of sexual trafficking."

I first met Michelle and her co-worker Susan when they asked Soohyun, a staff member of Sisterhood Center, for help running away from their club. Sitting in a dark corner of a pub near the camptown, Michelle gave a lengthy and passionate speech about how she came to South Korea to work as a singer and was deceived into the club trade. She asked Soohyun if the NGO could help sue the promoters on trafficking charges. In South Korea, migrant hostesses could file lawsuits against club owners and promoters, but the chances of winning were minimal; a successful legal precedent was set in 2006, but the majority of these cases were dismissed before going to court, due to lack of evidence. As victims of trafficking, women who sought legal redress were provided a special temporary visa, room and board at a migrant women's shelter, and legal and medical assistance during the course of the suit, but they could not work legally during this time. When the lawsuit ended, women had to return to their home countries immediately without an extended work permit or eligibility for permanent residency. At the time, Michelle seemed less concerned with these practical matters than with the issue of morality; she wanted all of the clubs shut down and all Filipina hostesses to return home because the camptown clubs were "shameful to all Filipinos." Michelle's determination to end trafficking in the clubs seemed to converge seamlessly with the antitrafficking project of South Korean feminist groups. For Michelle, claiming victimhood was a way to reclaim her compromised dignity and moral status.

But the status of trafficked victim also entailed moral costs. This became clear when Soohyun collected Michelle's and Susan's testimonies about their clubs' working conditions—documenting, for instance, how many hours they worked and whether the club had a bar fine. Assuming that I would not be familiar with the topic, Soohyun explained, "Bar fine is a system of prostitution in which customers take the women out for sex." Susan, who until then had been quiet, objected, "No, bar fines are not about sex. It's different from prostitution." She continued, "I went out on bar fine several times, but only with my boyfriend. When I am really tired, he took me out so that I can rest." Michelle also chimed in: "We all make boyfriends to protect ourselves because we don't want to go out with just about anybody."

This interchange revealed the frictions that emerged during negotiations between migrant hostesses and feminist NGOs as agents of human rights. For Sisterhood Center, the camptown club industry represented a clear case of prostitution and sexual trafficking, but this definition invalidated the more complex experiences of migrant hostesses, even those like Michelle who actively wanted to claim victimhood. Migrant hostesses had devised a frame in which they understood the bar fine system as distinct from prostitution because monetary exchanges served not as payment for a sexual service but as an "intimate and relational exchange."[11] These exchanges occurred within a space of romance, where women received gifts and protection from their boyfriends. When Susan said, "Bar fines are not about sex," she asserted her place in the moral hierarchy by distancing herself from the stigma of prostitution and the sex trade.

Both Michelle and Susan stated that during their time in the club, they maintained their moral respectability by choosing one special customer as a boyfriend and asking him to come to their rescue. Claiming human rights on the basis of being victims of sexual trafficking would require them to renounce this script of romance and recount their victimhood as participants in (forced) sexual labor to themselves, in court, and on the public record. Accepting the definition of hostess work as trafficking thus posed a moral dilemma for migrant hostesses: it offered some women resources as victims and a moral status above that of prostitutes, but it also required them to accept and publically admit that they engaged in sex trade, which many were hesitant to do. The gendered stigma that sexual commerce carries was not just imposed by outsiders but also generally shared among migrant hostesses.

For the next few months, I frequently visited Michelle's apartment and became familiar with more complicated stories of force and victimhood. These women's experiences caused moments of rupture in the seemingly seamless narratives of victimhood described by Sisterhood Center counseling reports.

Although Michelle consistently expressed anger toward the promoter and club owner, the reasons for her anger were not fully captured by the language of forced trafficking. She felt violated when she first came to South Korea on the entertainer visa and was asked to do hostess work instead of singing onstage. Not wanting to return to the Philippines empty-handed to add to her parents' disappointment with her "failures," she acquiesced, thinking she might never have a chance to go abroad again. That was when she met her "true love" Brian, an American GI customer who visited the club every day to see her. With Brian's help, Michelle was able to manage Juice sales and bar fines. Then there came an unexpected disruption, for which Michelle blamed the promoter:

> Brian was my true love, and he begged to run away, but I didn't want to break the contract. But after six months, the promoter made me pack my bag and took me to the airport to go back to the Philippines. My contract was valid for another six months. How could they do that to me when I did everything right?

According to her, the disruption was a mistake on the part of the promoter, who wrongfully believed that her contract was for six months, not one year.

But because she had left South Korea, Michelle had to wait to get a new visa, and she worked hard to return to the same club. "I had to come back. For the first six months, I didn't earn much money because . . ." Michelle hesitated for a few seconds and went on, "You see . . . I had an operation [abortion] not long after I came. I never told my family, but he [the GI boyfriend] already left when I found out about the pregnancy, and I had no choice. The club owner paid for the operation and took $200 out of my paycheck every month."

After six months of desperately waiting in the Philippines, Michelle returned to Basetown. When she returned, her "true love" Brian was engaged to another Filipina woman. But another love came. Jack Brown, a twenty-two-year-old GI from Kansas, started courting her, and she thought he might be the one she and her sons could rely on. They planned her escape from the club, but as they approached the chosen date, something unexpected happened: her co-worker Tricia ran away from the same club on her day off, and the club owner became very angry. He accused Michelle, wrongfully in her opinion, of being a bad influence on Tricia, and brought her to the airport to send her away. "Again, they did that to me!" Michelle exclaimed. After the promoter took her to the departure gate, instead of going through immigration, she pretended she left something outside and exited to the terminal. Then her boyfriend, Jack, came and picked her up from the airport. "I can't allow things like this to happen. They shouldn't treat us like this." She was determined to do something about the mistreatment of migrant hostesses, which led her to seek help from Sisterhood Center.

Michelle and Susan initially wanted to pursue legal action against the club owner and the promoter, but for the next three months they faced real-life challenges. Sisterhood Center offered them free shelter, but both were reluctant to live there because they had already moved in with their American GI boyfriends. Michelle was also concerned that a legal case would make it difficult to support her children and parents in the Philippines without a work permit for the duration of the trial. Furthermore, several Filipina women who worked in the same club kept calling her to drop the case, saying, "If you do that, the club will close, and we don't want to go back." Even though Michelle said the club owner was making the women send those messages, she also knew that some women genuinely wanted to stay, because she herself had once fought her way back to Basetown.

She also realized that her previous return to the same club would hurt her legal claim of trafficking. In the meantime, Jack proposed, promising that he would move Michelle and her two children to the United States. Three months after contacting Sisterhood Center, with a cubic zirconia ring on her finger, Michelle let me know that she and Susan had given up the lawsuit. She said, "I'd still like to do it, but Jack doesn't want me to. He wants me to be safe in the Philippines and wait for him there."

Migrant hostesses' decision not to participate in human rights–based recourse against their employers should not imply passive acceptance of their labor conditions; instead, this refusal involved a decision-making process that took into account the material and moral costs of such action. Michelle and other women faced a reality in which romance with American GIs offered far greater benefits than the promise of temporary rights as trafficked victims in South Korea. Every migrant woman I met in the camptowns knew someone who had successfully married a GI and moved to the United States. By engaging in a romantic courtship and marrying an American GI, Filipina hostesses could achieve legal status in South Korea as a spouse of US military personnel, financial stability, the chance to emigrate to the United States, and the moral status of a wife. Romance with American GIs was not a guarantee of happiness; stories of abandonment, broken promises, and womanizers were equally common among the women I met. It was a risky pursuit, and migrant hostesses were aware of that. However, lacking other grounds on which to claim citizenship in the South Korean state and society, migrant hostesses' pursuit of romance and marriage operated as an alternate path to rights and recognition within the transnational space of US military camptowns.

Migrant women who immigrated to South Korea via cross-border marriages could rely on the model of mother-citizens to claim their rights and belonging through their South Korean children. But migrant hostesses had difficulty utilizing motherhood as a basis for citizenship. For migrant hostesses whose children resided in the Philippines, motherhood did not facilitate rights claims in either South Korea or the Philippines. Instead, motherhood was an individual responsibility that they tried to fulfill through migrant labor. When they became pregnant in South Korea in their encounters with American GI boyfriends or customers, some, like Michelle, chose to terminate their pregnancy. Other women gave birth in South Korea, but their attempts to seek rights and recognition as mothers were fraught with barriers because birth on South Korean soil does not confer citizenship under the state.

Amy Samiento, a Filipina woman in her late thirties, decided to migrate overseas to work as a hostess to support her daughter as a single mother. During her mid- to late twenties, she made eight rounds on six-month contracts in Japan, leaving her daughter in the care of her mother. But when she turned thirty, the promoter rejected her, saying she was too old for Japanese customers, so the next available choice was South Korea. Unlike Michelle, Amy was informed about the nature of her work with American GI customers, and she did not perceive herself as a victim of fraud or trafficking.

Amy recalled what had happened five years earlier, when a fellow hostess from her club ran away to report to a Filipino Catholic priest that the club was facilitating prostitution. The priest brought the police to the club to rescue the women, and they all went to the police station and later to the shelter. At first, she and the others were excited at the prospect of winning a large sum of money for compensation. But it turned out that even if the lawsuit were successful, the financial award would be trivial, not even coming close to covering her loss of income from missing the remainder of her contract. Amy and her co-workers decided not to participate in the suit or to testify as victims of sexual trafficking. Amy explained, "I told the police: You can't blame the club owner. He didn't force anyone to prostitute. I didn't do anything. Those young girls, they were doing it to buy leather boots and stuff like that." After a few days in the shelter, she recalled, a couple of the women went to live with their American GI boyfriends, and most of them, including Amy, returned to the club to work as before, continuing her efforts to provide for her daughter.

After her return, Amy met a serious boyfriend, an American GI named Tom, and she left the club to move in with him. However, they broke up soon after because Tom continued to see other women, and she returned to the club before finding out that she was pregnant. Working in the club and raising a child by herself felt impossible, and she made an appointment at the hospital to have an abortion. But one night, she had a dream that changed everything.

> A baby boy was calling me in the dark. Mama, mama, he kept calling. I didn't know the sex of the baby then, but it was definitely a boy's voice. When I woke up, instead of going to a hospital, I locked myself in

the room for two weeks. All I thought about was the baby, and I finally decided to have him.

When Amy told Tom that she was pregnant, they got back together. Tom was there when she gave a birth to Andy, a baby boy. Tom acknowledged paternity and got Andy an US passport. But he kept seeing other women, and when Andy was barely two months old, he married a Filipina neighbor and stopped providing any support for Andy. Tom then left South Korea to return to the United States. As Amy told this story, Andy, now three years old, was trying to grab the biscuit on the table next to our coffee in her small room in Basetown.

Amy tried to secure child support from Tom, with very little success. If she were legally married to Tom, she would have been entitled to a visa as a dependent of the American military in South Korea, as well as to access to facilities in the military camp, such as the medical clinic and legal services. When GIs were legally married and abandoned their wives, the women could seek assistance from the office for family support services on the American military base to secure child support, and the GIs were likely to face negative consequences for violating the code of conduct. Sofia Thomson, a social worker in charge of the US military's family support services in Basetown, told me:

> It is very unfortunate that some of our soldiers act irresponsibly and abandon their wives. That's why we have a hotline for abandoned wives and children in Tagalog and Russian, so that they can get help. We get them a military card and help them in the process of locating their husbands and making them fulfill their duties.

Because Amy was not Tom's wife, however, she remained undocumented and was denied assistance from the family support services as well as from the American embassy, which denied her help in locating Tom after he transferred to a military base in the United States. This made no sense to Amy: "My child is an American citizen. His father acknowledged that he's the father in the military legal office and got an American passport for him. And now that he deserted me and Andy, why shouldn't the family support services help us? Isn't my boy a military family?"

Without support from Tom, she provided for Andy by working at a pepper mill factory and later at another club in Basetown. One day, I went to her place to help her fill out the forms to send to the child support enforcement agency in the United States. We filled out the form to the best of our abilities; it would later be reviewed by a public lawyer she met through Sisterhood Center. Afterward we went to a diner with Andy, and three young American GIs were sitting next to our table. Andy went to their table and the men played with him, holding him up high as Andy giggled. When the men left the restaurant, Andy followed them and started crying. Consoling him, Amy turned her eyes away from me and said, "Whenever he sees soldiers, he follows them. Before, one guy asked him, 'Where's your daddy?' and he looked really confused and said, 'I don't know.' It breaks my heart to hear that." Her usually confident voice was shaken, and she sealed her lips tight. After a few moments, she continued, "I sometimes don't know whether this whole thing is worth it, you know?" She fell back into silence. A few months later, when she heard a negative decision from the child support agency because she was out of their jurisdiction, she started making plans to return to the Philippines with Andy.

For migrant hostesses—who work, face rights violations, and sometimes become mothers in military camptowns—few avenues existed to claim rights and belonging in South Korea. They could not assert membership as trafficked victims, workers, or even mothers because their moral legitimacy was rendered questionable and their attempt to gain standing through marriage and family was fraught with risks. Their contained presence in camptowns left little mark in South Korea, as they were not recognized as subjects of rights, either as migrant workers or as migrant women.

MIGRANT WOMEN'S HUMAN RIGHTS AND BEYOND

In this chapter, I examined the ruptures between the South Korean feminist advocacy discourse of protecting migrant women's human rights and the social worlds of migrant wives and hostesses. For migrant wives and migrant hostesses, taking up human rights based on victimhood involved moral dilemmas, even for those seeking redress for their abuse or exploitation. Their experiences reveal the hollowness of a notion of universal human rights that ignores rights as achieved through everyday interactions embedded in a moral community. The pursuit of citizenship is related not only to legal and political governance and the provision of formal rights but also to the construction of a moral landscape that situates the subjects of rights as full or marginal members of a polity.

For both groups of migrant women in South Korea, the institutions of heterosexual marriage and family, rather than victimhood, offered a potential pathway to material benefits, legal status, and moral recognition in a community. For migrant wives faced with the pressure to prove the sincerity of their marriage by assimilating to "the Korean way," motherhood was a basis to claim membership in South Korea. Migrant hostesses were hesitant to claim the status of trafficked victims because they wished to continue their work and pursue intimate relationships with American GIs, which offered a risky pathway to mobility, despite the lack of basis to claim rights and belonging in South Korea. Through interactive processes of claims-making, migrant women in South Korea emerged as subjects of rights only as mother-citizens, which left migrant hostesses in camptowns without a basis for citizenship claims in South Korea either as workers or as mothers.

Coda

Migrant Rights and a Politics of Solidarity

On June 1, 2011, Patricia Hana Ocampo was born in Factorytown to the delight of her parents, Florence and Rob. They decided to raise Patricia themselves, unlike many other Filipino parents who sent their babies to the Philippines after the baptism ceremony to be raised by their parents or sisters. Florence missed their two sons in the Philippines and wanted to bond with her daughter, unlike her own mother who had been absent for migrant work overseas. She still harbored a dream of emigrating to Canada, but was prepared to wait several years and save up money in South Korea. Rob agreed, and he wanted to give Patricia the Korean middle name of Hana. Raising Patricia in South Korea seemed feasible because they had a large extended family and neighbors who could look after her on days when both her parents were required to work overtime. There was also a reliable day-care center at Peace Center for the children of migrant workers and "multicultural families." Florence and Rob registered the birth at the Philippine embassy in Seoul, and Patricia became a Filipino citizen, but because of both parents' undocumented status in South Korea, Patricia has no legal status in her country of birth.

When I returned to South Korea in 2014, Patricia was three years old. If the saying "It takes a village to raise a child" was true anywhere, it was in Factorytown. Because Patricia was one of only a few children in a migrant community where parents and children are usually separated by an ocean, she had become the center of attention. Patricia had over two hundred godparents looking after her. Her birthday parties were an occasion for the whole Filipino community to come together in celebration. Patricia was a symbol for the migrant community in Factorytown, her photo appearing on the cover of Peace Center's newsletter for donors and the public. Florence was happy that Patricia was learning Korean words from teachers and other children during day care while speaking Tagalog in the Filipino community. From the perspective of the South Korean state, Patricia might have been "born out of place,"[1] but from the perspective of her parents, relatives, and the people of Factorytown, she was embedded in a strong community of kinship and support.

Yet as long as South Korea maintains its exclusionary policies against migrant workers, Patricia will someday lose her footing in this rich "village" of care, either through deportation or through exposure to the shadows of citizenship—discrimination and exclusion in her natal home of South Korea.

In April 2014, a group of National Assembly members in South Korea, spearheaded by the first immigrant assembly member Jasmine Lee, hosted a congressional hearing on the Migrant Children's Human Rights Act, a law that would extend rights to education, health, and personhood to undocumented migrant children. If it were to pass, this legislation would create fissures in the sturdy wall barring many migrants from citizenship, and would bring migrant children like Patricia out of the shadows. After the hearing, many South Koreans responded with the concern that the act would open up a floodgate of undocumented migration into South Korea. The act has not yet been proposed to the National Assembly, and its future remains uncertain. So does the border of citizenship in South Korea. As citizenship's promise of full membership and equality clashes with the realities of exclusion, struggles over migrant rights will continue, and new forms of solidarity and opposition will emerge, giving rise to new perils, promises, and possibilities.

REMAKING THE BORDERS OF CITIZENSHIP

This book took a journey into the paradox of citizenship—the allure of equality alongside its perpetually unfulfilled promise—by situating the pursuit of citizenship in the complex terrain where people come together to seek dignity and security in an unequal world. As an increasing number of women seek mobility overseas, they enter into the marginal spaces of a transnational landscape in which migrant labor is welcomed but full membership and rights are held out of reach. I attend to the margins of citizenship, the heart of the struggle for migrant rights in South Korea. Margins are not simply determined by structural forces and imposed exclusion; they are also full of vibrant contestation that shifts and remakes the borders of citizenship. This book revealed that struggles around citizenship do not begin and end with legislation but rather involve continuous on-the-ground negotiation and subject-making through labor processes, civil society mobilization, and the drawing of moral boundaries.

I followed three overlapping groups of Filipina migrant women in their everyday encounters with the South Korean state and civil society. The legal and policy regime in South Korea governed each group of migrants in distinct ways: through a short-term rotation policy for migrant factory workers, a multicultural integration policy for migrant wives, and an antitrafficking policy for migrant hostesses. Against this backdrop, I interrogated the discrepancy between citizenship on the books and the realities on the ground, moving beyond a narrow focus on the provision of rights through law and policy. I delved into the margins of citizenship where social inequalities of gender, race, class, and nation operated in the interactive process of making migrant rights and constituting migrant subjects. In this space, migrant women challenged the national and ethnic borders in South Korea, relying on the distinct resources produced by their labor and intimate relationships as factory workers, club hostesses, and wives and mothers to claim their rights and belonging.

The margins of citizenship were a place where Filipina migrant women's aspirations for transnational mobility butted up against the South Korean legal and social apparatus that hindered their settlement and claims-making. They were where the exclusionary and disciplinary projects of immigration crackdowns and deportations collided with tightly mobilized migrant communities and South Korean migrant advocates, creating a temporary border of containment and implicit safe zones for some undocumented migrants. The margins also offered a space where various groups of South Korean civil society actors, such as social workers, trade unionists, pastors, feminist activists, and university students and volunteers, enacted their own agendas as migrant advocates and agents of integration. At times, migrants welcomed these agendas, and at times they refused them. The margins are where migrant women negotiated their respective positions within the discourses of human rights, workers' rights, gendered victimhood, and maternal citizenship, the place where migrant subjects were produced and South Koreans' subjectivity was transformed.

The remaking of citizenship upon migrant encounter was not free from power relations, and migrant advocacy or integration efforts were implicated in reproducing inequalities as well as challenging them. South Korean advocates acted as mediators of rights who did not simply represent the voices and interests of migrants but also engaged in their own citizenship projects. The subjects of *migrant workers* and *migrant women* were constructed through the interactions of migrants and South Korean migrant advocates as separate groups, even though labor and marriage migrants belonged to a cohesive ethnic and religious migrant community. The organization of civil society in South Korea—with its institutionalized modes of civic engagement, including social movements, professional social work, and faith-based carework—provided migrants with different kinds of intervention and involvement depending on the evolution of their relations with advocates. Whereas paternalistic interaction norms between advocates and migrant factory workers restricted equal and full membership by reinforcing migrants' place lower in the hierarchy as recipients of care, advocates' maternal concern for migrant wives combined with the ideal of the mother-citizen to create conditions more conducive to the development of autonomous collective claims. The making of migrant subjects excluded migrant hostesses, who were often isolated from the ethnic community and were not targeted for political empowerment.

Under such conditions, migrant women in South Korea entered into multiple negotiations and alliances with South Korean civil society actors in the pursuit of rights, entitlements, and moral respect, which went hand in hand with, and at times extended beyond, claims for citizenship. Migrant struggles were closely intertwined with social movement legacies in South Korea, and intersecting social inequalities of gender, race, and nation affected the dynamics of civil society mobilization to offer unique opportunities and limitations to distinct migrant groups. Migrant factory workers, both men and women, were able to rely on the dignity of workers to claim labor rights, but this discourse was less effective in addressing gender-specific concerns, such as maternal health, as a matter of labor rights. Whereas women factory workers were considered as *workers* but not as women, migrant hostesses and migrant wives were construed as vulnerable *women* needing protection offered by South Korean feminist groups. The paths to citizenship diverged for these latter two groups as well, as migrant wives relied on their statuses as mothers of South Korean children to support their inclusion in South Korean society as moral and political equals, and migrant hostesses had access to neither the dignity of workers nor that of mothers, leading to their exclusion from the making of migrant subjects in South Korea.

Through comparative examination of three groups of migrant women in South Korea, the book illuminated the interactive processes involved in negotiations over the boundary of citizenship. Struggles for migrant rights reveal as much about South Korea as a host society as they do about migrants. Since the 1980s, migrant communities in South Korea have built a space of their own against the exclusionary migration regime through alliances with various corners of South Korean civil society. Like many other nation-states facing a recent wave of migration, South Korea is confronted with the question of how to recognize these migrant newcomers and long-term inhabitants, not just as "paper cups" to be used for their labor before being thrown away but as people with lives, desires, families, aspirations, and rights. What will the future of migrant citizenship be in South Korea, and how will it transform the borders of citizenship more broadly? How does the decentering of citizenship offer insight into these questions?

BUILDING A POLITICS OF SOLIDARITY

"[S]ince action is the political activity par excellence,
natality, and not mortality, may be the central category of political, as distinguished from metaphysical,
thought."

—HANNAH ARENDT,
THE HUMAN CONDITION[2]

This book opened with five hundred migrants and South Koreans marching on the streets of Seoul in 2008, protesting against immigration crackdowns and demanding radical reform of migrant labor policy. Collective
actions like this rally exemplified the high degree of mobilization among
migrant communities and South Korean migrant advocates, which led to
significant gains in labor and social rights for migrants over the past two
decades. Yet, despite these ongoing efforts, structural conditions in South
Korea severely constrained migrant agency. Immigrant raids, restrictions
on migrant workers' labor rights, and barriers to labor and marriage migration hamper migrant rights even in the face of fierce contestation from
migrant activists in the form of street protests, immigration van chases,
legal claims in the courts and before the National Human Rights Commission of Korea, and lobbying in the National Assembly.

The discriminatory practices of immigration raids targeting racially
conspicuous individuals in migrant-concentrated neighborhoods harm
the migrant community as a whole, including permanent residents and
naturalized citizens. Furthermore, under the Employment Permit System,
migrant workers are not guaranteed the freedom to choose their workplace.
They have been denied the full right of association, which serves as the
basis for workers' collective action in South Korea. Few of the migrants
who marched in the 2008 rally still remained in South Korea seven years
later; some left South Korea voluntarily, but many others, especially the
leaders of the migrant unions, were targeted for their political activism and
forcibly deported because they defied the boundaries of containment for
migrants in South Korea.

These key issues in the expansion of migrant rights and citizenship
have been at the forefront of migrant activism in South Korea for the past

decade. Activists demand a halt to immigration crackdowns; amnesty for undocumented migrants, especially migrant children; and legislation against discrimination on the basis of race, ethnicity, and national origin. Migrant activism successfully built alliances with labor movements, human rights groups, and women's movements—though stronger and more intersectional alliance building is still possible, especially for migrant hostesses—yet since 2008, the overall capacity of South Korean civil society has weakened under two consecutive conservative governments that prioritized economic development over distributive justice and democratic processes. Furthermore, in the aftermath of the global financial crisis, anti-immigrant sentiment is on the rise. As one South Korean migrant advocate lamented, "Average South Koreans are having a hard time with their livelihoods these days. They can't afford to care about human rights, about democracy, and certainly not about migrants."

There is a pervasive sense among migrant activists in South Korea that they are a voice without an echo. How do we work for the inclusion of newcomers when community and belonging are also eroding among citizens as a whole? When the language of rights is losing its appeal in popular political discourse, what other bases can be found on which to build a politics of solidarity with migrants? How can struggles for migrant rights become a fruitful site to rethink the meaning of belonging and human dignity and revitalize civil society with new alliances and a critical lens?

Throughout this book, I highlighted deep connections kindled in the margins of citizenship as a way to envision a possible foundation for migrant rights. We have seen South Korean trade unionists and student activists marching with migrant workers; pastors and priests serving migrants in their congregations as "the least of these"; and South Korean middle-aged women taking on the role of "maternal guardians" for migrant wives. We have also seen cross-ethnic solidarity among migrant workers and South Korean workers and managers on the shop floor. In some cases, South Koreans approached migrants with a paternalistic attitude, offering to "help" through a set of prescriptive answers. But in others, migrants and South Korean activists experienced moments of solidarity that broke down the walls of legal exclusion and interpersonal hierarchies.

For political theorist Hannah Arendt, the condition of natality, a distinctive human capacity to begin something anew, is at the heart of the political sphere. Migrant citizenship is not simply about inclusion in a preexisting polity; it is also about recognizing that the newcomer brings to the polity itself the radical possibility of transformation. Thinking of migrant newcomers as political equals who contribute new possibilities and new actors to the nation's future requires a profound respect for the human capacity of natality. The cultivation of this respect will be critical for reclaiming the political community in South Korea as well as globally—a community that will be open to those excluded from the conventional bases to claim rights and belonging, such as shared ethnicity, legal documents, the dignity of workers and mothers, and heteronormative marriages.

Migrant women and men in South Korea rarely encounter such a welcoming embrace. From a South Korean husband shouting "Go back to your country!" during a heated argument, to a stranger on the bus calling the immigration office to report the sighting of an "illegal," to a promoter escorting migrant hostesses to the airport even before their work contracts and visas expire, the threat of repatriation and denied belonging is a routine challenge in the lives of migrants in South Korea. Even sympathetic South Koreans sometimes enact exclusion, as when migrant advocates organize "happy return" programs for migrant workers or when well-meaning Christian volunteers ask migrants when they plan to return home. In response to the latter question, Katherine, a Filipina migrant in Factorytown, told me, "I just smile and say, 'hopefully soon.'" Lowering her voice, she confided, "But I am telling you, I am not going back." This confidence was Katherine's way of claiming South Korea as her home, a statement against the forces in South Korea that questioned her membership and belonging. As migrants like Katherine assert their place in South Korea by "not going back," they also propel the nation-state of South Korea forward, away from its migrant-free imagined past and deeper into the process of transformation that will remake its borders of citizenship. And perhaps this is where citizenship's persisting allure lies: not in the concrete promise, but in the transformative potential that can rekindle the polity.

Notes

1. Coethnic migrants in South Korea, such as North Koreans and *chosônjok* (Korean ethnic groups in China), negotiate national boundaries under separate legal and policy edifices (N. Kim 2008); their negotiations are beyond the scope of this study. For the complexity of the North Korean migrant case, see Chung (2008) and Choo (2006); for chosônjok migration to South Korea, see Freeman (2011) and J. Kim (2011).

2. http://www.mospa.go.kr/frt/bbs/type010/commonSelectBoardArticle.do?bbsId=BBSMSTR_000000000008&nttId=42487 (Last accessed on July 19, 2014)

3. The current nationality law in Korea grants foreign spouses—both men and women—spousal visas that include a work permit. Foreign spouses must reside in Korea with their Korean spouses for two years before applying for naturalization. In response to criticism from feminist advocacy groups about vulnerability arising from the legal dependency of migrant wives on their South Korean husbands, the state reformed the law in 2003 so that migrant wives could apply for permanent residency and naturalization even after a divorce if the divorce was the husband's fault.

4 http://www.mospa.go.kr/frt/bbs/type010/commonSelectBoardArticle.do?bbsId=BBSMSTR_000000000008&nttId=42487 (Last accessed on July 19, 2014)

5. The *Trafficking in Persons Report,* issued by the US Department of State in 2001, which ranked Korea as a Tier 3 country that failed to make efforts to prohibit trafficking, provided the discursive devices for South Korean feminist organizations to reform the antiprostitution law. For more detailed analysis of antitrafficking initiatives in South Korea, see Cheng (2011).

6. http://www.immigration.go.kr/HP/COM/bbs_003/ListShowData.do?strNbodCd=notio097&strWrtNo=141&strAnsNo=A&strOrgGbnCd=104000&strRtnURL=IMM_6070&strAllOrgYn=N&strThisPage=1&strFilePath=imm. (Last accessed on July 28, 2014).

7. Jacobson 1996; Soysal 1994.

8. Bloemraad 2004; Menjívar 2006.

9. Walia 2010; Walsh 2014.

10. Ong 1999.

11. Sadiq 2008.

12. Somers 2008.

13. Rodriguez 2010.

14. hooks 1990, 341.

15. Anderson 1983.

16. Brubaker 1996, 230.

17. Glenn 2004, 1.

18. Bloemraad, Korteweg, and Yurdakul 2008.

19. Although the polity is commonly assumed to be the nation-state, it could encompass other political communities of a different scale that possess a clear institutional structure and the capacity for governance, such as a city or region.

20. Clarke, Coll, Dagnino, and Neveu 2014.

21. Glenn 2004; Poole 2004; Monforte and Dufour 2011; Stasiulis and Bakan 1997.

22. Marshall 1950.

23. Bourdieu 1991; Goldberg 2008.

24. Stasiulis and Bakan 2005, 116.

25. Clarke, Coll, Dagnino, and Neveu 2014; Stasiulis and Bakan 2005; McNevin 2011.

26. For discussion of the interactive process of citizenship-making, see Korteweg (2006).

27. Gordon and Lenhardt 2008.

28. Glenn 2011.

29. Parreñas 2001b.

30. Agustin 2007; Choo 2013; Cheng 2010; Parreñas 2011.

31. Cheng 2010; Parreñas 2011; Brennan 2004.

32. Parreñas 2001a; Hondagneu-Sotelo 2007; Lan 2006.

33. Constable 2003; Freeman 2011; Faier 2009.

34. All interviews and conversations with Filipina migrant women were conducted in a mixture of Tagalog, English, and Korean, yet most of them preferred Tagalog as the main language of communication. Even though my Tagalog was far from fluent, because the interviewees and I had known each other for several months and had become familiar with each other's vocabularies and accents, we were able to communicate and understand one another. Many migrant wives were fluent in Korean and many hostesses were fluent in English, and we also spoke in those languages, but Tagalog became a secret language that we used in front of husbands, in-laws, and club owners.

All names of organizations in Factorytown and Basetown and those of individuals are pseudonyms, except in the case of public events and official documents. In the case of personal names, I chose pseudonyms that reflect the name the person used in South Korea (except public figures); for migrant wives who changed their names to Korean ones, I chose Korean pseudonyms. For Korean names, last names appear before first names. Some personal details of research participants have been altered to protect confidentiality. I translated all quotes into English.

35. These migration patterns create a gendered dynamic that differs from the one created by the migration of Filipina women who work as domestic workers, caretakers, and nurses in the United States, Europe, and other East Asian countries, whose cases are well documented (Constable 1997; Espiritu 2003; Parreñas 2001a). While only a small number of Filipina women in my study worked as domestic workers or nannies, at times going between live-in domestic work and factory work, many Filipina women in South Korea had worked as domestic workers in the Middle East and in Southeast and East Asia prior to their arrival to South Korea.

As of June 2014, among the 24,407 Filipina women residing in South Korea, 10,474 (43 percent) came via marriage with South Korean men, whereas 2,074 (8.5 percent) entered with industrial laborer visas for factory work, and 3,089 (12.7 percent) with "entertainer" visas used for hostess work. Of the total, 5,533 (22.7 percent) are undocumented; in large part, these women work in the factories and domestic homes. http://www.immigration.go.kr/HP/COM/bbs_003/ListShow-Data.do?strNbodCd=noti0097&strWrtNo=141&strAnsNo=A&strOrgGbnCd=1 04000&strRtnURL=IMM_6070&strAllOrgYn=N&strThisPage=1&strFilePath=imm. (Last accessed on July 28, 2014).

36. This book focuses mostly on churches' secular advocacy work. I have discussed the religious aspects of these churches in relation to their migrant advocacy work in Choo (2015).

37. These national organizations included the Joint Committee with Migrants in Korea (JCMK), a large umbrella organization of forty-one locally based migrant advocacy NGOs in Korea; I attended their international and national discussion forums, World Migrant's Day Festivals, and protests and press conferences, as well as other events. Other organizations whose gatherings and forums I attended included the Migrants' Trade Union, Migrant Worker's Television, and the Center for Migrant Women's Human Rights. In addition, I collected and analyzed various textual materials, including publications and pamphlets from migrant advocacy NGOs, textbooks and other educational materials used for migrant education programs, newsletters for donors and the public, and government legal and policy documents.

Chapter 2

1. Ehrenreich and Hochschild 2004.
2. Parreñas 2001a.
3. Lan 2007.
4. Espiritu 2003.
5. Parreñas 2010. The exclusionary model is predominant in Asia (Seol and Skrentny 2009), but short-term migrant systems are also becoming increasingly common in Europe and North America (Castles 2006).

6. Rodriguez 2010, 79.

7. Paul 2011.

8. Rodriguez 2010.

9. Parreñas 2001a; Pratt 2012.

10. Parreñas 2001b.

11. Seol 2005.

12. Kim 2003. Rather than legalize the majority of undocumented migrants, the state selectively granted one-year work permits only to migrants who had stayed in South Korea for less than four years.

13. This restriction was a main point of contention between faith-based advocacy organizations—which prioritized passing the reform despite constraints—and migrant trade unionists.

14. Pratt 2012.

15. Hyunok Lee (2012) finds that among marriage-migrant women from China and Southeast Asia in South Korea, the rate of living together with parents-in-law (27.5 percent) is significantly higher than among their South Korean women counterparts (4.36 percent), suggesting migrant wives' role in providing elder care.

16. The Unification Church, which promotes international marriage, also began working as a matchmaking agency in the 1990s to marry Korean men and women from Japan, the Philippines and Mongolia. At the same time, among those who came to Korea as migrant workers, some married locals and became involved in matchmaking activities themselves.

17. On the current nationality law in Korea regarding foreign spouses, see Chapter 1, n. 3 above.

18. Piper 2003.

19. Piper and Roces 2003.

20. Y. Lee 2015.

21. For an in-depth exploration of the romantic relationship between American GIs and Filipina migrant hostesses in American camptowns in South Korea, see Cheng (2010), Choo (2016), Yea (2005).

22. Höhn and Moon 2010.

23. J. Lee 2010.

24. N. Y. Lee 2006. Jin-kyung Lee (2010) also notes that the South Korean state played the role of labor broker in the camptown clubs. Grace Cho (2008) reports that more than one million South Korean women have worked as hostesses in camptown clubs since the 1950s, though this number is a conservative estimate.

25. Ong 2006.

26. The club industry shows striking similarities in organization and work practices across the Philippines, Okinawa, and South Korea. See Sturdevant and Stoltzfus (1992).

27. Cheng 2011.

28. The hierarchical, temporal division between American GIs and Asian migrant workers resonates with the legacy of racial segregation in the United States that played out in camptown clubs in South Korea until the 1970s; see

Moon (1997). During my fieldwork in Basetown, the American GIs were of diverse racial and ethnic groups, including whites, Latinos, African Americans, Filipinos, and Korean Americans, and there was no longer any explicit segregation in the clubs along racial lines.

On the shifting meaning of the US military in South Korea, Jin-kyung Lee (2010, 179) argues, "If South Korean military prostitution now includes a migrant workforce from overseas, due to the relative wealth of the South Korean national economy, there is a way in which the enlisted ranks of the American military, largely made up of the racialized working class, have become transnational migrant militarized labor, serving the South Korean state and capital."

29. The camptown clubs are exclusive to foreigners and do not allow Korean customers, but the owner of the club where Linda worked sometimes entertained his Korean friends in the club.

30. This optimistic vision about emigration to the United States does not necessarily map into the postimmigration reality. For an ethnographic account of South Korean women who emigrated to the United States following their American GI husbands, see Yuh (2002).

31. Rodriguez 2010.

Chapter 3

1. H.-K. Lee 2008.
2. Hondagneu-Sotelo 2008; Ong 2003; Newendorp 2008.
3. Honig 1998.
4. The South Korean actors in this chapter predominantly worked with migrant factory workers and migrant wives, and only a few advocated for migrant hostesses and farm workers. I chose not to highlight the specific experiences of South Korean feminist activists working with migrant hostesses in this chapter. Because the South Korean actors had only limited reach among migrant hostesses on a day-to-day level, the sample of these activists was so small that it was not possible to tell their personal stories and protect confidentiality. Instead, I discuss the activities and public statements of South Korean feminist organizations for migrant hostesses in Chapters 6 and 7.
5. N. Lee 2007.
6. Yang 2012.
7. Moon 2005.
8. Parreñas 2008.
9. See Choo (forthcoming) for a more detailed analysis of the race, gender, and class dynamics of maternal guardianship.
10. The gross enrollment rate for tertiary education in South Korea increased from 7 percent in 1970 to 39 percent in 1980 and then to 68 percent in 1997; the gender composition of universities also changed from 27 percent women in 1970 to 43 percent in 1998 (Park 2007).

11. Song 2009; Y. Lee 2015.

12. Chang 2012.

Chapter 4

1. Coutin 2000.

2. Willen 2007; Abrego 2011.

3. Calavita 1998; Coutin 2000; De Genova 2002.

4. Calavita 2003.

5. De Genova 2002, 429.

6. De Genova 2013.

7. Joon Kim 2003.

8. The most recent statistics on undocumented migrants in South Korea (December 31, 2013) record their number as 183,106, or 11.6 percent of all migrants (Ministry of Justice 2014, 283).

Chapter 5

1. Piper and Roces 2003.

2. Rodriguez 2002.

3. D. Kim 2011.

4. N. Lee 2007.

5. Migration scholars Danièle Bélanger and Hongzen Wang studied integration programs in South Korea and Taiwan and found that although these programs tended to infantilize migrants, they also had the potential to open up "hidden spaces of resistance" for migrant women's community formation (Bélanger 2007; Wang 2007; Wang and Bélanger 2008).

6. This glorification of "helping" work—whether in the form of colonial missionary work, contemporary volunteerism, or contemporary global development projects—involves a gendered moral imperative based on the notion of women's "natural" compassion, benevolence, and caring capacities. This gendered valuation of caring is tied to an essentialized notion of motherhood in what Mindry (2001) calls "a politics of feminine virtue."

7. B. Lee 2009.

Chapter 6

1. Lamont 2002.

2. Parreñas 2011.

3. For detailed analysis of the conditions of camptown clubs in the 1970s, especially during the "the Camptown Clean-up Campaign" in the early 1970s, see Moon (1997).

4. Choo 2016; Cheng 2010; Parreñas 2011.

5. Similarly, Hagan's study (1998) in the United States finds that immigrant women concentrated in domestic work experienced isolation from coethnic networks due to their live-in arrangements as opposed to men in the same community whose labor process was more conducive to building migrant social networks.

6. Joon Kim 2003; Koo 2001.

7. E. Kim 2000; H. Kim 2001.

8. Koo 2001; Chun 2009.

9. D. Kim 2011.

10. Because most of the workplaces that hire migrant workers are small in size and not unionized, the MTU does not engage in collective bargaining, but operates like an advocacy organization in coalition with faith-based groups.

11. D. Kim 2011.

12. Seol 2012.

13. Gordon and Lenhardt 2008.

14. Chun 2009.

15. Cheng 2011.

16. Moon 1999.

17. Moon 1999.

18. Agustín 2007.

Chapter 7

1. Feminist scholars critically interrogate the discourse of human rights (Hesford and Kozol 2005). The portrayal of women as helpless victims can legitimize the state as their protector (Brown 1995), harm their mobilization (Ally 2008), and undermine their citizenship.

2. In 1983, Women's Hotline United mobilized against domestic violence. The South Korean feminist movement subsequently achieved additional legal reforms, including the Sexual Violence Special Act (1993), the Domestic Violence Prevention Act (1998), and the Anti-Prostitution Act (2004) (S. Moon 2002).

3. See Yea (2004) for a detailed description of marital negotiations and troubles among American GI–Filipina women couples in the camptowns.

4. Seol et al. 2003, xv.

5. Brennan 2004; Faier 2009; Parreñas 2011.

6. Lan 2008.

7. Friedman 2012.

8. The trafficking discourse presumes migrant women's victimhood and calls on the state to provide protection, which can undermine the rights of migrant women in sexual commerce by restricting their mobility while doing little to improve their conditions (Agustin 2007; Chapkis 2003; Parreñas 2011). In the case of migrant wives, this reliance on the state results in the heightened control and surveillance of women involved in cross-border marriages (Constable 2003; Freeman 2011).

A significant body of critical feminist scholarship critiques this simplistic narrative of victimhood by documenting the agency of migrant women in navigating the complex realities of work, romance, and border-crossing in the global political economy. For marriage migration, see Constable (2003), Faier (2009), Suzuki (2003); for sex work, see Brennan (2004), Cheng (2010), Parreñas (2011).

9. H. Cho 2002.

10. Cheng 2011; H. M. Kim 2007.

11. Bernstein 2007; Hoang 2011.

Coda

1. Constable 2014.

2. Arendt 1998, 9.

Works Cited

Abrego, Leisy J. 2011. "Legal Consciousness of Undocumented Latinos: Fear and Stigma as Barriers to Claims-Making for First- and 1.5-Generation Immigrants." *Law & Society Review* 45:337–70.

Agustin, Laura. 2007. *Sex at the Margins: Migration, Labour Markets and the Rescue Industry.* London: Zed Books.

Ally, Shireen. 2008. "Domestic Worker Unionisation in Post-Apartheid South Africa: Demobilisation and Depoliticisation by the Democratic State." *Politikon* 35:1–21.

Anderson, Benedict. 1983. *Imagined Communities : Reflections on the Origin and Spread of Nationalism.* London: Verso.

Arendt, Hannah. 1998. *The Human Condition.* Chicago: University of Chicago Press.

Bélanger, Danièle. 2007. "The House and the Classroom: Vietnamese Immigrant Spouses in South Korea and Taiwan." *Population and Society* 3 (1): 1–38.

Bernstein, Elizabeth. 2007. *Temporarily Yours: Intimacy, Authenticity, and the Commerce of Sex.* Chicago: University of Chicago Press.

Bloemraad, Irene. 2004. "Who Claims Dual Citizenship? The Limits of Postnationalism, the Possibilities of Transnationalism, and the Persistence of Traditional Citizenship." *International Migration Review* 38:389–422.

Bloemraad, Irene, Anna Korteweg, and Gökçe Yurdakul. 2008. "Citizenship and Immigration: Multiculturalism, Assimilation, and Challenges to the Nation-State." *Annual Review of Sociology* 34:153–79.

Bourdieu, Pierre. 1991. *Language and Symbolic Power.* Cambridge, Mass.: Harvard University Press.

Brennan, Denise. 2004. *What's Love Got to Do with It? Transnational Desires and Sex Tourism in the Dominican Republic.* Durham, NC: Duke University Press.

Brown, Wendy. 1995. *States of Injury: Power and Freedom in Late Modernity.* Princeton, NJ: Princeton University Press.

Brubaker, Rogers. 1996. *Nationalism Reframed: Nationhood and the National Question in the New Europe.* Cambridge: Cambridge University Press.

Calavita, Kitty. 1998. "Immigration, Law, and Marginalization in a Global Economy: Notes from Spain." *Law and Society Review* 32:529–66.

———. 2003. "A Reserve Army of Delinquents: The Criminalization and Economic Punishment of Immigrants in Spain." *Punishment & Society* 5:399–413.

Castles, Stephen. 2006. "Guestworkers in Europe: A Resurrection?" *International Migration Review* 40 (4): 741–66.

Chang, Kyung-Sup. 2012. "Economic Development, Democracy and Citizenship Politics in South Korea: The Predicament of Developmental Citizenship." *Citizenship Studies* 16 (1): 29–47.

Chapkis, Wendy. 2003. "Trafficking, Migration, and the Law: Protecting Innocents, Punishing Immigrants." *Gender & Society* 17:923–37.

Cheng, Sealing. 2010. *On the Move for Love: Migrant Entertainers and the U.S. Military in South Korea.* Philadelphia: University of Pennsylvania Press.

———. 2011. "Sexual Protection, Citizenship and Nationhood: Prostituted Women and Migrant Wives in South Korea." *Journal of Ethnic and Migration Studies* 37:1627–48.

Cho, Grace. 2008. *Haunting the Korean Diaspora: Shame, Secrecy, and the Forgotten War.* Minneapolis: University of Minnesota Press.

Cho, Haejoang. 2002. "Living with Conflicting Subjectivities: Mother, Motherly Wife, and Sexy Woman in the Transition from Colonial-Modern to Postmodern Korea." In *Under Construction: The Gendering of Modernity, Class, and Consumption in the Republic of Korea,* edited by Laura Kendall, 165–95. Honolulu: University of Hawai'i Press.

Choo, Hae Yeon. 2006. "Gendered Modernity and Ethnicized Citizenship: North Korean Settlers in Contemporary South Korea." *Gender & Society* 20 (5): 576–604.

———. 2013. "The Cost of Rights: Migrant Women, Feminist Advocacy, and Gendered Morality in South Korea." *Gender & Society* 27 (4): 445–68.

———. 2015. "The Needs of Others: Revisiting the Nation in North Korean and Filipino Migrant Churches in South Korea." In *Multiethnic Korea? Multiculturalism, Migration, and Peoplehood Diversity in Contemporary South Korea,* edited by John Lie, 119–41. Berkeley: Institute for East Asian Studies, University of California, Berkeley.

———. 2016. "Selling Fantasies of Rescue: Intimate Labor, Filipina Migrant Hostesses, and US GIs in a Shifting Global Order." *positions: asia critique* 24 (1): 179–203.

———. Forthcoming. "Maternal Guardians: Intimate Labor and the Pursuit of Gendered Citizenship among South Korean Volunteers for Migrant Women." *Sexualities.*

Chun, Jennifer J. 2009. *Organizing at the Margins: The Symbolic Politics of Labor in South Korea and the United States.* Ithaca, NY: Cornell University Press.

Chung, Byung-Ho. 2008. "Between Defector and Migrant: Identities and Strategies of North Koreans in South Korea." *Korean Studies* 32 (1): 1–27.

Clarke, John, Kathleen Coll, Evelina Dagnino, and Catherine Neveu. 2014. *Disputing Citizenship.* Bristol, UK: Policy Press.

Constable, Nicole. 1997. *Maid to Order in Hong Kong: Stories of Filipina Workers.* Ithaca, NY: Cornell University Press.

———. 2003. *Romance on a Global Stage: Pen Pals, Virtual Ethnography, and "Mail Order" Marriages.* Berkeley: University of California Press.

———. 2014. *Born Out of Place: Migrant Mothers and the Politics of International Labor.* Berkeley: University of California Press.

Coutin, Susan B. 2000. *Legalizing Moves: Salvadoran Immigrants' Struggle for U.S. Residency.* Ann Arbor: University of Michigan Press.

De Genova, Nicholas P. 2002. "Migrant 'Illegality' and Deportability in Every-day Life." *Annual Review of Anthropology* 31:419–47.

———. 2013. "Spectacles of Migrant 'Illegality': The Scene of Exclusion, the Obscene of Inclusion." *Ethnic and Racial Studies* 36 (7): 1180–98.

Ehrenreich, Barbara, and Arlie Russell Hochschild, eds. 2004. *Global Woman: Nannies, Maids, and Sex Workers in the New Economy.* New York: Metropolitan Press.

Espiritu, Yen Le. 2003. *Home Bound: Filipino American Lives across Cultures, Communities, and Countries.* Berkeley: University of California Press.

Faier, Lieba. 2009. *Intimate Encounters: Filipina Women and the Remaking of Rural Japan.* Berkeley: University of California Press.

Freeman, Caren. 2011. *Making and Faking Kinship: Marriage and Labor Migration between China and South Korea.* Ithaca, NY: Cornell University Press.

Friedman, Sara L. 2012. ". Adjudicating the Intersection of Marital Immigration, Domestic Violence, and Spousal Murder: China-Taiwan Marriages and Competing Legal Domains." *Indiana Journal of Global Legal Studies* 19:221–55.

Glenn, Evelyn Nakano. 2004. *Unequal Freedom: How Race and Gender Shaped American Citizenship and Labor.* Cambridge, Mass.: Harvard University Press.

———. 2011. *Forced to Care: Coercion and Caregiving in America.* Cambridge, Mass.: Harvard University Press.

Goldberg, Chad. 2008. *Citizens and Paupers: Relief, Rights, and Race from the Freedmen's Bureau to Workfare.* Chicago: University of Chicago Press.

Gordon, Jennifer, and Robin A. Lenhardt. 2008. "Rethinking Work and Citizenship." *UCLA Law Review* 55:1161–1238.

Hagan, Jacqueline M. 1998. "Social Networks, Gender, and Immigrant Incorporation: Resources and Constraints." *American Sociological Review* 63:55–67.

Hesford, Wendy S., and Wendy Kozol, eds. 2005. *Just Advocacy? Women's Human Rights, Transnational Feminisms, and the Politics of Representation* New Brunswick, NJ: Rutgers University Press.

Hoang, Kimberly K. 2011. "She's Not a Low-Class Dirty Girl! Sex Work in Ho Chi Minh City, Vietnam." *Journal of Contemporary Ethnography* 40:367–96.

Höhn, Maria, and Seungsook Moon, eds. 2010. *Over There: Living with the US Military Empire from World War Two to the Present.* Durham, NC: Duke University Press.

Hondagneu-Sotelo, Pierrette. 2007. *Doméstica: Immigrant Workers Cleaning and Caring in the Shadows of Affluence.* Berkeley: University of California Press.

————. 2008. *God's Heart Has No Borders: How Religious Activists Are Working for Immigrant Rights.* Berkeley: University of California Press.

Honig, Bonnie. 1998. "Immigrant America? How Foreignness 'Solves' Democracy's Problems." *Social Text* 56:1–27.

hooks, bell. 1990. "marginality as site of resistance." In *Out There: Marginalization and Contemporary Cultures,* edited by Russell Ferguson, Martha Gever, Trinh T. Minh-ha and Cornel West, 341–43. Cambridge, MA: MIT Press.

Jacobson, David. 1996. *Rights across Borders: Immigration and the Decline of Citizenship.* Baltimore and London: Johns Hopkins University Press.

Kim, Denis. 2011. "Catalysers in the Promotion of Migrants' Rights: Church-Based NGOs in South Korea." *Journal of Ethnic and Migration Studies* 37:1649–67.

Kim, Eunshil. 2000. "The Cultural Logic of the Korean Modernization Project and Its Gender Politics." *Asian Journal of Women's Studies* 6 (2): 50–77.

Kim, Hyun Mee. 2001. "Work, Nation and Hypermasculinity: The 'Woman' Question in the Economic Miracle and Crisis in South Korea." *Inter-Asia Cultural Studies* 2 (1): 53–68.

————. 2007. "The State and Migrant Women: Diverging Hopes in the Making of 'Multicultural Families' in Contemporary Korea." *Korea Journal* 47:100–22.

Kim, Jaeeun. 2011. "Establishing Identity: Documents, Performance, and Biometric Information in Immigration Proceedings." *Law and Social Inquiry* 36 (3): 760–86.

Kim, Joon. 2003. "Insurgency and Advocacy: Unauthorised Foreign Workers and Civil Society in South Korea." *Asian and Pacific Migration Journal* 12:237–69.

Kim, Nora Hui-Jung. 2008. "Korean Immigration Policy Changes and the Political Liberals' Dilemma." *International Migration Review* 42 (3): 576–96.

Koo, Hagen. 2001. *Korean Workers: The Culture and Politics of Class Formation.* Ithaca, NY: Cornell University Press.

Korteweg, Anna. 2006. "The Construction of Gendered Citizenship at the Welfare Office: An Ethnographic Comparison of Welfare-to-Work Workshops in the United States and the Netherlands." *Social Politics: International Studies in Gender, State & Society* 13 (3): 314–40.

Lamont, Michèle. 2002. *The Dignity of Working Men: Morality and the Boundaries of Race, Class, and Immigration.* Cambridge, MA: Harvard University Press.

Lan, Pei-Chia. 2006. *Global Cinderellas: Migrant Domestics and Newly Rich Employers in Taiwan.* Durham, NC: Duke University Press.

————. 2007. "Legal Servitude and Free Illegality: Migrant 'Guest' Workers in Taiwan." In *Asian Diasporas: New Formations, New Conceptions,* edited by Rhacel S. Parreñas and Lok C. D. Siu, 153–277. Stanford, Calif.: Stanford University Press.

————. 2008. Migrant Women's Bodies as Boundary Markers: Reproductive Crisis and Sexual Control in the Ethnic Frontiers of Taiwan." *Signs* 33:833–61.

Lee, Byungju. 2009. "Dreaming of Obama in Korea: Migrant Women Pursuing Politics." *Kuki News,* http://news.kukinews.com/article/view.asp?page=1&gC ode=kmi&arcid=0001630778&cp=nv.

Lee, Hye-Kyung. 2008. "International Marriage and the State in South Korea: Focusing on Governmental Policy." *Citizenship Studies* 12 (1): 107–23.

Lee, Hyunok. 2012. "Political Economy of Cross-Border Marriage: Economic Development and Social Reproduction in Korea." *Feminist Economics* 18 (2): 177–200.

Lee, Jin-kyung. 2010. *Service Economies: Militarism, Sex Work, and Migrant Labor in South Korea.* Minneapolis: University of Minnesota Press.

Lee, Namhee. 2007. *The Making of Minjung: Democracy and the Politics of Representation in South Korea.* Ithaca, NY: Cornell University Press.

Lee, Na Young. 2006. "The Construction of U.S. Camptown Prostitution in South Korea: Trans/formation and Resistance." PhD Diss., University of Maryland, College Park.

Lee, Yoonkyung. 2015. "Labor after Neoliberalism: The Birth of the Insecure Class in South Korea." *Globalizations* 12 (2): 184–202.

Marshall, T. H. 1950. *Citizenship and Social Class.* Cambridge: Cambridge University Press.

McNevin, Anne. 2011. *Contesting Citizenship: Irregular Migrants and New Frontiers of the Political.* New York: Columbia University Press.

Menjívar, Cecilia. 2006. "Liminal Legality: Salvadoran and Guatemalan Immigrants' Lives in the United States." *American Journal of Sociology* 111:999–1037.

Mindry, Deborah. 2001. "Nongovernmental Organizations, 'Grassroots,' and the Politics of Virtue." *Signs* 26 (4): 1187–1211.

Ministry of Justice of South Korea. 2014. "Korean Immigration Service Statistics 2013" http://www.moj.go.kr.

Monforte, Pierre, and Pascale Dufour. 2011. "Mobilizing in Borderline Citizenship Regimes: A Comparative Analysis of Undocumented Migrants' Collective Actions." *Politics & Society* 39 (2): 203–32.

Moon, Katharine. 1997. *Sex among Allies: Military Prostitution in U.S.-Korea Relations.* New York: Columbia University Press.

———. 1999. "South Korean Movements against Militarized Sexual Labor." *Asian Survey* 39:310–27.

———. 2007. "Resurrecting Prostitutes and Overturning Treaties: Gender Politics in the 'Anti-American' Movement in South Korea." *Journal of Asian Studies* 66:129–57.

Moon, Seungsook. 2002. "Carving Out Space: Civil Society and the Women's Movement in South Korea." *Journal of Asian Studies* 61:473–500.

———. 2005. *Militarized Modernity and Gendered Citizenship in South Korea.* Durham, NC: Duke University Press.

Newendorp, Nicole DeJong. 2008. *Uneasy Reunions: Immigration, Citizenship, and Family Life in Post-1997 Hong Kong.* Stanford, Calif.: Stanford University Press.

Ong, Aihwa. 1999. *Flexible Citizenship: The Cultural Logics of Transnationality.* Durham, NC: Duke University Press.

———. 2003. *Buddha Is Hiding: Refugees, Citizenship, the New America.* Berkeley, Calif.: University of California Press.

———. 2006. *Neoliberalism as Exception: Mutations in Citizenship and Sovereignty.* Durham, NC: Duke University Press.

Park, Hyunjoon. 2007. "South Korea: Educational Expansion and Inequality of Opportunity in Higher Education." In *Stratification in Higher Education: A Comparative Study, Studies in Social Inequality,* edited by Yossi Shavit, Arum Richard, and Adam Gamoran, 87–112. Stanford, Calif.: Stanford University Press.

Parreñas, Rhacel Salazar. 2001a. *Servants of Globalization: Women, Migration, and Domestic Work.* Stanford, Calif.: Stanford University Press.

———. 2001b. "Transgressing the Nation-State: The Partial Citizenship and 'Imagined (Global) Community' of Migrant Filipina Domestic Workers." *Signs* 26:1129–54.

———. 2008. *The Force of Domesticity: Filipina Migrants and Globalization.* New York: NYU Press.

———. 2010. "Homeward Bound: The Circular Migration of Entertainers between Japan and the Philippines." *Global Networks* 10 (3): 301–23.

———. 2011. *Illicit Flirtations: Labor, Migration, and Sex Trafficking in Tokyo.* Stanford, Calif.: Stanford University Press.

Paul, Anju Mary. 2011. "Stepwise International Migration: A Multistage Migration Pattern for the Aspiring Migrant." *American Journal of Sociology* 116 (6): 1842–86.

Piper, Nicola. 2003. "Wife or Worker? Worker or Wife? Marriage and Cross-Border Migration in Contemporary Japan." *International Journal of Population Geography* 9 (6): 457–69.

Piper, Nicola, and Mina Roces, eds. 2003. *Wife or Worker? Asian Women and Migration.* New York: Rowman & Littlefield.

Poole, Deborah. 2004. "Between Threat and Guarantee: Justice and Community in the Margins of the Peruvian State." In *Anthropology in the Margins of the State,* edited by Veena Das and Deborah Poole, 35–66. Santa Fe, NM: School of American Research Press.

Pratt, Geraldine. 2012. *Families Apart: Migrant Mothers and the Conflicts of Labor and Love.* Minneapolis: University of Minnesota Press.

Rodriguez, Robyn M. 2002. "Migrant Heroes: Nationalism, Citizenship and the Politics of Filipino Migrant Labor." *Citizenship Studies* 6 (3): 341–56.

———. 2010. *Migrants for Export: How the Philippine State Brokers Labor to the World.* Minneapolis: University of Minnesota Press.

Sadiq, Kamal. 2008. *Paper Citizens: How Illegal Immigrants Acquire Citizenship in Developing Countries.* Oxford: Oxford University Press.

Seol, Dong-Hoon. 2005. "Global Dimensions in Mapping the Foreign Labor

Policies of Korea: A Comparative and Functional Analysis." *Development and Society* 34:75–124.

———. 2012. "The Citizenship of Foreign Workers in South Korea." *Citizenship Studies* 16:119–33.

Seol, Dong-Hoon, Hyun-Mee Kim, Geonsu Han, Hyunwoong Go, and Sallie Yea. 2003. *Final Report of the Commissioned Research on Prostitution of Foreign Women.* Seoul: Ministry of Gender Equality.

Seol, Dong-Hoon, and John D. Skrentny. 2009. "Why Is There So Little Migrant Settlement in East Asia?" *International Migration Review* 439:578–620.

Somers, Margaret R. 2008. *Genealogies of Citizenship: Markets, Statelessness, and the Right to Have Rights.* Cambridge: Cambridge University Press.

Song, Jesook. 2009. *South Koreans in the Debt Crisis: The Creation of a Neoliberal Welfare Society.* Durham, NC: Duke University Press.

Soysal, Yasemin N. 1994. *Limits of Citizenship: Migrants and Postnational Membership in Europe.* Chicago: University of Chicago Press.

Stasiulis, Daiva, and Abigail B. Bakan. 1997. "Negotiating Citizenship: The Case of Foreign Domestic Workers in Canada." *Feminist Review* 57:112–39.

———. 2005. *Negotiating Citizenship: Migrant Women in Canada and the Global System.* Toronto: University of Toronto Press.

Sturdevant, Saundra Pollock, and Brenda Stoltzfus. 1992. *Let the Good Times Roll: Prostitution and the US Military in Asia.* New York: New Press.

Suzuki, Nobue. 2003. "Transgressing 'Victims': Reading Narratives of 'Filipina Brides' in Japan." *Critical Asian Studies* 35:399–420.

Walia, Harsha. 2010. "Transient Servitude: Migrant Labour in Canada and the Apartheid of Citizenship." *Race & Class* 52 (1): 71–84.

Walsh, James. 2014. "From Nations of Immigrants to States of Transience: Temporary Migration in Canada and Australia." *International Sociology* 29 (6): 584–606.

Wang, Hong-zen. 2007. "Hidden Spaces of Resistance of the Subordinated: Case Studies from Vietnamese Female Migrant Partners in Taiwan." *International Migration Review* 41 (3): 706–27.

Wang, Hong-zen, and Danièle Bélanger. 2008. "Taiwanizing Female Immigrant Spouses and Materializing Differential Citizenship." *Citizenship Studies* 12 (1): 91–106.

Willen, Sarah S. 2007. "Toward a Critical Phenomenology of 'Illegality': State Power, Criminalization, and Abjectivity among Undocumented Migrant Workers in Tel Aviv, Israel." *International Migration* 45:8–38.

Yang, Myungji. 2012. "The Making of the Urban Middle Class in South Korea (1961–1979): Nation-Building, Discipline, and the Birth of the Ideal National Subjects." *Sociological Inquiry* 82 (3): 424–45.

Yea, Sallie. 2004. "Runaway Brides: Anxieties of Identity for Trafficked Filipinas in South Korea. *Singapore Journal of Tropical Geography* 25 (2): 180–97.

————. 2005. "Labour of Love: Filipina Entertainer's Narratives of Romance and Relationships with GIs in US Military Camp Towns in Korea." *Women's Studies International Forum* 28 (6): 456–72.

Yuh, Ji-Yeon, 2002. *Beyond the Shadow of Camptown: Korean Military Brides in America.* New York: New York University Press.

Index

activists and advocates. *See* feminist
  advocacy organizations; migrant
  advocates; political activists
age-appropriate respect, 103
Americans. *See* Canada; GIs; United
  States; US military camptowns
amnesty, for undocumented migrant
  workers, 24, 122, 170
Amnesty International, 109
Arendt, Hannah, *The Human
  Condition*, 169, 170–71

Bangladeshis, 11, 41, 98–99, 121, 123;
  activism continued after deportation
  to, 69, 110; communities, 88, 98;
  immigration raids, 72, 76, 77,
  83; MTU, 88, 106; South Korean
  advocates and, 64, 104–6, 153
banmal, 33, 103–6
"bar fines," 39, 41–42, 125–30, 143–44,
  155–57
Basetown, 11, 12–14, 17, 40, 174n34;
  club hostesses, 2–3, 13–16, 38–39, 42,
  119, 120, 125–31, 137–63; club owners
  and managers, 121, 125, 127–28,
  145, 154–56. *See also* US military
  camptowns
bonding: hostesses with female club
  owners and managers, 127–29;
  male factory owners/managers and
  workers, 123–25. *See also* friendships;
  marriages

borders: of citizenship, 166–68;
  of containment, 74–75, 83–92,
  104, 109, 167, 169. *See also*
  marginalization; social boundaries;
  spatial boundaries
boundaries. *See* borders
Brubaker, Rogers, 6

Calavita, Kitty, 74
camptowns. *See* US military
  camptowns
Canada: migrant destination, 4, 29–30,
  164; Toronto as "sanctuary city," 4
capitalism, global, 8, 51, 69, 102
carework, 9, 85, 178n6; faith-based, 102,
  107, 114–15, 167; volunteer, 56. *See
  also* domestic work
Catholic Church: activism, 28, 133;
  Filipino community, 12, 96, 97, 140;
  and hostess work, 13, 15, 130, 140;
  Migrant Mission, 13; motherhood
  glorified by, 151; sanctity of
  marriage, 150; Tagalog mass, 16, 28,
  97, 130. *See also* faith-based migrant
  advocacy organizations
Catuira, Michel, 107, 109, 110
children of migrants: citizenship, 161,
  164, 165; education, 32, 36–37,
  59–61; Migrant Children's Human
  Rights Act, 165
Cho, Haejoang, 151
Christians: Protestant, 12, 133, 134;

social justice for hostesses, 139; view of migrants, 8; view of Unification Church, 33. *See also* Catholic Church; faith-based migrant advocacy organizations

churches: Basetown, 130; Factorytown, 12, 13, 20, 85, 88, 90, 97, 101, 131–34; and hostesses, 140; Jesus Church, 25, 131–33; migrant, 12, 13, 17, 20, 48, 53, 55, 85, 88, 90, 92, 95–97, 101, 106; migrant advocates, 8, 12–13, 16–17, 53, 78, 106, 131, 133, 134, 175n36; Protestant, 12, 133, 134. *See also* Catholic Church; faith-based migrant advocacy organizations; Unification Church

"circular" migrants, 21

citizenship, 4–10, 24, 162–63; advocacy and, 71, 120; children of migrants, 161, 164, 165; concept, 6–7; decentering, 1–18, 95; equality project of, 7, 10, 166; gendered, 56–60, 118–42; "margins of," 6, 10, 18, 166–67, 170; mother-citizens, 10, 57–60, 143–63, 167, 168; paradox of, 6–10, 166; "postnational," 4; remaking borders of, 166–68; rules, 1–2, 3; shadows of, 4–10, 74, 92, 165; worker-citizens, 9, 10, 118–42

City Hall Center, 101, 111–13, 115–16

civil society, 101–10, 116–17, 131–42, 167–69. *See also* migrant advocates; political activists; social workers

claims-making, 167–68; exclusion from, 2–3, 74, 166; interactive process of, 3, 154, 163

class, social, 36–37, 48–49, 56, 63, 103. *See also* labor

club hostesses, 18, 22, 23, 118–42, 167, 170; "bar fines," 39, 41–42, 125–30, 143–44, 155–57; club owners and managers, 41, 121, 125, 127–29, 145, 154–58; competing, 121, 130, 142; dignity, 140, 141, 142, 156, 168;

"easy work," 140; English language use, 174n34; entertainer visas, 3, 38, 40, 119, 138, 143, 157, 175n35; feminist advocates and, 13–14, 16, 41, 137–44, 155, 156, 162–63, 168, 177n4; Filipinas, 13–14, 41, 121, 125, 137–63, 175n35; GIs as customers, 41–43, 121, 125, 157–60; GIs marrying, 39–40, 42–43, 130, 138, 140, 146, 154, 159, 161; hours, 126; human rights, 9–10, 137–39, 144–51, 154–62; Juice sales, 125–27, 130, 143, 157; labor rights, 9, 10, 18, 119–21, 125, 128–30, 131, 138–42, 154, 179–80n8; leaving for factory work, 75; migrant workers as customers, 41–42, 125; moral status, 9, 129–30, 131, 140–41, 154–59; motherhood, 159–62, 168; new, 129; quota systems, 126; rotation system, 129, 130, 141; running away, 127, 129, 130, 155, 157; sexual trafficking policy, 3, 137–39, 142, 144–49, 155–60, 163, 166; social isolation, 129–30; South Korean, 176n24; subcontracting system, 129; tips and commissions, 39, 119, 126, 130; US military camptowns, 2–3, 13–16, 38–39, 40–43, 119, 120, 125–31, 137–63; victimhood, 3, 10, 18, 41, 137–63, 166, 168. *See also* sexual commerce

coalition building, 101–2, 110, 117, 138, 179n10

coethnic communities, 2, 85, 173n1, 179n5; Bangladeshi, 88, 98; hostesses lacking support of, 141; migrant wives and factory workers, 34, 95–96, 123; mutual help within networks of, 122–23, 125; Nepalese, 90, 98; social boundaries of containment, 90–91. *See also* Filipino community; migrant communities

"comfort women," 139

communities: advocates and workers, 99; home connections in Philippines, 21, 27–28, 97, 122; "imagined," 6; political and global, 171. *See also* churches; coethnic communities; migrant communities

Confucianism, 151

containment, 17–18, 82–92; borders of, 74–75, 83–92, 104, 109, 167, 169

cosmopolitan desires, younger generation, 47, 62–69

Coutin, Susan, 73

cross-border marriages, 2, 9–11, 18, 43; romantic love, 150; as sexual trafficking, 145–49, 179–80n8; Unification Church, 31–32, 34, 150, 176n16. *See also* migrant wives

cross-ethnic solidarity, 123–25, 170

cross-ethnic subject-making, migrant women and migrant workers, 95, 96, 98–100, 111–17, 170

curiosity, transnational mobility for, 62, 63, 66–67

decentering citizenship, 1–18, 95

De Genova, Nicholas, 74, 76

deportation, 2, 32, 42, 74, 87; activism continued after, 69, 110; detention center, 82, 89, 124; Factorytown migrants, 76, 82, 84, 109, 165; friendships continuing after, 124–25; migrant families, 4; mobilization of migrant communities and migrant advocacy groups complicating, 78, 92, 166–67; politically active migrants targeted for, 88–89, 92, 109, 110, 125, 169; protection from, 84, 85; report to the immigration office causing, 89–91

detention center, 82–84, 89, 124

"developmental generation": men, 47–54, 55, 58–59, 62; women, 55–63; younger generation and, 63–66

dignity, 47, 69–71, 144–45, 151;

hostesses, 140, 141, 142, 156, 168; worker, 9, 18, 71, 131, 132, 134–37, 140, 141, 142, 168

discrimination, 165; club owner, 41; "foreign" appearance targeted by immigration raids, 77, 86–87, 92, 169; gender, 9, 55–56, 136; by marital families, 60–61; migrant advocacy organizations and, 50, 136, 170; South Koreans toward Filipinas, 32–33, 35–36. *See also* rights

domestic violence, 145, 147–48, 179n2

domestic work, of wives, 56–62

domestic workers, 28, 175n35; Canada, 30; factory work preferred, 31; Hong Kong, 22, 27, 85; South Korea, 9–10, 21–22, 23, 85; Taiwan, 29, 73, 85, 122; US, 175n35, 179n5. *See also* carework

economics: migration driven by need, 50–51; postsocialist economy, 5–6; South Korean economic development, 51, 55, 56, 170. *See also* financial crises; funding; income

education: attendance statistics, 113–14; children of migrants, 32, 36–37, 59–61; "developmental generation," 55–56, 59–60, 62–63; multicultural programs, 12, 35–36, 45–46, 99–100, 111–17; tertiary, 177n10. *See also* language education

88 *Manwon Sede (the* 880,000 *Won Generation)*, 66

elections, migrant women, 116–17, 153

Employment Permit System. *See* EPS (Employment Permit System)

entertainer visas, 3, 38, 40, 119, 138, 143, 157, 175n35

EPS (Employment Permit System), 169; short-term guest workers, 27–29, 75, 84, 122, 133

equality: Ministry of Gender Equality, 99, 117, 137, 146; project of citizenship, 7, 10, 166

Equality Trade Union, 102
ethnic groups: GIs, 176–77n28; myth
    of ethnic homogeneity, 1–2. *See
    also* coethnic communities; cross-
    ethnic…; multicultural policy; race;
    individual ethnic groups
exclusionary policies, South Korea,
    17–18, 21, 52, 111, 165–68, 175n5

Factorytown, 11–17, 101–10, 120,
    131–37, 174n34; churches, 12, 13, 20,
    85, 88, 90, 97, 101, 131–35; cross-
    ethnic male bonding of workers
    and owners, 123–25; deportation
    of migrants, 76, 82, 84, 109, 165;
    factory owners vs. raids, 78, 81, 121;
    fear of raids, 75–78, 82, 85–87, 109;
    Filipino community, 12, 20, 32, 131,
    140, 164–65; labor rights advocacy,
    131–37, 140; massive crackdown
    (2008), 76–77, 84, 87–88; migrant
    journey to, 20–21, 24, 26–32, 73;
    migrant wives, 34, 95–96, 123,
    143–63; population of migrants, 75,
    76, 122; raids, 76–87; safe space,
    84–92; women workers, 121–25. *See
    also* Peace Center
factory workers, 3, 10–12, 22–24,
    177n4; becoming, 26–31; factory
    work preferred over domestic work,
    31; Filipinas, 121, 175n35; gender
    divisions, 121; hostesses becoming,
    75; labor activism, 48–49; labor
    rights, 10, 18, 119–21, 125, 129–30,
    131–37, 140–42, 168; men, 121,
    132; migrant wives in community
    with, 34, 95–98, 123; paternalism
    of advocates, 103–7, 110, 116, 167,
    170; rotation system, 2, 3, 27, 129,
    130, 141, 166; "trainees," 26–27,
    75, 118, 133; women, 119–25, 132,
    135–37, 141–42, 168; worker dignity,
    9, 18, 71, 131, 132, 134–37, 140, 141,
    142, 168; working visa, 12, 73, 85,

98–99, 109, 122, 136, 175n35. *See also*
    Factorytown
faith-based migrant advocacy
    organizations, 53, 110, 116–17, 170,
    175n36; carework, 102, 107, 114–15,
    167; coalition building, 101–2,
    179n10; Factorytown, 11–12, 16–17,
    78, 101–8; and hostesses, 140;
    labor rights, 120, 131–35, 176n13;
    maternal care, 113, 114–15; *minjung*
    movement, 8, 110, 132. *See also*
    Christians; churches; Peace Center
families: deportation of, 4;
    "multicultural families" *(damunhwa
    gajok)*, 2, 35, 59, 99, 111, 116–17,
    164; patriarchal conception of,
    35; reunification, 29, 30. *See also*
    children of migrants; migrant
    wives; motherhood
Families Apart (Pratt), 30
farm workers, 41, 141, 177n4
feminist advocacy organizations,
    179n2; antiprostitution law, 41, 137,
    138–39, 173n5, 179n2; hostesses,
    13–14, 16, 41, 137–44, 155, 156,
    162–63, 168, 177n4; maternity rights
    of women workers, 136; migrant
    wives, 144, 149, 153, 162–63, 173n3;
    rhetoric of motherhood, 153;
    Sisterhood Center, 13–14, 16, 137–
    41, 146, 155–59, 162; victimhood
    of women, 3, 8, 137–47, 156, 168,
    179n1, 179–80n8
ferry disaster, *Sewol*, 5, 54
fieldwork. *See* research
Filipinas, 11, 17, 19–44; factory work,
    121, 175n35; hostesses, 13–14, 41, 121,
    125, 137–63, 175n35; migrant wives,
    95–97, 143–63, 175n35, 176n16;
    Philippines experiences, 23–24, 31,
    37, 44; population in South Korea,
    175n35
Filipino community: Catholic Church,
    12, 96, 97, 140; Factorytown, 12, 20,

32, 131, 140, 164–65; Jesus Church, 131–33; MTU reaching out to, 106; Philippine home communities, 21, 27–28, 96–97, 122

financial crises: global (2008), 69, 170; IMF crisis (late 1990s), 37, 65, 68, 69

"Four Asian Tigers," 6, 22

freedom: to choose workplace, 169; transnational mobility associated with, 47, 62–63, 66–67

friendships: cross-ethnic, 124–25; risk assumed by South Korean and migrant "comrades," 107–10. See also bonding

funding: advocacy organizations, 107; immigrant integration projects, 2, 46, 111, 114; returnees' continuing political activism, 110; "victims of sexual trafficking," 137. See also income

gender: anxiety surrounding women's migration from the Philippines, 25; citizenship, 56–60, 118–42; club owners and managers, 121, 125; discrimination, 9, 55–56, 136; factory worker rights, 132, 135–37, 168; generation and, 47, 55–56; labor based on, 9, 46, 56, 62, 120, 121; Ministry of Gender Equality, 99, 117, 137, 146; university composition, 177n10; victimhood, 3, 8, 10, 18, 41, 137–63; worker-citizens, 9, 118–42. See also men; women

generation: gender and, 47, 55–56. See also "developmental generation"

GIs, 125; hostess customers, 41–43, 121, 125, 157–60; hostesses comparing migrant workers with, 41–42; hostesses competing in service to, 121, 130; hostesses marrying, 39–40, 42–43, 130, 138, 140, 146, 154, 159,

161; and new hostess arrivals, 129; racial and ethnic groups, 176–77n28; segregation from migrants, 41, 176–77n28

Glenn, Evelyn Nakano, 6

global capitalism, 8, 51, 69, 102

global financial crisis (2008), 69, 170

"guest workers," 8, 51–52, 119–20; EPS workers (short-term guest workers), 27–29, 75, 84, 122, 133

health care: factory workers, 119, 120; hostesses, 119, 138, 139; maternity, 135–37, 168; Migrant Workers' Mutual Aid for Health Care, 133; national health insurance, 4, 133; for undocumented migrants, 4, 119, 133, 165

"helping" work: glorification of, 178n6. See also carework

hierarchical interaction styles, 103–5, 116, 167, 170, 178n5

Hong Kong, 6, 22, 27, 35

Hong Sehwa, 66–67

Honig, Bonnie, 46

hooks, bell, 6

hostesses. See club hostesses

The Human Condition (Arendt), 169, 170–71

human rights, 4, 145, 162–63; dignity preferred over, 144–45; hierarchical interaction and, 106; hostesses, 9–10, 137–39, 144–51, 154–62; marriage and family preferred over, 163; migrant advocates working for, 50, 101–2, 106, 144, 145–47, 156, 169–70; Migrant Children's Human Rights Act, 165; National Human Rights Commission of Korea, 77, 93, 169; protests, 26–27, 77, 93–94, 169; rhetoric of motherhood vs., 151–62; women's victimhood, 137–39, 144–51, 154–63, 179n1

I Am a Taxi Driver in Paris (Hong Sehwa), 66–67

IMF crisis/Asian financial crisis (late 1990s), 37, 65, 68, 69

immigrant integration, 116–17, 167, 178n5; funding, 2, 46, 111, 114; migrant advocates and, 51–54, 58–59, 111; multicultural education, 12, 35–36, 45–46, 99–100, 111–17; projects, 2, 34–35, 46, 48

immigration laws, 74, 79, 104, 152, 165

immigration officers, 3, 12, 89; mobilization of migrant community and migrant advocacy groups against, 10, 78–82, 92, 166–67, 169; raiding, 10, 75–82, 86–87; reporting to, 83–84, 89–92, 171; safe space from, 84–92; strategies to avoid, 74. *See also* deportation; immigration raids

immigration raids, 17, 21, 32–33, 72–92, 166–67; advocates mobilized against, 10, 76–82, 92, 166–67, 169; after EPS, 27; fear of, 75–78, 82, 83, 85–87; "foreign" appearance targeted by, 77, 86–87, 92, 169; halted, 133; political activists targeted by, 88–89, 92, 109, 169; protests against, 77–82, 94, 102, 134, 169–70; purposes, 87, 89. *See also* containment; deportation; immigration officers

income: hostesses, 126; men and women factory workers, 121, 122; "migrant" wage, 96; minimum wage, 26, 27, 126, 133; severance pay, 27, 89, 107, 108, 119, 133, 135

Indonesia, working abroad in, 68, 69

Industrial Trainee System (ITS), 26–27, 75, 118, 133

integration. *See* immigrant integration

interviews, 10–11, 66, 174–75n34

ITS. *See* Industrial Trainee System (ITS)

Japan: "comfort women," 139; hostess work in, 22, 38–39, 126, 127, 160; migrant advocacy, 79

Japanese migrants, 32, 33, 36, 176n16

Jehovah's Witnesses, 14

Jesus Church, 25, 131–33

Joint Committee with Migrants in Korea (JCMK), 175n37

Juice sales, hostess, 125–27, 130, 143, 157

KOICA (Korean Overseas International Community Development Agency), 67, 68

labor: activists, 48–49, 102, 107–10, 131–37, 140–42, 176n13; counseling, 12, 67, 97, 102, 107, 111, 140; gendered, 9, 46, 56, 62, 120, 121; immigration laws creating, 74; irregular employment, 65–66; "labor brokerage state," 6, 44, 176n24; laws, 1–2, 131, 133; massive layoffs, 66–67; unemployment and underemployment, 66; US transnational migrant militarized labor, 176–77n28; volunteer work, 55–62, 115–16. *See also* carework; domestic work; labor rights; migrant trade unions; migrant workers

labor contracts, 17, 22, 27, 30, 119, 120; after expiration, 34, 95; factory workers, 22, 136; health care, 139; hostess, 22, 119, 126, 139, 157–58; and pregnancy, 135–36

labor rights, 9, 26–27, 63, 102, 169; advocates for, 108, 120, 131–37, 140–42, 176n13; factory workers, 10, 18, 119–21, 125, 129–30, 131–37, 140–42, 168; hostesses, 9, 10, 18, 119–21, 125, 128–30, 131, 138–42, 154, 179–80n8; maternity, 135–37, 168; right of association, 89, 133, 169; severance pay, 27, 89, 107, 108, 119, 133, 135; worker-citizens, 9, 10,

118–42; worker dignity, 9, 18, 71,
131, 132, 134–37, 140, 141, 142, 168;
workers' compensation, 27, 105, 120,
133, 136. *See also* labor contracts
Lamont, Michéle, 124
Lan, Pei-Chia, 21
language education, 61; Korean, 12,
35–36, 45–46, 99–100, 111–15, 165;
multicultural education programs,
12, 35–36, 45–46, 99–100, 111–17
language use: advocates' hierarchical
interaction styles, 103–5, 116, 167;
banmal, 33, 103–6; English, 1, 12,
36, 107, 174n34; interviews, 174n34;
Jehovah's Witnesses, 14; *jondaemal*,
107; Korean, 1, 12, 94, 103, 107, 115,
174n34; MTU, 107; Vietnamese, 61.
See also Tagalog
laws: illegality of undocumented
migrant workers, 21, 73–92, 119–20,
132, 152, 171; immigration, 74, 79,
104, 152, 165; labor, 1–2, 131, 133;
legalization of undocumented
migrant workers, 80, 119, 133,
176n12; against prostitution, 40, 41,
137, 138–39, 173n5, 179n2. *See also*
police; rights; visas
Lee, Jasmine, 117, 165
Lee, Namhee, 110
Lee, Yoonkyung, 37
legality. *See* laws; passports; rights; visas

marginalization: gender, 55; "margins of
citizenship," 6, 10, 18, 166–67, 170;
social class, 36–37, 48–49. *See also*
borders; discrimination
Marriage Migrant Women as
Politicians project, 117
marriages: arranged (*jungmae*), 58;
"fake," 58, 100, 148, 149; GIs and
hostesses, 39–40, 42–43, 130, 138,
140, 146, 154, 159, 161; "marriage
of convenience," 75; "marriage
migrant" category, 95, 96, 98–101,

111–17, 169, 170; preferred over
rights, 163; respect for women in,
60–61; sanctity of, 150; younger
generation, 66. *See also* cross-border
marriages
Marshall, T. H., 7
matchmaking, 23, 176n16; commercial
agencies, 34, 96, 145, 146; cross-
ethnic male bonding and, 124;
and state regulation, 93–94, 145;
Unification Church, 31–32, 34, 150,
176n16; and women's victimhood,
145
maternalism: advocates with migrant
women, 58–59, 112–17, 167, 170;
rhetoric of motherhood, 151–62
maternity rights, 135–37, 168. *See also*
motherhood
men: coethnic community, 123, 179n5;
cross-ethnic male bonding, 123–25;
"developmental generation," 47–54,
55, 58–59, 62; factory workers, 121,
132, 135; worker-citizen associated
with, 9, 118–42
middle class, 56, 63
migrant advocates, 9, 12–18, 45–71,
101–2, 167, 169–70, 175n36, 177n4;
boundaries between migrants and
South Korean advocates, 102, 103;
"developmental generation," 47–62;
health care for undocumented
migrants, 4; hierarchical interaction
styles, 103–5, 116, 167, 170, 178n5;
and hostesses, 14, 140–41, 177n4;
vs. immigration raids, 10, 76–82,
92, 166–67, 169; labor rights, 108,
120, 131–37, 140–42, 176n13; male
leadership, 55; migrant wives'
activism, 94, 116–17; *minjung*
movement, 8, 48–49, 110, 132,
142; mobilization with migrant
community, 9, 10, 78–82, 92,
166–67, 169; modes of political
mobilization, 94, 169; multicultural

education, 12, 36, 45–46, 99–100, 111–17; Nepalese factory owner, 124–25; paternalism, 103–7, 110, 116, 167, 170, 178n5; for regularization of undocumented migrants, 80; van chases, 10, 80–81, 169; younger generation, 47, 62, 65–69. *See also* faith-based migrant advocacy organizations; feminist advocacy organizations; migrant trade unions; Peace Center

Migrant Children's Human Rights Act, 165

migrant communities, 87, 166–67, 168; integration programs and, 178n5; mobilization with advocates, 9, 10, 78–82, 92, 166–67, 169. *See also* coethnic communities

Migrante International, 110

migrant trade unions, 1, 18, 101, 169, 170, 176n13; absent in Factorytown, 123; Equality Trade Union, 102; Sisterhood Center receiving little support from, 140. *See also* MTU (Migrants' Trade Union)

migrant wives, 3, 22, 112; collective representations, 94–95, 99–100, 117; in community with factory workers, 34, 95–98, 123; domestic work asked of, 56–62, 176n15; "fake marriage," 58, 100, 148, 149; feminist advocates and, 144, 149, 153, 162–63, 173n3; Filipina, 95–97, 143–63, 175n35, 176n16; illegality, 152; Korean language use, 174n34; maternal care, 58–59, 112–17, 167, 170; mother-citizens, 10, 57–60, 143–63, 167, 168; mothers-in-law, 58, 112, 148; multicultural educational programs, 12, 35–36, 45–46, 99–100, 111–17; official category of "marriage migrant" or "migrant woman," 95, 96, 98–101, 111–17, 169, 170; political activism, 94, 116–17, 152;

social boundaries of containment, 91, 92; spousal visas, 28, 32, 42, 86, 87, 94–95, 138, 143, 151–52, 161, 173n3; victimhood, 93–94, 143–63, 168, 179–80n8; Vietnamese, 36, 37–38, 45, 57–58, 61, 86, 93, 100, 152; volunteer work, 115–16. *See also* cross-border marriages; motherhood

"migrant woman" category, 95, 96, 98–101, 111–17, 140, 167, 170. *See also* migrant wives

migrant workers: beginning (late 1980s), 26, 84, 101; collective representations, 94–95, 99–100, 117; farm workers, 41, 141, 177n4; migrant women distinguished from, 95, 96, 98–101, 111–17, 140, 167, 170; rotation system, 2, 3, 27, 129, 130, 141, 166. *See also* club hostesses; domestic workers; factory workers; "guest workers"; labor; undocumented migrant workers

minimum wage, 26, 27, 126, 133

Ministry of Gender Equality, 99, 117, 137, 146

minjung movement, 8, 48–49, 110, 132, 142

Mongolians, 14, 32, 45, 50–51, 77, 176n16

moral status: hostesses, 9, 129–30, 131, 140–41, 154–59; motherhood, 151–54; victimhood, 155, 162–63; wife, 159

motherhood, 118; factory worker, 135–36; hostesses, 159–62, 168; maternity rights, 135–37, 168; miscarriage, 136–37; mother-citizens, 10, 57–60, 143–63, 167, 168; mothers-in-law, 58, 112, 148; rhetoric of, 151–62

MTU (Migrants' Trade Union), 101, 102, 107–10, 133, 175n37, 179n10; Bangladeshis, 88, 106; vs. immigration raids, 78, 134; immigration raids targeting, 88–89, 92, 109; official status, 89, 107;

risk assumed by South Korean and migrant "comrades," 107–10, 116; women, 28–29

"multicultural families" *(damunhwa gajok)*, 2, 35, 59, 99, 111, 116–17, 164

Multicultural Family Support Centers, 111

multicultural policy, 34–36, 46, 166; educational programs, 35–36, 45–46, 99–100, 111–17

mutual help: migrant worker networks, 122–23, 125, 133. *See also* coalition building; solidarity

names: fake name passports, 83; pseudonyms, 174–75n34

natality, Arendt on, 169, 170–71

National Assembly, South Korea, 117, 153, 165, 169

National Human Rights Commission of Korea, 77, 93, 169

naturalization process, 100

neoliberalism, 5–6, 65–66, 69

Nepal: activism continued after deportation to, 69, 110; returning to, 14, 69, 125; traveling and working abroad in, 63, 68

Nepalese: communities, 90, 98; Factorytown, 11, 109, 121; immigration raids, 83, 90; male bonding with South Koreans, 124–25; MTU, 109, 110; Peace Center parish, 101, 106; reporting troublemakers to the immigration office, 90; South Korean advocates and, 1, 64, 106; women's work, 121

nonsettlement policy, South Korea, 3, 73, 79, 91–92

Olympics, Seoul (1988), 63

Ong, Aihwa, 40

Park Jung-Hee, 56

Parreñas, Rhacel, 21

passports: children of GIs and hostesses, 161; delivery after arrests, 82, 88; employers holding, 16, 118, 119, 120, 138, 145; fake name, 83; forged, 81; husbands and in-laws holding, 145, 149. *See also* visas

paternalism: employers of hostesses, 127, 142; migrant advocates, 103–7, 110, 116, 167, 170, 178n5

Peace Center, 70, 101–7; day-care center, 164; vs. immigration raids, 76–81, 87–88; migrant wife story, 149; multicultural education, 12, 36, 45–46, 99–100, 111–15; newsletter for donors and the public, 165; paternalism, 103–7, 110

Philippines: activism continued after deportation to, 110; compared with South Korea, 37; embassy in Seoul, 97, 164; as experienced by Filipina migrants, 23–24, 31, 37, 44; home communities in, 21, 27–28, 97, 122; "labor brokerage," 6, 44; "migrant citizenship," 24; migrant workers' connections with, 23–29; MTU head (2009–2010), 107; "national heroes," 24, 96–97; street safety, 31, 33. *See also* Filipinas; Filipino community

Piper, Nicola, 34

police: Basetown, 13; and criminalized migrants, 73–74. *See also* immigration officers

political activists: continuing after deportation, 69, 110; elections, 116–17, 153; labor, 48–49, 102, 107–10, 131–37, 142; migrant wives, 94, 116–17, 152; sex worker, 139; student, 8, 48–49, 110, 170; targeted by immigration raids and deportation, 88–89, 92, 109, 110, 125, 169. *See also* feminist advocacy organizations; migrant advocates; migrant trade unions; politics; protests

politics: of solidarity, 169–71; symbolic,
9, 46. *See also* political activists
population: entertaincr visas, 175n35;
Factorytown migrants, 75, 76, 122;
Filipinas coming via marriage with
South Korean men, 175n35; Filipinas
in South Korea, 175n35; hostesses
in US military clubs, 13–14, 41, 121,
125, 176n24; industrial laborer visas
for factory work, 175n35; migrants
in South Korea, 2, 14; South Korean
national, 2; South Korean tertiary
education gross enrollment rate,
177n10; undocumented migrant
workers, 26, 75, 76, 122, 133, 178n8;
US military camp, 12–13
Pratt, Geraldine, 30
prostitution: antiprostitution law,
40, 41, 137, 138–39, 173n5, 179n2;
victimhood of hostesses, 137–63. *See
also* sexual commerce
Protestant churches, 12, 133, 134
protests, 2, 102, 169–70; candlelight
vigil, 134; direct voices of migrant
workers, 93–94, 106–10; human
rights, 26–27, 77, 93–94, 169;
immigration raids, 77–82, 94,
102, 134, 169–70; legalization of
undocumented migrant workers,
119; march in Seoul (2008), 1, 169;
sit-in, 63–65

race: "foreign" appearance targeted by
immigration raids, 77, 86–87, 92,
169; GIs, 176–77n28. *See also* ethnic
groups; multicultural policy
research, 10–11; fieldwork, 11–17;
interviews, 10–11, 66, 174–75n34
rights, 7, 9, 18, 164–71; civil society
mobilization for migrant rights,
131–42, 169; dignity chosen over,
144–45; maternity, 135–37, 168; right
of association, 89, 133, 169; women
factory workers, 119–21, 125, 132.

See also citizenship; discrimination;
human rights; labor rights; laws
Rodriguez, Robyn, 6, 22, 24, 96
rotation system, migrant worker, 2, 3,
27, 129, 130, 141, 166

safety: safe space for undocumented
migrant workers, 84–92, 167; street,
31, 33. *See also* victimhood; violence
"sanctuary city," Toronto, 4
schooling. *See* education
segregation: GIs from migrants,
41, 176–77n28; hostesses, 155; of
migrants, 51–54, 85, 87, 120. *See also*
spatial boundaries
severance pay, 27, 89, 107, 108, 119, 133,
135
Sewol ferry disaster, 5, 54
sexual commerce, 9–10, 13, 40–41;
victimhood and, 3, 10, 18, 41, 137–
63, 179–80n8. *See also* club hostesses;
prostitution; sexual trafficking
sexual harassment, 28, 125, 128, 136
sexual morality, stigma for hostesses, 9,
129–30, 131, 140–41, 154–59
sexual relations, bar fines and, 39, 41,
128, 156
sexual trafficking, 9, 173n5; victims of,
3, 137–39, 142, 144–49, 155–60, 163,
166, 179–80n8
sex worker activism, 139
Sisterhood Center, 13–14, 16, 137–41,
146, 155–59, 162
social boundaries: of containment,
74–75, 84, 88–92, 109; between male
owners and factory workers, 124;
between migrants and South Korean
advocates, 102, 103
social class, 36–37, 48–49, 56, 63, 103.
See also labor
social transformation, 7, 49, 50, 65, 101,
116, 168, 171
social workers: "developmental
generation," 48; multicultural

education programs, 113–15;
    Sisterhood Center, 137–38, 139;
    view of migrants, 8
solidarity, 18, 164–71; building
    politics of, 169–71; cross-ethnic,
    123–25, 170; Factorytown migrants,
    82, 122–25, 164–65; hostess
    competition and, 130; MTU
    emphasis, 110; student activists, 64;
    transnational activist, 69. *See also*
    bonding; mutual help
Somers, Margaret, 5
South Korea, 168; achievement
    of parliamentary democracy,
    62; authoritarian regimes
    (1960s–1980s), 40, 47, 48, 51, 56,
    63, 132, 134; beginnings of labor
    migration (1980s), 26; compared
    with the West, 37; culpability for
    victimhood of women, 93–94,
    145–46; democratization of, 101;
    economic development, 51, 55,
    56, 170; exclusionary policies,
    17–18, 21, 52, 111, 165–68, 175n5;
    Filipina population, 175n35; labor
    broker in the camptown clubs,
    176n24; meanings for Filipinas, 23;
    National Assembly, 117, 153, 165,
    169; nonsettlement policy, 3, 73,
    79, 91–92; reform of migrant labor
    policy (2003–2004), 26–27, 84,
    133; relocation experiences within,
    57; travel ban, 62, 63. *See also* civil
    society; state
spatial boundaries ("home, factory,
    and church"/zone of containment),
    74–75, 83–88, 92, 104. *See also*
    segregation
"standard track," 65–66
state: "labor brokerage state," 6, 44,
    176n24; primary actor shaping
    migrant citizenship, 17–18;
    protection of women, 93–94,
    145–46. *See also* citizenship; laws

street safety, 31, 33
student activists, 8, 48–49, 110, 170
subject-making, migrant, 167;
    collective, 94–95, 99–110, 117, 154;
    cross-ethnic, 95, 96, 98–100, 111–17,
    170; subjects of rights, 10, 99, 142,
    162–63
symbolic politics, 9, 46

Tagalog, 12, 75, 165, 174n34; hotline
    for abandoned wives and
    children, 161; mass, 16, 28, 97, 130;
    multicultural library, 36; TNT, 39,
    83
Taiwan, 6, 20, 22; domestic workers,
    29, 73, 122; factory workers, 22, 31;
    integration programs, 178n5
Toronto, "sanctuary city," 4
trade unions. *See* migrant trade unions
"trainees," 26–27, 75, 118, 133
transformation, 167; personal, 7, 44;
    social, 7, 49, 50, 65, 101, 116, 168,
    171
travel ban, overseas, 62, 63

undocumented migrant workers:
    advocacy for, 133, 136; amnesty,
    24, 122, 170; Filipina population,
    175n35; health care, 4, 119, 133, 165;
    illegality, 21, 73–92, 119–20, 132,
    152, 171; legalization of, 80, 119, 133,
    176n12; Migrant Children's Human
    Rights Act and, 165; population,
    26, 75, 76, 122, 133, 178n8; safe
    space, 84–92, 167; TNT, 39, 83.
    See also deportation; immigration
    raids; visas
Unification Church, 12, 33; cross-
    border marriages, 31–32, 34, 150,
    176n16; motherhood glorified by,
    151
unions: women's, 136. *See also* migrant
    trade unions
United States: domestic workers,

175n35, 179n5; embassy in South
Korea, 89, 161; migration to, 29–
30, 37–38, 177n30; segregation of
migrants, 52. *See also* US military
camptowns
US military camptowns, 2–3, 11,
12–14, 15, 40, 176–77nn28,29;
club hostesses, 2–3, 13–16, 38–39,
40–43, 119, 120, 125–31, 137–63. *See
also* Basetown; GIs

victimhood, migrant women, 8, 143–
63, 168; blame for, 145; feminists
and, 3, 8, 137–47, 156, 168, 179n1,
179–80n8; hostesses, 3, 10, 18,
41, 137–63, 166; motherhood
and, 154–63; sexual trafficking, 3,
137–39, 142, 144–49, 155–60, 163,
166, 179–80n8; state culpability
for, 93–94, 145–46
Vietnamese, 11, 98, 115–16; migrant
wives, 36, 37–38, 45, 57–58, 61, 86,
93, 100, 152
violence: street, 31; against women,
16, 137, 144–48, 151, 152, 179n2
visas: entertainer visa, 3, 38, 40, 119,
138, 143, 157, 175n35; "industrial
trainee," 118; spousal visa, 28, 32,
42, 86, 87, 94–95, 138, 143, 151–52,
161, 173n3; working visa, 12, 73, 85,

98–99, 109, 122, 136, 175n35. *See
also* passports
volunteer work, 55–62, 115–16

wages. *See* income
women: coethnic community, 122–23;
"developmental generation,"
55–63; factory workers, 119–25, 132,
135–37, 141–42, 168; "helping" work,
178n6; before and after marriage,
56; "migrant woman" category, 95,
96, 98–101, 111–17, 140, 167, 170;
unions, 136; violence against, 16, 137,
144–48, 151, 152, 179n2. *See also* club
hostesses; domestic work; feminist
advocacy organizations; marriages;
migrant wives; motherhood;
victimhood
worker-citizens, 9, 10, 118–42
workers' compensation, 27, 105, 120,
133, 136
working class. *See* labor; migrant
workers
working visa, 12, 73, 85, 98–99, 109,
122, 136, 175n35

younger generation: cosmopolitan
desires, 47, 62–69; and
"developmental generation," 63–66;
student activists, 8, 48–49, 110, 170